COMPLETE WILD GAME COOKBOOK

COMPLETE
WILD GAME
Cookbook
190+ RECIPES
FOR HUNTERS AND ANGLERS

Bri Van Scotter

Photography by
Marija Vidal

ROCKRIDGE
PRESS

For general information on our other products and services or to obtain technical support, please contact our Customer Care Department within the United States at (866) 744-2665, or outside the United States at (510) 253-0500.

Rockridge Press publishes its books in a variety of electronic and print formats. Some content that appears in print may not be available in electronic books, and vice versa.

Interior and Cover Designer: Sean Doyle
Art Producer: Tom Hood
Editor: Pam Kingsley
Photography ©2020 Marija Vidal, food styling by Karen Shinto. Author photo courtesy of Leticia Andrade

ISBN: Print 978-1-64739-733-3
eBook 978-1-64739-435-6
R0

To my husband, my best friend, and biggest supporter.
For without you, this all wouldn't have been possible.
Je t'aime bel homme.

CONTENTS

← Ahi Tuna Poke Bowl, page 231

INTRODUCTION

MY PASSION for food has played a huge role in my life. It's my career, my hobby, my source of comfort, and my medicine.

When college came around, I had wanted to attend culinary school but opted to go to university. Two degrees later, I found myself in a cubicle, hating life.

I ended up getting a second job as a hostess in a restaurant and soon talked my way into the pastry department. I never worked harder, and I absolutely loved every minute of it. Soon, I found myself walking into the Culinary Institute of America in Napa, California.

One day at a catering event, I met a local farmer who had raised the chickens I had so carefully prepared for that evening. I found myself at his farm the next day, and a week later I had my own set of eggs that I would hatch, raise as chickens, and slaughter myself. For weeks, I tended my brood, and then came the day for me to harvest them. It was in that moment that I decided, as a chef, if I can cook an animal, I should be able to harvest it myself. That evening, as I sat on my apartment floor in tears, eating the most delicious roast chicken I had ever had, my life changed.

After working in fine dining, I ended up in Georgia, where I discovered hunting. My husband bought me a bow, and six months later I was in a tree stand on opening day harvesting my first doe.

With a freezer that was full of venison, I wanted to show folks that there was so much more to cooking wild game than grilling a backstrap or making a popper. So, I created *Wilderness to Table*, my website where I teach people about the versatility of wild game and just how delicious it can be.

Now I hunt all over the world, free-dive the deep seas to spearfish, and fly-fish the rivers of Georgia, and I love every minute of it. Hunting has shown me what real food should taste like. I know exactly where my food comes from, I have a deeper respect for what I prepare and enjoy, and I know I'm providing the best protein possible for my family. I hope you enjoy these recipes.

Eat wild!

← Venison Tamales, page 26

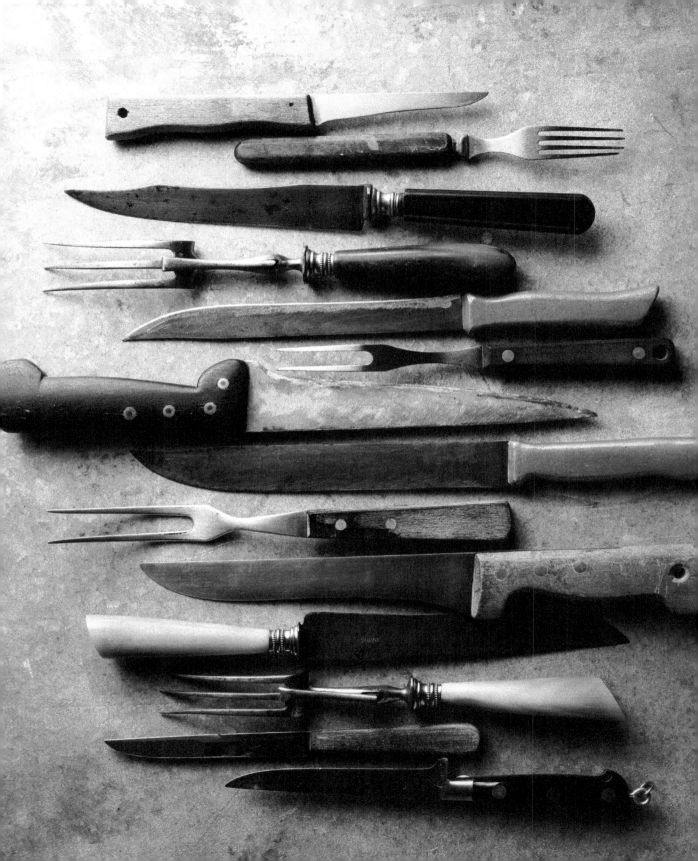

CHAPTER 1

Your Wild Game Kitchen

Wild game is absolutely beautiful protein; versatile, and delicious. And it's even more delicious when you have a well-stocked kitchen to help you cook it. The right ingredients can make all the difference in the field and in the kitchen. Unlike farmed protein, wild game can require a bit more care. With the right tools and techniques, you can transform a "gamey" piece of meat into something marvelous.

Tools and Equipment

"You're only as good as your tools." I'm sure you have heard this saying, and it's true. The quality of your cooking equipment is as important as the tools themselves.

KNIVES

Knives are basic building blocks of good cooking. Look at them as an investment—quality is better that quantity. The three knives every kitchen should have are: a chef's knife, paring knife, and serrated bread knife.

Chef's knives vary from 6 to 12 inches with a blade that tapers upward to a point. This shape allows you to rock the knife back and forth for mincing. It is the workhorse of your knives and will be useful for almost all the cutting you'll need to do.

A paring knife is short-bladed and used for intricate cutting, peeling, and dicing. It is useful when you're working with small items.

Serrated, or bread knives, have saw-like blades. This makes them efficient at cutting through a thick or resistant outer surface, like a crusty loaf of bread or the tough skin of a tomato.

COOKWARE

For every pot, there is a purpose. There are six pieces of cookware that I find indispensable:

→ 8-quart or larger stockpot with a lid, for boiling pasta or making soups
→ 3-quart oven-safe sauté pan with a lid, for frying, deglazing, and sautéeing
→ 3-quart saucepan with a lid (I love copper because it conducts heat so well, but it is pricey)
→ Cast-iron skillet—durable, cheap, and great for handling high heat
→ 6- to 8-quart Dutch oven with a lid, for braises and stews
→ Nonstick skillet, for searing and more delicate preparations, like eggs

Cooking Techniques

Different cooking methods bring out different flavors and textures that impact your final dish. Understand and master them and cooking will become easier and produce better results.

PAN-SEARING

Pan-searing is about building flavor. Use a stainless steel or cast-iron skillet over high heat. Add a thin coating of oil; 2 or 3 teaspoons. Pat the meat or fish dry to prevent steaming when it hits the hot pan. Place it in the skillet and let it be; moving it will interfere with browning. To ensure even cooking and avoid steaming, don't crowd the pan.

FRYING

Panfrying adds rich, caramelized flavor while retaining moisture and tenderness. It relies on oil or fat as the heat-transfer medium. Direct contact with the pan results in greater browning and crisping of the food. When panfrying it's important to maintain constant medium-high heat or else the coating will get soggy, not crispy. Deep-frying submerges the food in hot oil. Foods that are deep-fried cook faster than when panfried.

ROASTING

Roasting is a dry-heat cooking method that results in browning and sweet caramelized flavors. It's great for larger cuts of meat.

BRAISING

Braising is most often employed for tough cuts. When braising, meat is usually first seared at a high temperature to form a nice crust. Then, liquid is added, and the meat is cooked for a long time at low heat. Braising breaks down the connective tissues and softens the muscle fibers, resulting in an incredibly moist, tender dish.

GRILLING AND SMOKING

Grilling food directly over a hot fire (400°F to 550°F) for a short period of time is perfect for tender cuts like steaks, chops, and burgers, and fish like salmon and tuna that you want to give a deep sear while keeping the center rare to medium.

Grilling using indirect heat works like roasting in an oven. The food isn't placed directly over the heat source; it's positioned off to the side, with the lid down. To create an indirect setup on a gas grill, preheat it with all the burners on high, then turn half of them off; that will be your cool spot. In a charcoal grill, build the fire; when it's ready, push the coals to one side to create the cool space. Indirect heat is great for large cuts of meat that need longer cooking times, like roasts and brisket, or smaller cuts that would end up burnt on the outside by the time the interior was properly cooked, like duck legs.

Liquid Gold

When processing your harvest, there is one "cut" you might overlook: fat. Not all fat is created equal; deer fat, for instance, is too gamey to use. But the rendered fat of ducks, geese, and wild boar? Nothing tops it for bringing silky, rich flavor to whatever you panfry, sauté, or deep-fry. Try my Duck-Fat French Fries on page 108, and you'll be hooked! I also use it to replace butter in baked goods, like my shortbread cookies on page 110.

To render wild boar fat, take the fattiest pieces of meat, dice them, and put them in a large, heavy pot like a Dutch oven. Add ½ to ¾ cup water and set over medium-low heat. Rendering takes time, usually about an hour; gently stir the pot every 10 minutes while the meat simmers. The cracklings will start to float to the surface; you may think they're done at this point, but they're not—keep stirring occasionally. You may hear popping; that's just moisture evaporating. You will know the fat is done rendering when the cracklings fall back to the bottom of the pot. Remove the pot from the heat and let it cool a bit. Strain the rendered fat through a colander lined with cheesecloth. Transfer it to a glass jar and store it in the refrigerator; it will keep for up to 3 months.

To render duck or goose fat, trim off the extra fat and skin from either end of the bird's cavity and cut into smaller pieces. Render the fat in a saucepan over low heat, pressing on the pieces occasionally with the back of a spoon. Within an hour, it should be melted and clear. Let it cool down a bit, then pour into a cheesecloth-lined colander to strain. Transfer to an airtight jar; refrigerate up to 6 months or freeze up to a year.

You can also use your grill, with an indirect setup, to smoke food (though I prefer an electric wood smoker). On a gas grill, use wood chips or pellets, soaked or dry. (I soak them if adding them directly to the fire.) Or wrap 2 to 3 cups of wood chips or pellets in foil. Poke holes in the pouch so the smoke can escape and set it on the grates. Be careful not to block the propane or natural gas jets; never impede the flow of gas.

To smoke on a charcoal grill, place an aluminum tray filled with water in the middle of the grill, with the coals on either side. The water regulates the temperature and catches fat. Add soaked wood chips or chunks directly to the coals.

Different woods produce different flavors; hickory, oak, and mesquite are deep and bold and best for red meats like venison. Lighter woods such as applewood, cherry, pecan, and alder work well with white meats like rabbit and fish.

If smoking slow and low, you will need to replenish the coals to keep the fire burning. The best way is to add unlit charcoal, briquettes, or wood chunks to your grill or smoker when the temperature starts dropping. The coals will light the fresh fuel and keep the fire going. Note that every time the lid is opened, heat is released, causing temperature swings. So as tempting as it may be to check on your meat's progress, keep the lid closed as much as possible. Also, if the temperature in the grill gets too high, close the vents to reduce the amount of oxygen, which will lower the temperature.

DRYING AND DEHYDRATING

Drying and dehydrating use very low heat (generally 130°F to 155°F) to remove almost all the moisture from food; this is how jerky is made. Once the water is removed, the food will not spoil as quickly. It can be done in an oven or a dehydrator.

When I make jerky, I often add curing salt to help preserve it. The brands I use are Prague Powder #1, Instacure #2, and Morton Tender Quick, which can be found on Amazon; almost all supermarkets carry Morton Tender Quick. Four ounces of Prague Powder #1 will cure 100 pounds of meat—it's best for making bacon, cured ham or fish, and jerky. Instacure #2 is best used for charcuterie meats like pepperoni and dry sausages. Morton Tender Quick is a less concentrated curing salt and works well for small batches; you'll use 1 tablespoon for every pound of meat. It's best for poultry, salmon, sausage, and jerky.

You do not have to use curing salts when making jerky. But if you don't use them in a recipe that calls for them, you do need to raise the dehydration temperature to 160°F to kill any bacteria. It's also important to consume jerky not made with curing salt within 2 to 3 days of dehydrating. If you are making jerky from any kind of fowl, you must dehydrate at 165°F to kill bacteria.

Please note that nitrates and nitrites can be toxic when not used in the recommended proportions, so it is extremely important to follow the package and recipe directions.

When storing jerky, you can purchase silica packets and add them to the airtight container to help decrease moisture.

Freezing Meat for Thin Slices

When making jerky or other dishes that require very thinly sliced pieces of meat, freeze the meat ahead of time for 30 to 45 minutes. Doing so will allow the meat to firm up just enough to make slicing it by hand or on a slicer much easier.

The recipes in this book focus on fresh sausage. If you'll be making sausage on a regular basis, invest in a grinder (it can also be the grinder attachment for a stand mixer) and a stuffer if you plan on using casings. You can also use a food processor to grind meat; however, you must be very careful not to overprocess the meat or your sausage will come out tough.

The ratio of fat to meat is key to achieving the proper texture. I recommend 20 percent fat to 80 percent meat. Shank, shoulder, brisket, and other fatty cuts work best.

It's important to keep everything cold—the equipment, bowls, mixing spoons, and meat—because the heat produced by the friction of grinding can cause the fat to melt. For best results, you want the fat to remain in its solid state. Cut the meat into 1-inch pieces and put it in the freezer for 20 to 30 minutes; you want it to firm up but not freeze. If you are using a grinder, run the meat through a large die, then again through a medium die.

If you are using a food processor, freeze the food processor bowl and blade. Fill the bowl only halfway with meat and pulse 8 to 10 times, just 1 second for each pulse because the food processor creates a lot of friction. Take your time, work in small batches, and only pulse—never run the food processor continuously.

No matter how you grind your meat, it should look coarsely ground, not smooth.

Once the meat is processed, form it into patties or stuff it into casings. Casings come in different diameters. I prefer to use natural hog or sheep casings, but you can use collagen casings, which are typically used for snack sticks and hot dogs. Casings can be purchased from your local butcher or online.

To fill casings, you need a sausage stuffer. It is simple to use; place the ground meat in the stuffer and attach a casing to the port. Slowly press the meat through the port, making sure not to overstuff the casing or it will burst during cooking. You can make a single long sausage or twist the sausage every 5 to 7 inches to create links.

Food Safety

Food safety is one of the most important parts of healthy eating. To prevent cross-contamination, practice these easy steps.

1. **Clean:** Wash your hands and surfaces often. Do not rinse seafood, meat, or poultry, since rinsing can spread more germs. Wipe up drips or spills immediately.

2. **Separate:** Don't cross-contaminate! Separate raw animal proteins from other foods. Use a dedicated cutting board. Never place cooked meat back on the same surface that was in contact with raw food.

3. **Cook:** Cook to the correct temperature. Food is safely cooked when the internal temperature gets high enough to kill harmful microbes. To ensure the proper temperature, use an instant-read food thermometer and place it in the thickest part of the food without touching any bone, fat, or gristle.

4. **Chill or Heat:** Keep the refrigerator at 40°F or below. Hot foods should be held at 140°F or above. Food is no longer safe to eat when it's been between 40°F to 140°F for more than two hours; one hour if the ambient temperature is above 90°F.

What You Need to Know About CWD

Chronic Wasting Disease (CWD) is a contagious neurological disease that affects deer, elk, and moose. It causes degeneration of the brain, eventually resulting in death. It may take more than a year before an infected animal develops symptoms. The Centers for Disease Control and Prevention recommend that you do not eat meat from an animal that has CWD.

Before you go hunting, contact your state's Department of Natural Resources to see if CWD has been found in your chosen area. If it has been, it is best to have your harvest tested after hunting. If that isn't possible, but your harvest shows no physical signs of CWD, avoid eating the brain, spinal cord, lymph glands, tonsils, eyes, and spleen. Avoid these parts when butchering to prevent possible contamination. Wear rubber gloves when field-dressing and processing. Avoid sawing through bones like the spinal cord and do not use a knife that has been used to cut bone to cut edible meat. Removing as much fatty tissue as possible will help remove the lymph glands, which lie in fat deposits under the skin and between muscles.

Storage

It's highly important to get your wild game or any meat under refrigeration as quickly as possible to preserve its quality. Wild game will keep in the freezer for 8 to 12 months. I prefer to vacuum-seal my meat, which removes all the air, preventing freezer burn.

THAWING

The absolute best way to thaw frozen meats is by leaving them in the refrigerator until completely thawed. Do not thaw meat on the countertop. You can thaw meat in a microwave, but be careful not to cook the meat before it's completely thawed.

CHAPTER 2

Venison, Elk, and Moose

My quest for organic protein led me to hunting. Whitetail deer was the very first big game I ever hunted and is probably the one I won't ever forget. That whitetail has led me to hunt elk and moose, and each of these animals has provided amazing meat. Venison is hands down the most common meat found in a hunter's freezer, and for good reason. From stews to jerky, there is an endless array of recipes that highlight the delicious qualities of venison. I guarantee you will change the way you think about venison, elk, and moose after you cook your way through this chapter.

← Porcini-Crusted Venison Rack, page 22

Venison

Venison is adored for its rich, spicy, and earthy flavors. Many deer enjoy a diet of acorns, berries, and herbs, and those flavor notes can be found in their meat as well. The most prized cut of a deer is the backstrap, where these flavors are well highlighted. The backstrap is lean and tender, whereas the hindquarter is the toughest part of a deer. Don't let that deter you from cooking it; because of its high fat content, it can be one of the most delicious cuts and is best when braised. The meat from the neck and shoulders is better suited for grinding, whereas the ribs and brisket are wonderful for braising and stewing.

The "gamey" flavor that venison is often said to have has a lot to do with how quickly the harvest died and was field-dressed. It is best to field-dress your harvest as fast as possible to avoid the buildup of lactic acid in the muscles, the culprit behind gaminess. The single most important thing to do to ensure the best-tasting meat is to cool down the meat as quickly as you can.

AGING VENISON

Just like aging beef, aging venison improves flavor, so consider hanging and aging your harvest. Hanging a deer (elk and moose are too large to make this feasible), whole or in quarters, in a refrigerator or a walk-in cooler is best. Make sure there is adequate airflow and the temperature is kept between 34°F to 37°F to prevent bacteria growth. Hanging allows cold air to completely circulate throughout the aging process. During this time, a "cap" forms on the skin that is actually a type of fungus that must be removed prior to cooking. The amount of time your harvest ages is up to you. I like to hang my harvest for one week, test it for flavor (the gamey flavor decreases with time) and then continue to test every other day until I get the desired result. I recommend aging for 18 to 21 days if possible. Aging produces a smoother and firmer texture and a very earthy flavor with hints of sage, acorns, and herbs.

Elk

Elk is prized for its rich, almost beefy flavor. With a texture that is similar to its whitetail cousin, elk tends to be much leaner and carry less gamey flavor, making it a favorite among hunters. When field-dressing an elk, the best thing you can do to preserve that elegant flavor is to bleed out the carcass as best you can. This will keep any gamey flavor at bay.

Since elk is tremendously lean, it is always best to cook it in fat; also, fat should be added when grinding elk meat.

Moose

Moose is another excellent game meat, tasting much like beef. Like elk, moose meat is extremely lean and lacks a lot of fat; it also lacks virtually any gamey flavor. It tends to be a bit sweeter than elk, which makes it pair well with berries and red wine.

The prized cut on a moose is the tenderloins. Because of the size of the animal, a moose tenderloin is about the same as a beef tenderloin. These precious cuts are often destroyed when mechanically processing a moose but can easily be removed by hand by pulling them free from the section where the ribs meet the spine.

Field-Dressing

Generally, quartering the animal in the field, then processing those quarters down to edible portions when you get home is best. Be sure to work as fast as possible and keep the meat as cool as possible. To quarter the animal, you will need a sharp knife and bone saw. Quartering consists of removing the head, cutting the animal in half across the stomach (just under the ribs), then cutting or sawing in between the spinal cord. Finally, removing the two front quarters gives you four pieces. If these pieces are still too large to pack out, the carcass can be cut down further, but check your state's laws. Some states require the carcass be delivered to a checking station for examination. Be sure to label each piece with the name, address, and hunting license number of the person who shot it.

The Cuts

The main cuts of deer, moose, and elk consist of the neck, shoulder or chuck, ribs, shanks, flank, loin or backstrap, tenderloin, rump, and leg or round. From these large pieces you can break them down even further to best suit your cooking needs. Each large piece can be used for different dishes and cooking methods. It's important to understand that tender cuts need a different cooking method from those that are tougher. For example, backstrap is best prepared as a steak cooked over direct heat; on the other hand, the round is best cooked at a lower temperature for a longer time.

Here is how the cuts break down:

Neck: stews, braises, soups, ground meat

Shoulder or Chuck: braises, stews, soups, roasts, ground meat, jerky, sausage

Ribs: braises and ground meat

Shanks: soups, stews, osso buco and other braises, roasts, sausage, ground meat

Flank: stews, sausage, jerky, ground meat

Tenderloin or Backstrap: steaks or fillets, kebabs, chops

Rump: braises, stews, roasts, jerky, ground meat, sausage

Leg or Round: braises, stews, roasts, kebabs, jerky, ground meat

VENISON

Venison au Vin

PREP TIME: 30 MINUTES / **COOK TIME:** 1 HOUR 45 MINUTES / **YIELD:** 6 SERVINGS
OTHER GAME YOU CAN USE: ELK, MOOSE, BEAR

This is a game take on the classic French chicken stew, coq au vin. It's delicious served over a bed of mashed potatoes laced with butter.

3 tablespoons olive oil, divided

6 ounces bacon, diced

2½ pounds venison stew meat

2¾ teaspoons kosher salt, divided

1 teaspoon freshly ground black pepper

2 medium carrots, cut into 1-inch pieces

3 stalks celery, thinly sliced

1 large yellow onion, diced

4 cloves garlic, minced

½ cup brandy

3 cups red wine

3 cups Venison Stock (page 264) or beef broth

⅓ cup tomato paste

¼ cup balsamic vinegar

2 tablespoons packed light or dark brown sugar

8 sprigs thyme

1 teaspoon chopped fresh rosemary

3 bay leaves

3 cups sliced cremini mushrooms

2 tablespoons unsalted butter, softened

1½ tablespoons all-purpose flour

1½ cups frozen peas

1 cup cipolline onions

1. In a large Dutch oven, warm 1 tablespoon of olive oil over medium heat. Line a plate with paper towels.

2. Add the bacon and cook until crispy, for 5 to 6 minutes. Using a slotted spoon, transfer to the prepared plate, leaving the fat in the pot.

3. Season the venison with 2 teaspoons of salt and the pepper.

4. Increase the heat to medium-high. Add half of the venison and cook, turning occasionally, until golden brown, for 4 or 5 minutes. Transfer to a plate. Repeat with the remaining venison. Pour off all but about 2 tablespoons of the fat.

5. Reduce the heat to medium-low. Add the carrots, celery, and yellow onion; cook, stirring occasionally, until the vegetables brown, for 3 to 5 minutes.

6. Add the garlic and cook, stirring, until fragrant, for 1 minute.

7. Add the brandy and, using a wooden spoon, scrape up any browned bits from the bottom of the pot until the brandy has evaporated.

8. Add the wine, stock, tomato paste, vinegar, brown sugar, thyme, rosemary, bay leaves, and ½ teaspoon of salt; bring to a boil.

9. Reduce the heat to medium. Gently boil for 20 minutes.

10. Reduce the heat to low. Cover, and simmer for 30 minutes, or until the venison has cooked through.

11. Meanwhile, in a large sauté pan, heat the remaining 2 tablespoons of olive oil over medium heat.

12. Add the mushrooms and remaining ¼ teaspoon salt; cook, stirring frequently, until the mushrooms are golden brown, for about 5 minutes. Remove from the heat.

13. In a small bowl, mash the butter and flour to make a smooth paste.

14. Using a slotted spoon, transfer the cooked venison to a plate.

15. Increase the heat to medium. Stir in ¾ of the butter paste. Gently boil until the sauce has thickened, for 5 to 7 minutes; add the remaining paste for a thicker sauce. Discard the bay leaves.

16. Add the venison and any accumulated juices, peas, and cipolline onions; simmer for about 20 minutes.

17. Right before serving, stir in the browned mushrooms and bacon. Remove from the heat. Taste and adjust the seasoning, if needed.

Braised Venison over Red Wine Risotto

PREP TIME: 30 MINUTES / **COOK TIME:** 2 HOURS 30 MINUTES / **YIELD:** 6 TO 8 SERVINGS
OTHER GAME YOU CAN USE: ELK, MOOSE

Risotto has always been the comfort food I turn to when I need a special dish to make me happy. Throw in some wine, and now I'm completely happy. Mix that with braised venison, and it's the perfect combo. Start making the risotto about 50 minutes before the braised venison would be ready; risotto is at its best when served ultra-creamy and hot.

FOR THE VENISON:

3 pounds venison stew meat

2 tablespoons all-purpose flour

1 tablespoon olive oil

3 ounces pancetta or
bacon, chopped

1 medium onion, finely diced

1½ cups dry red wine

8 sprigs parsley

4 cloves garlic, minced

4 sprigs thyme

2 sprigs rosemary

4 cups Venison Stock (page 264)
or beef broth

1 tablespoon tomato paste

1. Preheat the oven to 350°F.

2. **To make the venison:** Put the venison in a large bowl, sprinkle with the flour, and toss to coat.

3. In a large Dutch oven, heat the olive oil over medium heat. When it's hot, add the pancetta and onion; cook, stirring, for about 10 minutes.

4. Add one-third of the venison and cook until golden brown on all sides, for 4 to 5 minutes. Transfer to a plate. Repeat with remaining venison.

5. To the pot, add the wine, parsley, garlic, thyme, and rosemary; bring to a boil. Cook for 5 minutes to reduce the wine slightly.

6. Stir in the stock and tomato paste; bring to a boil.

7. Return the venison to the pot, cover, and put in the oven. Cook until the venison is fork tender, for 1½ to 2 hours. Remove from the oven. Let sit for 10 minutes.

FOR THE RISOTTO:

3 tablespoons unsalted butter

1 cup minced onion

1 clove garlic, minced

1 cup Arborio rice

½ cup dry red wine

3½ cups chicken broth

½ cup grated
   Parmesan cheese

8. **To make the risotto:** In a large sauté pan, melt the butter over medium-high heat.

9. Add the onion and cook until translucent, for about 5 minutes.

10. Stir in the garlic and cook for 2 minutes.

11. Add the rice and cook, stirring, until toasted, for about 3 minutes.

12. Add the wine and, using a wooden spoon, scrape up any browned bits from the bottom of the pan. Cook until the wine has almost evaporated, for 3 to 5 minutes.

13. Add the broth, 1 cup at a time, stirring after each addition, until completely absorbed. Continue until all the broth is used, which will take 30 to 40 minutes. Remove from the heat.

14. Stir in the Parmesan cheese until melted.

15. Serve the braised venison over the risotto.

West African–Inspired Stew

PREP TIME: 20 MINUTES / **COOK TIME:** 1 HOUR 30 MINUTES / **YIELD:** 6 SERVINGS
OTHER GAME YOU CAN USE: ELK, MOOSE, BEAR, WILD BOAR

Africa has some of the most stunning landscapes, as well as a delicious food scene. What I loved best in my travels there were the dishes that have been passed down through generations. I was at a hunting lodge in Namibia and had this stew, made with gemsbok, served over rice. I like to double the recipe and freeze the leftovers.

2 teaspoons vegetable oil

2 pounds venison stew meat, cut into 1-inch cubes

2 medium onions, sliced

3 stalks celery, thinly sliced

2 cloves garlic, minced

5 cups Venison Stock (page 264) or beef broth

1 tablespoon beef bouillon granules

5 cups shredded napa cabbage

2 medium green bell peppers, thinly sliced

2 medium zucchini, cut into ¼-inch-thick slices

¼ cup creamy peanut butter

½ teaspoon curry powder

½ teaspoon cayenne pepper

4 cups hot cooked white rice

½ cup chopped roasted peanuts

1. In a large Dutch oven, heat the vegetable oil over medium-high heat until hot.

2. Add the venison, and cook, turning, until browned on all sides, for 5 to 7 minutes. Transfer to a plate.

3. Add the onions and celery to the pot; cook until lightly golden, for 6 to 8 minutes.

4. Add the garlic and cook, stirring, for 2 minutes.

5. Add the stock and, using a wooden spoon, scrape up any browned bits from the bottom of the pot.

6. Stir in the bouillon granules and return the venison and any accumulated juices to the pot; bring to a boil.

7. Reduce the heat to low. Cover, and simmer for 45 minutes.

8. Stir in the cabbage, bell peppers, and zucchini; simmer until the vegetables are tender, for 20 minutes.

9. Stir in the peanut butter, curry powder, and cayenne pepper; cook until incorporated, for 2 minutes. Remove from the heat.

10. Serve the stew over the rice and garnish with the peanuts.

Braised Smoked Venison Shanks

PREP TIME: 20 MINUTES / **COOK TIME:** 4 HOURS 40 MINUTES / **YIELD:** 2 SERVINGS

OTHER GAME YOU CAN USE: ELK

This dish is worth the time it takes to cook. The shank is made up of active muscles with a lot of connective tissues. When cooked properly, those tissues break down and add great richness to the dish. This dish is delicious served with mashed potatoes drizzled with the sauce.

2 venison shanks

2 teaspoons kosher salt

1 teaspoon freshly ground black pepper

2 tablespoons vegetable oil

1 cup white wine

2 heads garlic, halved

3 cups Venison Stock (page 264) or beef broth, plus more as needed

3 sprigs rosemary

1 teaspoon red pepper flakes

Small pinch dried thyme

1. Using a small paring knife, cut slits into the shanks all over. Season with the salt and pepper.

2. Set an electric smoker to 250°F.

3. Put the shanks in the smoker and smoke for 1½ hours. Remove from the smoker.

4. Preheat the oven to 350°F.

5. In a large, cast-iron skillet, heat the vegetable oil over medium-high heat until hot.

6. Add the shanks and cook until browned on all sides, for about 10 minutes. Transfer to a plate.

7. Add the wine and, using a wooden spoon, scrape up any browned bits from the bottom of the pan. Simmer until the wine is reduced by half, for 6 to 8 minutes.

8. Add the garlic, stock, rosemary, red pepper flakes, thyme, and shanks with any accumulated juices.

9. Put the skillet in the oven and braise, turning the shanks every 30 minutes, until the meat is falling off the bone, for 3 hours. If the liquid reduces before the shanks are done, add more stock as needed. Remove from the oven and serve.

Stuffed Backstrap

PREP TIME: 20 MINUTES / **COOK TIME:** 1 HOUR 5 MINUTES / **YIELD:** 8 TO 10 SERVINGS
OTHER GAME YOU CAN USE: ELK, MOOSE

This is an easy and beautiful way to serve a backstrap. If you don't want to roast it, feel free to grill it. Just follow the recipe and grill at 300°F to 350°F, for the same amount of time.

1 (3- to 5-pound) venison backstrap, trimmed of silverskin

1 pound bacon, chopped

2 cups chopped cremini mushrooms

1 onion, finely diced

2 cloves garlic, minced

8 ounces cream cheese

1 cup panko bread crumbs

¼ cup chopped scallions, green and white parts

1. Preheat the oven to 325°F.

2. Butterfly the backstrap lengthwise, making sure not to cut all the way through so that it is still in one piece and opens like a book.

3. In a large, cast-iron skillet, cook the bacon, mushrooms, and onion over medium-high heat until the onion is translucent and the bacon is cooked, for about 5 minutes.

4. Add the garlic and cook for 2 minutes. Remove from the heat. Let cool for about 10 minutes.

5. Stir in the cream cheese, bread crumbs, and scallions.

6. Spread the cheese mixture evenly over the open backstrap to 2 inches from the edge.

7. Roll up the backstrap jelly-roll-style, using 5 pieces of butcher's twine to secure it; 2 from end to end and 3 across. Place on a rack set in a roasting pan.

8. Put the roasting pan in the oven and bake until the internal temperature (of the meat, not the filling) reaches 165°F, for 30 to 45 minutes. Remove from the oven. Transfer to a cutting board. Let rest for 10 minutes, then remove the twine, slice, and serve.

GAME TIP: If you are cooking an elk backstrap, increase the cooking time to 40 to 50 minutes. For a moose backstrap, increase it to 45 to 55 minutes.

Chicken-Fried Venison with Shiitake Gravy

PREP TIME: 30 MINUTES / **COOK TIME:** 30 MINUTES / **YIELD:** 6 SERVINGS

OTHER GAME YOU CAN USE: ELK, MOOSE, BEAR

This dish is crunchy, creamy, and oh-so-savory all at once. If you want to change things up, try adding waffles to the mix. Oh yeah!

FOR THE STEAKS:

4 cups peanut oil or vegetable oil

6 (6- to 8-ounce) boneless
    venison steaks

2 teaspoons kosher salt, plus
    more to taste

1 cup all-purpose flour

1 teaspoon ground nutmeg

½ teaspoon garlic powder

½ teaspoon onion powder

½ teaspoon freshly ground black
    pepper, plus more to taste

½ teaspoon paprika

1 large egg

½ cup heavy cream

FOR THE GRAVY:

4 tablespoons (½ stick) unsalted
    butter, divided

1 cup chopped shiitake
    mushrooms

3 shallots, minced

⅓ cup all-purpose flour

3 to 4 cups whole milk

½ teaspoon kosher salt

¼ teaspoon freshly ground
    black pepper

1. **To make the steaks:** In a large Dutch oven, heat the peanut oil over medium-high heat to 300°F to 325°F.

2. Meanwhile, using a meat tenderizer or mallet, pound the steaks evenly until ½ to ¼ inch thick. Season both sides with the salt. Set a wire rack over a sheet pan.

3. In a medium bowl, whisk together the flour, nutmeg, garlic powder, onion powder, pepper, and paprika. In another medium bowl, whisk together the egg and cream.

4. Dredge 1 steak at a time in the flour mixture, then place in the egg mixture to coat. Return to the flour mixture and dredge again. Transfer to a platter. Once the oil has come to temperature, fry 2 steaks at a time until golden brown, for 2 or 3 minutes per side. Transfer to the prepared wire rack. Season with salt and pepper. Turn off the heat.

5. **To make the gravy:** In a medium saucepan, melt 2 tablespoons of butter over medium-high heat.

6. Add the mushrooms and shallots; cook, stirring, until the mushrooms are golden, for 4 or 5 minutes. Add the remaining 2 tablespoons of butter and cook until melted.

7. Sprinkle in the flour and cook, stirring constantly, for 2 minutes.

8. Pour in 3 cups of milk, whisking constantly. If the gravy is too thick, add more milk and whisk until it has the desired consistency. Stir in the salt and pepper. Remove from the heat.

9. Serve the gravy on top of the chicken-fried venison steaks.

GAME TIP: If you are preparing this dish with bigger game such as elk, moose, or bear, increase the cooking time to 3 or 4 minutes per side.

Porcini-Crusted Venison Rack

PREP TIME: 10 MINUTES / **COOK TIME:** 40 MINUTES / **YIELD:** 4 TO 6 SERVINGS
OTHER GAME YOU CAN USE: ELK, MOOSE

This dish is simple to make, but it's a showstopper. The earthy flavors of wild game and mushrooms pair beautifully. Serve it with a hearty red wine like merlot or cabernet franc.

2 ounces dried porcini mushrooms, rehydrated in hot water, drained, and minced

3 tablespoons finely grated Parmesan cheese

2 tablespoons unsalted butter, softened

1 tablespoon Dijon mustard

2 teaspoons minced garlic

2 teaspoons fresh thyme leaves, chopped

1 (2½-pound) venison rack, at room temperature, trimmed of fat and membranes

1. Preheat the oven to 425°F.

2. In a small bowl, stir together the mushrooms, Parmesan cheese, butter, mustard, garlic, and thyme to form a paste.

3. Apply the paste over the meat (not the bones) in an even layer. Transfer to a roasting pan.

4. Roast until the internal temperature of the meat reaches 145°F for medium-rare, for 30 to 40 minutes. If the rack is browning too quickly, cover it with aluminum foil. Remove from the oven. Let rest for 15 to 20 minutes. Slice into individual portions and serve.

PRO TIP: For an elegant presentation, you can French the rack before roasting it. Using a paring knife, carve away the meat and connective tissue between the first few inches of the long bones.

Venison Wellington Pie

PREP TIME: 45 MINUTES / **COOK TIME:** 3 HOURS / **YIELD:** 4 TO 6 SERVINGS
OTHER GAME YOU CAN USE: ELK, MOOSE, BEAR, WILD BOAR

This dish has all the flavors of beef Wellington but in a pie and made with venison. Less expense, less fuss, and who doesn't love a pie?

Nonstick cooking spray, for
  greasing
2 strips bacon, diced
2 pounds venison stew meat, cut
  into 2-inch cubes
8 ounces cremini
  mushrooms, cubes
8 ounces porcini mushrooms,
  sliced (or use more cremini)
8 tablespoons (1 stick)
  unsalted butter
½ cup all-purpose flour
2 cups Venison Stock (page 264)
  or beef broth
1 cup dry red wine
1 tablespoon freshly squeezed
  lemon juice
2 teaspoons Dijon mustard
2 teaspoons Worcestershire sauce
2 teaspoons chopped fresh thyme
1 (12- to 14.4-ounce) bag frozen
  pearl onions
Kosher salt
Freshly ground black pepper
1 frozen puff pastry sheet, thawed
1 large egg, beaten
3 tablespoons chopped
  fresh parsley

1. Set a rack in the middle position in the oven. Preheat the oven to 325°F. Grease an 8-inch square baking dish with nonstick cooking spray.

2. In a large Dutch oven, cook the bacon over medium-high heat until just crispy, for about 5 minutes. Using a slotted spoon, transfer to a paper towel.

3. Add one-third of the venison and cook until golden brown on all sides, for 4 to 6 minutes. Transfer to a plate. Repeat with the remaining venison.

4. Add the cremini mushrooms and porcini mushrooms to the pot; cook, stirring, until golden brown, for 6 to 8 minutes. Transfer to the plate with the venison.

5. Add the butter and melt it. Whisk in the flour and cook, stirring constantly, for 2 minutes.

6. Whisk in the stock and wine; bring to a simmer.

7. Add the lemon juice, mustard, Worcestershire sauce, thyme, onions, bacon, and venison and mushrooms with any accumulated juices. Season with salt and pepper. Stir to combine.

8. Put the pot in the oven and bake for 2 hours. Remove from the oven.

9. Increase the oven temperature to 400°F. Carefully transfer the stew to the prepared baking dish.

10. Gently roll out the puff pastry to a 9-inch square.

11. Brush the top of the pastry and the top ½ inch of the baking dish with the egg wash. Gently press the pastry over the top of the dish. Using a paring knife, cut 3 small slits in the pastry to vent.

12. Put the baking dish in the oven and bake until the pastry is golden brown and the crust is fully cooked, 20 to 25 minutes. Remove from the oven.

13. Serve the pie immediately, garnished with the parsley.

Venison Tamales

PREP TIME: 1 HOUR 30 MINUTES / **COOK TIME:** 50 MINUTES, PLUS 9 HOURS ON LOW
YIELD: 28 TO 30 SERVINGS
OTHER GAME YOU CAN USE: ELK, MOOSE

Tamales are a Christmas tradition in my house. My mom is Mexican, and every year our Christmas morning was filled with tamales of all varieties. Now I make them with my daughter, or we throw a tamale party. This recipe will yield extra meat you can use in quesadillas, tacos, or enchiladas! Serve the tamales with enchilada sauce and sour cream.

FOR THE FILLING:

1 (3- to 4-pound) venison roast

1 large onion, coarsely chopped

4 large cloves garlic, chopped

2 (28-ounce) cans green enchilada sauce, plus more for serving

2 cups chicken broth

1 teaspoon kosher salt

1 teaspoon freshly ground black pepper

FOR THE DOUGH:

3½ cups masa harina, plus more as needed

1⅓ cups rendered wild boar fat (see page 4)

1½ teaspoons kosher salt

1½ teaspoons baking powder

2½ cups chicken broth

FOR ASSEMBLING THE TAMALES:

1 (8-ounce) package dried corn husks

12 ounces Cheddar-Jack cheese, shredded

Sour cream, for serving

1. **To make the filling:** In a slow cooker, combine the roast, onion, garlic, enchilada sauce, broth, salt, and pepper; cook on low for 9 hours.

2. Turn off the slow cooker. Use 2 forks to shred the meat in the sauce.

3. **To make the dough:** In a stand mixer fitted with the paddle attachment, combine the masa harina, fat, salt, baking powder, and 1 cup of broth; blend on low speed until well combined. Slowly add just enough of the broth, until the dough is firm. You want a soft, pliable dough that does not stick to the side of the bowl. If the dough is sticky, stop adding the broth and add 3 tablespoons of masa harina to firm it up. If the dough is firm, add more broth, about 2 tablespoons at a time.

4. **To assemble the tamales:** Place the husks in a large pot of water so they are fully submerged. Use a plate to weigh them down so they stay in the water. Let the husks soak for 30 minutes.

5. Remove the husks from the water and lightly dry using a clean towel. Put enough water in the bottom of a steamer pot or pasta pot until it reaches just below the steamer basket.

6. Place 1 husk at a time on a work surface with the narrow end closest to you. Spread ¼ cup of the dough into a 2½-by-4-inch rectangle in the center of the wide portion of the husk, leaving a 2- to 3-inch border at the sides of the husk. Spoon 1 heaping tablespoon of the filling in a strip down the center of the dough and top with scant 1½ tablespoons of cheese. Fold the long sides of the husk around the dough, bringing the dough over the filling to cover. Fold up the narrow end of the husk. Place the tamale, filled-side up, in the steamer basket. Repeat to make the remaining tamales.

7. Once the pot is filled with tamales, cover and bring to a boil over high heat.

8. Reduce the heat to medium and steam for 45 minutes, checking the water about halfway through and adding more if needed. Remove from the heat. Let sit for 10 minutes before serving.

The Ultimate Venison Chili

PREP TIME: 20 MINUTES / **COOK TIME:** 2 HOURS 30 MINUTES / **YIELD:** 10 TO 12 SERVINGS
OTHER GAME YOU CAN USE: ANY GROUND BIG GAME

I won a chili cook-off with this recipe. Yes, it's that good! It's one of those recipes that is better the next day, and even better if you double the batch and freeze for last-minute meals. The longer the flavors of the chili can mingle together, the better.

3 tablespoons olive oil or avocado oil

2 onions, diced

2 pounds ground venison

1 green bell pepper, finely diced

8 ounces Hatch chiles, finely diced, or canned diced green chiles

1 tablespoon minced jalapeño

1 poblano chile, charred and finely diced

1 (14-ounce) can diced tomatoes, preferably San Marzano

1 (8-ounce) can tomato sauce

2 tablespoons ground cumin

2 tablespoons chile molido powder or chili powder

1 teaspoon kosher salt

½ teaspoon cayenne pepper

½ teaspoon smoked paprika

2 cups Venison Stock (page 264) or beef broth

½ (15.5-ounce) can black beans, drained and rinsed

½ (15.5-ounce) can kidney beans, drained and rinsed

4 cloves garlic, minced

Kosher salt

Freshly ground black pepper

Shredded Cheddar cheese, sour cream, diced avocado, and sliced scallions, for serving

1. In a large Dutch oven, heat the olive oil over medium-high heat.

2. Add the onions and cook until golden brown, for about 5 minutes.

3. Add the venison and cook, stirring with a wooden spoon to break into small pieces, until browned and no longer pink, for about 5 minutes.

4. Add the bell pepper, Hatch chiles, jalapeño, and poblano chile; cook, stirring occasionally, for about 10 minutes.

5. Stir in the tomatoes with their juices, tomato sauce, cumin, chile molido powder, salt, cayenne pepper, and paprika; cook for 10 minutes.

6. Add the stock, black beans, kidney beans, and garlic; bring to a simmer.

7. Reduce the heat to low. Cover, and simmer for 2 hours. Remove from the heat. Taste for salt and pepper.

8. To serve, top a bowl of chili with the cheese, sour cream, avocado, and scallions.

PRO TIP: If you are in a hurry, simmer the chili in step 7 for just 1 hour.

Roman-Style Venison and Wild Boar Meatballs

PREP TIME: 25 MINUTES / **COOK TIME:** 1 HOUR 20 MINUTES / **YIELD:** 6 TO 8 SERVINGS
OTHER GAME YOU CAN USE: ANY GROUND, WILD GAME MEAT

I am very particular with meatballs; they must be completely tender, they must be big enough to require a fork, fresh herbs are a must, and they must be topped with Parmesan. Through my years of making meatballs I finally came up with my perfect version, inspired by some I had in Rome. I added wild boar because venison is so lean that it needs some fat to help make the meatballs tender. Serve with creamy polenta and you have a to-die-for meal.

½ cup bread crumbs

½ cup milk

1 pound ground venison

1 pound ground wild boar or pork

4 ounces thick-cut bacon, finely diced

2 large eggs, beaten

½ cup grated Parmesan cheese

3 tablespoons chopped fresh basil

2 tablespoons chopped fresh flat-leaf parsley

2 tablespoons chopped garlic

2 teaspoons minced fresh oregano

2 teaspoons kosher salt, plus more to taste

1 teaspoon freshly ground black pepper, plus more to taste

12 ounces mozzarella cheese, cut into ½-inch cubes

⅓ cup olive oil

1 large yellow onion, finely diced

1 (28-ounce) can crushed tomatoes

Chopped fresh basil, for garnish

1. In a small bowl, combine the bread crumbs and milk; let sit for 10 minutes.

2. In a large bowl, combine the venison, boar, bacon, eggs, Parmesan cheese, basil, parsley, garlic, oregano, salt, pepper, and the bread crumb mixture.

3. Scoop ¼-cup portions of the meat roll into balls with your hands.

4. Insert a piece of mozzarella cheese inside each meatball and gently close the hole. Put on a sheet pan.

5. In a large skillet, heat the olive oil over medium-high heat until hot.

6. Add half of the meatballs, and cook, turning occasionally, until browned on all sides, for about 8 minutes. Transfer to a plate. Repeat with the remaining meatballs.

7. Add the onion to the same skillet and cook until translucent and slightly brown, for 8 to 10 minutes.

8. Stir in the tomatoes with their juices. Season with salt and pepper. Bring to a simmer.

9. Reduce the heat to medium-low. Cover and simmer for 20 minutes.

10. Add the meatballs, cover, and simmer until cooked through, for about 30 minutes. Remove from the heat.

11. Serve the meatballs immediately, garnished with basil.

Venison Sausage–Stuffed Shells

PREP TIME: 50 MINUTES / **COOK TIME:** 1 HOUR 25 MINUTES / **YIELD:** 8 SERVINGS
OTHER GAME YOU CAN USE: ANY GROUND WILD GAME MEAT

Stuffed shells are the perfect weeknight dinner. All that cheesy goodness tucked inside pasta shells, then topped with marinara and more cheese; what's not to love? If you don't have venison sausage, any Italian sausage will do just fine.

Nonstick cooking spray, for greasing

2 teaspoons kosher salt, plus more for cooking the pasta

1 (16-ounce) package jumbo pasta shells

2 tablespoons olive oil

1 cup chopped onion

4 cloves garlic, chopped

1 pound Italian-Inspired Venison and Pork Sausage (page 32), without casings

3 cups spinach

1 (15-ounce) container ricotta cheese

2 cups shredded mozzarella cheese, divided

1½ cups grated Parmesan cheese, divided, plus more for serving

2 large eggs, beaten

1 tablespoon dried oregano

1 teaspoon freshly ground black pepper

1 (16-ounce) jar marinara sauce

Fresh basil leaves, cut into thin ribbons, for garnish

1. Preheat the oven to 350°F. Grease a 9-by-13-inch baking dish with nonstick cooking spray. Line a sheet pan with paper towels.

2. Bring a large pot of salted water to a boil over high heat. Cook the pasta as the package directs. Remove from the heat. Drain and submerge in a bowl of ice water to stop the cooking. Drain and arrange in a single layer on the prepared sheet pan.

3. In a large sauté pan, heat the olive oil over medium-high heat until hot.

4. Add the onion and cook until softened, for about 5 minutes.

5. Add the garlic and cook for 2 minutes.

6. Add the sausage and cook, stirring, until cooked through, for 8 to 10 minutes.

7. Stir in the spinach and cook until wilted, for 3 minutes. Remove from the heat. Let cool.

8. While the sausage mixture cools, in a medium bowl, stir together the ricotta cheese, 1 cup of mozzarella cheese, 1 cup of Parmesan cheese, the eggs, oregano, salt, and pepper until well combined. Stir in the cooled sausage mixture.

9. Spread half of the marinara sauce over the bottom of the prepared baking dish. Using a spoon, fill the pasta shells with the sausage-ricotta mixture. Set the filled shells on top of the sauce in the baking dish. Top the shells with the remaining marinara sauce and sprinkle with the remaining 1 cup of mozzarella cheese and ½ cup of Parmesan cheese.

10. Cover the baking dish with aluminum foil. Put the baking dish in the oven and bake until the shells are heated through, for 20 to 25 minutes. Remove the foil and bake for 10 minutes. Remove from the oven.

11. Garnish the shells with basil and extra Parmesan cheese if desired. Serve immediately.

PRO TIP: Double the recipe and freeze an extra batch to cook.

Italian-Inspired Venison and Pork Sausage

PREP TIME: 20 MINUTES, LONGER IF USING CASINGS / **YIELD:** 10 POUNDS
OTHER GAME YOU CAN USE: ANY GROUND BIG GAME MEAT

Making sausage is the perfect use for leftover trim pieces or really tough pieces that you would end up just tossing.

7 pounds chilled venison, coarsely ground (see page 6)

3 pounds chilled pork butt, finely ground

½ cup red-wine vinegar

¼ cup kosher salt

3 tablespoons paprika

2 tablespoons freshly ground black pepper

2 tablespoons onion powder

2 tablespoons fennel seeds

1 tablespoon dried marjoram

2 tablespoons chopped fresh rosemary

1 tablespoon chopped fresh thyme

2 teaspoons red pepper flakes

2 teaspoons cayenne pepper

10 cloves garlic, minced

Hog casings, for stuffing (optional)

1. In a large bowl, combine the venison, pork, and vinegar, using your hands to mix well.

2. To make the spice mixture, in a small bowl, whisk together the salt, paprika, black pepper, onion powder, fennel seeds, marjoram, rosemary, thyme, red pepper flakes, and cayenne pepper.

3. Stir in the garlic. Sprinkle the spice mixture over the meat mixture and use your hands to fully combine.

4. Stuff the sausage mixture into hog casings (if using; see page 6) or shape into patties.

STORAGE: Refrigerate for up to 6 days or vacuum-seal in 1-pound portions and freeze for up to 3 months.

Teriyaki Venison Jerky

PREP TIME: 15 MINUTES, PLUS 24 TO 48 HOURS TO MARINATE / **COOK TIME:** 4 HOURS

YIELD: 50 TO 60 PIECES

OTHER GAME YOU CAN USE: ELK, MOOSE

When in doubt, make jerky, right? Here's the recipe that I use most in my kitchen.

1 cup soy sauce

½ cup packed dark brown sugar

¼ cup rice vinegar

4 cloves garlic, sliced

1 tablespoon grated fresh ginger

1 tablespoon sesame oil

1 tablespoon sesame seeds

1 teaspoon freshly ground
black pepper

¼ teaspoon Instacure 2
(see page 5)

1 (2- to 3-pound) venison eye of
round, thinly sliced against
the grain

1. In a large bowl, whisk together the soy sauce, brown sugar, vinegar, garlic, ginger, sesame oil, sesame seeds, pepper, and Instacure.

2. Add the venison and toss to fully coat. Cover and refrigerate for 24 to 48 hours.

3. Set the dehydrator to 160°F.

4. Lightly shake off any excess liquid and place the venison slices on the dehydrator trays so they do not touch. Dehydrate for 2 hours.

5. Reduce the temperature to 145°F. Continue to dehydrate for about another 2 hours. Your finished jerky should be pliable like leather and should fray and crack slightly at the point at which you bend it. Remove from the dehydrator.

STORAGE: Refrigerate in an airtight container for up to 2 months or store at room temperature for up to 1 month.

Venison Biltong

PREP TIME: 30 MINUTES, PLUS 12 HOURS TO CURE / **COOK TIME:** 12 HOURS / **YIELD:** 40 TO 50 PIECES

OTHER GAME YOU CAN USE: ANY BIG GAME

I was in Namibia when I ate this jerky for the very first time. If you want to enjoy it as it's traditionally eaten, dip it first in softened butter before popping it in your mouth—it's absolutely delicious.

3 cups apple cider vinegar

¼ cup kosher salt

1½ tablespoons packed light or dark brown sugar

1 tablespoon garlic powder

1 tablespoon freshly ground black pepper

5½ pounds venison backstrap

¼ cup coriander seeds

1. In a small saucepan, whisk together the vinegar, salt, brown sugar, garlic powder, and pepper over medium-high heat. Bring to a low boil. Remove from the heat. Let cool to room temperature.

2. Cut the backstrap into strips about ¾ inch wide and 1¼ inches thick.

3. Heat a small skillet over medium-high heat until hot.

4. Add the coriander seeds and toast until slightly golden, for about 2 minutes. Remove from the heat. Crush the seeds in a mortar and pestle or with a cast-iron pan.

5. Sprinkle the bottom of a glass baking dish with some of the crushed coriander.

6. Arrange a layer of venison strips evenly on top. Then sprinkle with a layer of coriander. Repeat this process until all the venison and coriander are used. Cover and refrigerate for 12 hours. Turn and rub the venison slices with the salt mixture a couple of times throughout the curing process.

7. Set the dehydrator to 155°F.

8. Place the venison slices on the dehydrator trays so they do not touch. Dehydrate for 12 hours. Your finished jerky should be pliable like leather and should fray and crack slightly at the point at which you bend it. Remove from the dehydrator.

STORING: Refrigerate in an airtight container for up to 2 months or store at room temperature for up to 1 month.

ELK

Slow-Cooker Elk French Dip Sliders

PREP TIME: 20 MINUTES / **COOK TIME:** 30 MINUTES, PLUS 9 HOURS ON LOW / **YIELD:** 12 SERVINGS
OTHER GAME YOU CAN USE: VENISON

If you are having a party and want something fantastic to serve, these sliders are for you. They are made in the slow cooker and finished in the oven. If you want to go all out, make a large batch of caramelized onions and use them in place of the store-bought fried onions. If you have any extra meat, refrigerate in a container with the jus poured over the meat for up to 4 days.

1 (3-pound) elk rump roast

1 teaspoon kosher salt

½ teaspoon freshly ground
black pepper

2 large onions, sliced

2 cups beef broth or Venison
Stock (page 264)

2 tablespoons Worcestershire
sauce

1 bay leaf

1 clove garlic, minced

¼ teaspoon dried thyme

1 tablespoon sesame seeds

Nonstick cooking spray, for
greasing

1 (12-roll) package Hawaiian rolls

12 provolone cheese slices

1½ cups French fried onions

2 tablespoons unsalted butter

¾ teaspoon minced garlic

½ teaspoon onion powder

1. Season the roast with the salt and pepper. Place in a slow cooker.

2. Add the onions, broth, Worcestershire sauce, bay leaf, garlic, thyme, and sesame seeds. Cook on low for 9 hours.

3. Turn off the slow cooker. Transfer the roast to a clean platter and shred the meat using 2 forks.

4. Strain the cooking liquid to remove the solids. Pour it into a medium saucepan and cook over medium heat to reduce, for 20 minutes. Remove from the heat.

5. Meanwhile, preheat the oven to 350°F. Grease a 9-by-13-inch baking dish with nonstick cooking spray.

6. Place the bottoms of the rolls in the prepared baking dish and top with shredded elk meat. Top the meat with 1 slice of provolone cheese and 2 tablespoons of French fried onions. Place the roll tops over the onions.

7. In a small saucepan, combine the butter, garlic, and onion powder. Heat over medium-low heat until the butter has melted. Remove from the heat.

8. Brush the tops of the rolls with the butter mixture.

9. Put the baking dish in the oven and bake until the cheese melts, for 15 to 20 minutes. Remove from the oven.

10. Divide the sandwiches among individual plates and serve with the reduced jus.

Pan-Seared Elk Steaks with Blueberry-Poblano Sauce

PREP TIME: 20 MINUTES / **COOK TIME:** 20 MINUTES / **YIELD:** 2 SERVINGS

OTHER GAME YOU CAN USE: VENISON

This recipe is an ode to New Mexico, where the elk hunting is stunning and the food is spicy. I love this recipe for its blend of New Mexico culture and traditions. And the sauce is so good, you might want to make a large batch and can a few jars for friends.

FOR THE ELK STEAKS:

2 (6- to 8-ounce) elk steaks

2 teaspoons kosher salt

2 teaspoons freshly ground
   black pepper

4 tablespoons (½ stick)
   unsalted butter

2 tablespoons olive oil

3 cloves garlic, crushed

3 sprigs thyme

1 sprig rosemary

FOR THE SAUCE:

3 tablespoons unsalted butter

1 teaspoon minced garlic

1 cup blueberries

½ cup red wine

1 poblano chile, roasted and
   finely diced

1 teaspoon chopped fresh
   rosemary

Kosher salt

Freshly ground black pepper

1. **To make the elk steaks:** Let the steaks come to room temperature. Season both sides with the salt and pepper.

2. In a large, cast-iron skillet, heat the butter and olive oil over medium-high heat until hot.

3. Add the elk steaks, garlic, thyme, and rosemary. Using a large spoon, baste the steaks with the hot butter. Cook, flipping once, until the internal temperature of the steaks reaches 135°F, for about 8 minutes. Remove from the heat. Transfer to a clean plate, cover with aluminum foil, and let rest.

4. **To make the sauce:** In a medium sauté pan, cook the butter and garlic over medium-high heat until the butter has melted.

5. Add the blueberries and cook until they burst, for about 5 minutes. Using the back of a wooden spoon, gently crush the blueberries.

6. Add the wine, poblano chile, and rosemary; cook for 5 minutes. Season with salt and pepper if needed. Remove from the heat.

7. Serve the steaks topped with the sauce.

Sourdough and Sweet Potato Elk Stuffing

PREP TIME: 20 MINUTES / **COOK TIME:** 50 MINUTES / **YIELD:** 12 SERVINGS

OTHER GAME YOU CAN USE: ANY BIG GAME GROUND MEAT

Your go-to Thanksgiving stuffing is right here. This recipe has some ingredients that you may not think are worthy of stuffing, but when you try it, you will realize you should have been putting sweet potatoes in stuffing years ago. The sweet potatoes and elk are quite the dynamic duo. With the sour flavor from the sourdough and the sweetness from the cranberries, this stuffing is everything and more.

Nonstick cooking spray, for greasing

¼ cup olive oil

3 stalks celery, finely diced

2 large sweet potatoes, finely diced

2 carrots, finely diced

1 onion, finely diced

3 cloves garlic, minced

1½ teaspoons kosher salt

1 teaspoon freshly ground black pepper

12 ounces ground elk

4 ounces pork breakfast sausage or venison sausage

1 tablespoon chopped fresh rosemary leaves

1 tablespoon fennel seeds

1 teaspoon cayenne pepper

1 teaspoon ground coriander

4 cups cubed sourdough bread

1 cup dried cranberries

2 cups Venison Stock (page 264) or beef broth

1. Preheat the oven to 350°F. Grease a 9-by-13-inch baking dish with nonstick cooking spray.

2. In a large, cast-iron skillet, heat the olive oil over medium-high heat.

3. Add the celery, sweet potatoes, carrots, onion, garlic, salt, and pepper. Cook, stirring, until the onion is translucent and the sweet potatoes are cooked halfway through, for 5 to 7 minutes.

4. Add the elk and sausage. Cook, stirring with a wooden spoon to break meat into small pieces, until browned and no longer pink, for about 5 minutes.

5. Add the rosemary, fennel seeds, cayenne pepper, and coriander. Cook, stirring occasionally, for 5 minutes. Remove from the heat.

6. Stir in the bread, dried cranberries, and stock; toss to combine well. Evenly spread the mixture into the prepared baking dish.

7. Put the baking dish in the oven and bake until the stuffing is heated through and golden brown, for 25 to 30 minutes. Remove from the oven. Let cool for 5 minutes before serving.

Korean-Style BBQ Elk Jerky

PREP TIME: 10 MINUTES, PLUS 24 HOURS TO MARINATE / **COOK TIME:** 6 TO 8 HOURS
YIELD: 40 TO 50 PIECES
OTHER GAME YOU CAN USE: VENISON, MOOSE

This jerky blends all the elements that make Korean BBQ so craveable. It's so good, you will have to use all your hiding skills to keep it from your friends and family. Try this recipe with wild boar as well; it's amazing.

1 (3-pound) boneless elk roast, semi-frozen (see page 5)

½ cup soy sauce

¼ cup sesame oil

3 tablespoons packed light or dark brown sugar

2 tablespoons Worcestershire sauce

1 tablespoon gochujang or sriracha

1 tablespoon onion powder

1 tablespoon garlic powder

1 teaspoon liquid smoke

1. Cut the roast into ⅛-inch-thick slices, and put them inside a large zip-top bag.

2. In a medium bowl, whisk together the soy sauce, sesame oil, brown sugar, Worcestershire sauce, gochujang, onion powder, garlic powder, and liquid smoke to combine well. Pour over the roast and toss to fully coat. Seal and refrigerate for 24 hours.

3. Set the dehydrator to 155°F.

4. Lightly shake off any excess liquid and place the elk slices on the dehydrator trays so they do not touch. Dehydrate for 6 to 8 hours. Your finished jerky should be pliable like leather and should fray and crack slightly at the point at which you bend it. Remove from the dehydrator.

STORAGE: Refrigerate in an airtight container for up to 2 months or at room temperature for up to 1 month.

Tandoori-Spiced Elk Jerky

PREP TIME: 10 MINUTES, PLUS 24 HOURS TO MARINATE / **COOK TIME:** 2 TO 4 HOURS
YIELD: 30 TO 40 PIECES
OTHER GAME YOU CAN USE: ANY BIG GAME MEAT

Jerky may not be an Indian dish, but Indian spices pair really well with wild game jerky. This jerky dehydrates for a much shorter time than other recipes because the yogurt marinade dries more quickly.

2 pounds elk flank steak, semi-frozen (see page 5)

1 cup whole-milk yogurt

½ cup apple cider vinegar

2 tablespoons Worcestershire sauce

¼ cup Indian-Style Spice Rub (page 248)

2 tablespoons packed light or dark brown sugar

1. Cut the steak against the grain into ⅛-inch-thick strips.

2. In a large bowl, combine the yogurt, vinegar, Worcestershire sauce, spice rub, and brown sugar; whisk to combine.

3. Add the elk strips and mix well to fully coat. Put inside a large zip-top bag, seal, and refrigerate for 24 hours.

4. Set the dehydrator to 145°F to 155°F.

5. Place the elk slices on the dehydrator trays so they do not touch. Dehydrate for 2 to 4 hours. Your finished jerky should be pliable like leather and should fray and crack slightly at the point at which you bend it. Remove from the dehydrator.

STORAGE: Refrigerate in an airtight container for up to 2 months or store at room temperature for up to 1 month.

MOOSE

Moose Crying-Tiger Salad

PREP TIME: 20 MINUTES / **COOK TIME:** 10 MINUTES / **YIELD:** 6 SERVINGS

OTHER GAME YOU CAN USE: VENISON, ELK

The most requested salad in my household is this one. This salad has the cooling effects of mint to balance the heat and is jam-packed with additional herbs that make everything come together perfectly. If I could only eat one salad, it would be this one, and I have a feeling you will be saying the same thing.

1 (1½-pound) moose steak

Kosher salt

Freshly ground black pepper

2 tablespoons avocado oil

5 cups mixed greens

4 scallions, green and white parts, chopped

1 cucumber, peeled and cut into ribbons

1 bird's eye (Thai) chile, thinly sliced

¼ cup chopped fresh mint

¼ cup chopped fresh Italian parsley

¼ cup chopped fresh cilantro

¼ cup chopped fresh basil

½ cup soy sauce

2 tablespoons freshly squeezed lime juice

2 tablespoons rice vinegar

1 tablespoon sambal oelek or 1 teaspoon red pepper flakes

1 tablespoon honey

1. Using a clean towel, pat the steak dry. Season with salt and pepper.

2. In a cast-iron skillet, heat the avocado oil over medium-high heat until hot.

3. Add the steak and cook, flipping once, until browned on both sides, for 6 to 8 minutes. Remove from the heat. Transfer to a clean plate.

4. In a large salad bowl, combine the mixed greens, scallions, cucumber, chile, mint, parsley, cilantro, and basil. Toss well to combine.

5. To make the dressing, in a small bowl, whisk together the soy sauce, lime juice, vinegar, sambal oelek, and honey to combine.

6. Cut the steaks against the grain into ¼-inch-thick slices. Arrange over the greens and drizzle with the dressing. Serve immediately.

Classic Moose Meatloaf

PREP TIME: 20 MINUTES / **COOK TIME:** 55 MINUTES / **YIELD:** 6 TO 8 SERVINGS

OTHER GAME YOU CAN USE: ANY BIG GAME GROUND MEAT

Everyone needs a delicious meatloaf recipe in their life, and this one checks all the meatloaf perfection boxes. I find that it works exceptionally well with moose meat, because moose has a bit more fat, which makes a tender and juicy meatloaf. Serve this with a side of garlic mashed potatoes and roasted asparagus and you have yourself a winner, my friend!

Nonstick cooking spray, for greasing

1 pound ground moose

1 cup bread crumbs

½ cup diced onion

½ cup whole milk

1 large egg, beaten

½ cup grated Parmesan cheese

1 tablespoon tomato paste

1 tablespoon minced garlic

1 tablespoon Worcestershire sauce

1 teaspoon chopped fresh parsley

1 teaspoon kosher salt

¼ teaspoon freshly ground black pepper

½ cup tomato sauce

2 tablespoons packed light or dark brown sugar

1 tablespoon red-wine vinegar

1. Preheat the oven to 350°F. Grease a 9-inch loaf pan with nonstick cooking spray.

2. In a large bowl, combine the moose, bread crumbs, onion, milk, egg, Parmesan cheese, tomato paste, garlic, Worcestershire sauce, parsley, salt, and pepper, using your hands to mix well. Transfer to the prepared pan and pat down for an even layer.

3. In a small bowl, stir together the tomato sauce, brown sugar, and vinegar. Spread evenly over the top of the meatloaf.

4. Put the loaf pan in the oven and bake until the internal temperature of the meatloaf reaches 160°F, for 55 minutes. Remove from the oven. Let rest for 10 minutes before serving.

Moose Baked Ziti

PREP TIME: 30 MINUTES / **COOK TIME:** 50 MINUTES / **YIELD:** 12 SERVINGS
OTHER GAME YOU CAN USE: ANY BIG GAME GROUND MEAT

If cozy were a pasta dish, it would be a baked ziti. It's meaty, cheesy, saucy, and filled with pasta. The great thing about this dish is you can use whatever ground meat you have in the freezer.

Nonstick cooking spray, for greasing

4 tablespoons olive oil, divided, plus more for drizzling

1 onion, finely diced

1 pound ground moose

1½ teaspoons kosher salt, divided, plus more for cooking the ziti

1 teaspoon freshly ground black pepper, divided

4 cups marinara sauce

2½ cups ricotta cheese

3 cloves garlic, minced

1 tablespoon grated lemon zest

1 teaspoon dried oregano

¼ teaspoon red pepper flakes

1 pound ziti

1 pound fresh spinach

1½ cups mozzarella cheese

½ cup grated Parmesan cheese

3 tablespoons chopped fresh basil

1. Preheat the oven to 425°F. Grease a 9-by-13-inch baking dish with nonstick cooking spray.

2. In a medium cast-iron skillet, heat 2 tablespoons of olive oil over medium-high heat. Add the onion and cook, stirring, until translucent, for about 4 minutes.

3. Add the moose, ½ teaspoon of salt, and ½ teaspoon of pepper. Cook, stirring, using a wooden spoon to break up the meat, until cooked and no longer pink, for 8 to 10 minutes. Add the marinara sauce and stir to combine. Remove from the heat.

4. In a medium bowl, combine the ricotta cheese, garlic, lemon zest, oregano, red pepper flakes, and remaining 1 teaspoon of salt and ½ teaspoon of pepper.

5. Bring a large pot of salted water to a boil over high heat. Cook the ziti as the package directs until al dente; drain. Set aside.

6. Return the pot to the stove over medium-high heat. Pour in the remaining 2 tablespoons of olive oil and add the spinach. Cook, stirring, until just wilted, for 2 to 3 minutes. Add the ziti and meat marinara. Stir until combined well.

7. Pour half of the pasta mixture into the prepared baking dish. Dollop the ricotta mixture over the pasta layer. Pour the remaining pasta mixture over the ricotta. Top with the mozzarella cheese and Parmesan cheese. Drizzle with a bit of olive oil.

8. Put the baking dish in the oven and bake until the cheese is golden brown, for 22 to 25 minutes. Remove from the oven.

9. Garnish the ziti with the basil and serve immediately.

Moose Bangers

PREP TIME: 1 TO 1 ½ HOURS / **COOK TIME:** 10 MINUTES / **YIELD:** 20 (6-INCH) LINKS

OTHER GAME YOU CAN USE: ANY BIG GAME GROUND MEAT

Bangers are a classic British sausage, similar to what we call breakfast sausage here in the States. Traditional bangers include rusk in the mixture, a wheat-based filler that makes them pop when they cook, which is how they got their name. I skipped the rusk for these, but otherwise tried to keep them as close to traditional as possible. If you've got duck fat on hand (not rendered), I highly recommend using it above all other fats for this.

4 pounds moose stew meat

1 pound pork fat, wild boar fat, or duck fat, cut into ½-inch pieces, then frozen

1 cup crushed ice

2 cups ice-cold water

1 cup panko bread crumbs

½ cup chopped cooked bacon

3 tablespoons kosher salt

2 tablespoons freshly ground black pepper

2 tablespoons chopped fresh sage

2 teaspoons onion powder

2 teaspoons ground ginger

1 teaspoon ground mace

1 teaspoon ground nutmeg

½ teaspoon ground allspice

Hog casings, for stuffing

1. In a large bowl, combine the moose, fat, and ice. Working quickly, grind the meat (see page 6).

2. Put the ground meat in a stand mixer fitted with a paddle attachment. Add the water, bread crumbs, bacon, salt, pepper, sage, onion powder, ginger, mace, nutmeg, and allspice. Mix on low speed until threads begin to appear in the meat, for 3 to 4 minutes. (If you take a clump of meat and pull it apart with your fingers, you will see tiny threads; this tells you the meat is ready and done mixing.)

3. Turn off the mixer. Thread your sausage through a stuffer fitted with the hog casings (see page 6).

STORAGE: Store the sausage fresh in an airtight container for up to 6 days. Or vacuum-seal the sausage and store in the freezer for up to 3 months.

Sweet-and-Spicy Moose Jerky

PREP TIME: 15 MINUTES, PLUS 24 HOURS TO MARINATE / **COOK TIME:** 10 TO 10 ½ HOURS

YIELD: 30 TO 40 PIECES

OTHER GAME YOU CAN USE: ANY BIG GAME MEAT

This jerky has a great sweet flavor followed by a delicious hint of spice.

1 cup soy sauce

¼ cup pineapple juice

2 tablespoons honey

2 tablespoons minced garlic

2 tablespoons sambal oelek or
  1 tablespoon red pepper flakes

1 tablespoon packed light or dark
  brown sugar

1 teaspoon onion powder

1 teaspoon ground cumin

½ teaspoon ground cloves

2 small shallots, minced

2 pounds lean moose meat, such
  as backstrap or tenderloin, cut
  into ⅛-inch pieces

1. In a large bowl, whisk together the soy sauce, pineapple juice, honey, garlic, sambal oelek, brown sugar, onion powder, cumin, cloves, and shallots.

2. Add the moose meat and toss until fully coated. Put inside a zip-top bag, seal, and refrigerate for 24 hours.

3. Set the dehydrator to 145°F to 155°F.

4. Lightly shake off any excess liquid and place the moose slices on the dehydrator trays so they do not touch. Dehydrate for 2 to 2½ hours.

5. Reduce the temperature to 145°F. Dehydrate for another 8 to 10 hours. Your finished jerky should be pliable like leather and should fray and crack slightly at the point at which you bend it. Remove from the dehydrator.

STORAGE: Refrigerate in an airtight container for up to 2 months or store at room temperature for up to 1 month.

CHAPTER 3

Bear and Wild Boar

Bear and boar are two of my favorite wild game meats. Bear is not only fun to hunt, but also a delicious protein. I always save as much bear fat as I possibly can because it is really wonderful to cook with.

If you have ever hunted boar, you know how grumpy they can be and that they will charge at you at a moment's notice, but that's hunting, right? Wild boar may not be the prettiest animals to hunt, but they are fantastically tasty. My favorite part of the boar is the belly—it's oh-so-fatty and scrumptious!

Bear 52
Wild Boar 60

← Wild Boar Porchetta, page 65

Bear

Bear meat is an underrated protein. It's similar to venison, with a slightly sweeter taste, though there are differences between spring bear and fall bear. The meat of fall bears is the sweetest and has more fat because they have been feasting on berries to fatten up for hibernation. Spring bear is slightly less sweet and milder in flavor, but is much more tender because of the bear's lack of activity during hibernation.

FIELD-DRESSING

This should be done as quickly as possible, since other bears will come out to feast on your harvest as well. It's also important to do so in order to reduce the weight of the bear, making it easier to pack out. Field-dressing also removes the bits that can potentially ruin the meat. Plus, it allows the meat to start cooling down, which is vital to preserving its quality.

To quickly field-dress a bear, it's best to gut it to prevent contamination and spoilage of the meat. Then skin the bear and remove the hide. Finally, break the bear down into quarters, which will be easier to transport back to camp. I highly recommend stowing game bags in your pack; they'll help keep your meat clean. Once you're at camp, get the bear meat into a cooler. Once it is fully chilled, you can break it down into small cuts.

Wild Boar

Wild boars may be seen as a pest by farmers but are a delicious source of protein, with a flavor that is like a combination of beef and pork. Boar meat has a bright-red coloring from the high iron content of a boar's diet. Boars that are feeding on nuts like acorns and peanuts will tend to have a nutty, earthy taste.

The most tender cuts on a wild boar are the tenderloin, rib back, loin, and strip loin, which also takes well to low and slow roasting. Shanks, stew meat, and short ribs are best cooked on low temperatures for long periods of time. The belly is my favorite cut, which works well for high-temperature cooking.

Just like all wild animals, wild boars are prone to parasites and diseases. The best way to ensure those parasites and diseases don't end up on your plate is to make sure not to damage the boar's digestive organs while field-dressing.

Hogs are fairly easy to field-dress. First, you want to remove the organs and gut the hog. Wild hogs can carry parasites and disease, so it is important to avoid slicing or damaging the digestive organs when gutting. I recommend wearing gloves throughout the process. After gutting the hog, remove the skin; this can be done in one shot but usually it's easier to remove it in strips. Next, remove the head and quarter the hog; this will make packing out much easier. Get back to camp as quickly as you can and get the meat into a cooler; let it fully chill before breaking it down further.

The Cuts

Butchering a bear is very similar to butchering a wild boar. The following are the prime sections and their uses:

Neck: ground meat

Ribs: rib roasts, steaks, ground meat

Chest muscles: brisket

Shoulders: chuck and shoulder roasts (cook slow and low in the oven or on the grill), ground meat, stew meat

Plate and Flank: pot roast, ground meat

Loin: steaks, chops, roasts (back half of loin can be used for stew meat, kebabs, ground meat), jerky

Hind legs: large roasts, ham, stew meat, jerky, ground meat

Side or Belly (for wild boar): bacon, spareribs

For both bear and wild boar, you can also harvest their fat. Come fall, a bear's weight will be 60 percent fat. Bear fat, however, spoils fast. To avoid this, field-dress and chill the bear as quickly as possible. For directions on rendering fat, see page 4.

BEAR

Shortcut Bear Pierogis

PREP TIME: 1 HOUR / **COOK TIME:** 35 MINUTES / **YIELD:** 24 PIEROGI
OTHER GAME YOU CAN USE: ANY BIG GAME GROUND MEAT

Made from scratch, pierogi are labor-intensive, but using wonton wrappers saves so much time. There are two ways to cook pierogi: You can boil them or panfry them. If you like a softer pierogi, then boil; if you want that crispy goodness, then panfry them. You know what, why not go a little crazy and boil half and fry half? Best of both worlds! And the bonus is pierogis freeze beautifully and will keep for up to 3 months.

2 tablespoons unsalted butter

1 small onion, finely diced

1 teaspoon sugar

1 teaspoon kosher salt, plus more for boiling the pierogi

½ teaspoon freshly ground black pepper

8 ounces ground bear meat

1 cup port wine (or any dry red wine)

1 large potato, cooked and cut into ¼-inch cubes

1 tablespoon minced garlic

1 teaspoon chopped fresh thyme

All-purpose flour, for dusting

1 (12- to 14-ounce) package wonton wrappers

2 large eggs, beaten

Sour cream, for serving

Chopped scallions, green and white parts, for serving

1. In a large, cast-iron skillet, melt the butter over medium-high heat.

2. Add the onion, sugar, salt, and pepper; cook until the onion is golden and caramelized, for about 10 minutes.

3. Add the meat and cook, stirring with a wooden spoon to break the meat into small pieces, until browned and no longer pink, for about 8 minutes.

4. Stir in the wine, potato, garlic, and thyme; cook until the wine has reduced by more than half, for 5 minutes. Remove from the heat.

5. Line a sheet pan with parchment paper and dust with flour.

6. Take a wonton wrapper and place 1 tablespoon of the filling in the middle of the wrapper.

7. Brush the edge of the wrapper lightly with the egg wash. Fold the wrapper in half, pressing the edges together and crimping them to seal. Put the pierogi on the prepared sheet pan and repeat with the remaining wonton wrappers and filling.

8. Bring a large pot of salted water to a boil over high heat.

9. Add 10 to 12 pierogi, one at a time. Cook for 2 to 3 minutes, then remove using a slotted spoon. Repeat with the remaining pierogi. (Or panfry the pierogi in a cast-iron skillet with ¼ inch of vegetable oil. Fry until both sides are golden brown and crispy, for about 4 minutes.)

10. Serve the pierogi with sour cream and scallions.

Mini Bear-Meat Pies

PREP TIME: 40 MINUTES / **COOK TIME:** 1 HOUR 5 MINUTES / **YIELD:** 12 PIES
OTHER GAME YOU CAN USE: ANY BIG GAME GROUND MEAT

These savory bites are baked in a muffin tin, which makes them great travel snacks. They also freeze well for up to 1 month, and if you have little ones in the house, you will be thankful you froze some ahead of time for a quick snack.

2 tablespoons olive oil

1 onion, finely diced

1 tablespoon minced garlic

1 cup mushrooms, finely chopped

1 pound ground bear meat

1 teaspoon kosher salt

½ teaspoon freshly ground
  black pepper

½ teaspoon ground savory

¼ teaspoon ground cloves

¼ teaspoon ground nutmeg

1 large egg

½ cup milk

All-purpose flour, for rolling the
  pie crusts

2 (14.1-ounce) frozen pie
  crusts, thawed

1. Preheat the oven to 350°F.

2. In a medium, cast-iron skillet, combine the olive oil and onion; cook over medium-high heat until the onion is translucent, for about 5 minutes. Add the garlic and cook for 1 minute. Add the mushrooms and cook until light golden brown, for 7 or 8 minutes.

3. Add the meat and cook, stirring with a wooden spoon to break it into small pieces, until browned and no longer pink, for about 5 minutes. Add the salt, pepper, savory, cloves, and nutmeg; stir to combine. Remove from the heat.

4. In a small bowl, whisk together the egg and milk.

5. Dust a work surface and rolling pin with flour. Lightly roll out 1 pie crust. Using a 5-inch round cookie cutter, cut 12 circles from the dough. Line a muffin tin with the circles.

6. Spoon the filling into the dough and brush the edges with the egg wash mixture.

7. Lightly roll out the remaining pie crust. Using a 3½-inch round cookie cutter, cut 12 circles from the dough. Place on top of the meat pies to form a crust and gently press down to seal with the bottom portion. Using a paring knife, make a small cut in the middle of each pie. Brush the pies with the egg wash mixture.

8. Put the muffin tin in the oven and bake until the pastry is golden brown, for about 45 minutes. Remove from the oven. Immediately unmold the meat pies and serve.

Slow Cooker Persian Bear Stew

PREP TIME: 25 MINUTES / **COOK TIME:** 15 MINUTES, PLUS 4 HOURS ON HIGH / **YIELD:** 6 TO 8 SERVINGS
OTHER GAME YOU CAN USE: VENISON, MOOSE, ELK

Bear meat goes really well with warm spices like cinnamon and allspice, which are common spices in Persian food. Thus, this stew is warm and delicious with a worldly flair. I happen to love Persian food, I'm a sucker for rice dishes, and the delicious herbs and spices used for cooking, I find utterly amazing. This recipe is an easy take on one of my favorite Persian dishes called Khoresh-e Ghormeh Sabzi. I have taken all the guess-work out of this dish and made it so that you can easily replicate it in a slow cooker. Which makes it even better right? If you have any left over, emphasis on the "if," this stew freezes well when vacuum-sealed.

2 tablespoons vegetable oil

1½ pounds bear stew meat

2 onions, finely diced

2 cloves garlic, minced

¼ cup tomato paste

4 cups beef broth or beef
   bone broth

1 (28-ounce) can crushed
   tomatoes

1½ cups frozen peas

1 tablespoon ground cumin

½ teaspoon ground turmeric

¼ teaspoon ground cinnamon

¼ teaspoon ground allspice

Kosher salt

Freshly ground black pepper

¼ cup freshly squeezed
   lemon juice

3 cups hot, cooked basmati rice

2 tablespoons chopped fresh mint

1 tablespoon chopped fresh basil

1. In a large, cast-iron skillet, working in batches if needed, combine the vegetable oil and bear meat. Cook over high heat, turning the meat, until browned on all sides, for 7 or 8 minutes. Remove from the heat. Transfer to a clean plate.

2. Add the onions and cook, stirring, until golden brown, for about 5 minutes.

3. Add the garlic and tomato paste. Cook for 2 minutes.

4. Return the bear meat to the skillet, stirring to coat in the onion mixture. Remove from the heat. Transfer to a slow cooker, scraping the skillet well.

5. Stir in the broth, crushed tomatoes, peas, cumin, turmeric, cinnamon, and allspice. Season with salt and pepper. Cook on high for 4 hours.

6. Turn off the slow cooker. Stir in the lemon juice.

7. Serve the stew on a bed of the basmati rice and garnish with the mint and basil.

Bear Bánh Mì Burgers

PREP TIME: 20 MINUTES / **COOK TIME:** 30 MINUTES / **YIELD:** 4 SERVINGS
OTHER GAME YOU CAN USE: ANY BIG GAME GROUND MEAT

If you have ever had a bánh mì, the Vietnamese sandwich with French influences, you know it's the most incredible sandwich around. I take it to a new level, keeping the same flavors of the traditional version, except using bear burgers, and it's purely delightful.

2 small carrots, shredded

½ cup rice vinegar

2 teaspoons sugar

3 tablespoons mayonnaise

2 tablespoons ketchup

1 teaspoon sriracha

1 clove garlic, minced

¼ teaspoon kosher salt, plus more to taste

¼ teaspoon freshly ground black pepper, plus more to taste

1½ pounds ground bear meat

1½ teaspoons curry powder

2 tablespoons vegetable oil

2 tablespoons salted butter, softened

1 baguette, quartered and split crosswise

Pickled jalapeños, for serving

Sprigs from 1 small bunch fresh cilantro, for garnish

1. Preheat the oven to 400°F.

2. To make the pickled carrots, in a small bowl, stir together the carrots, vinegar, and sugar.

3. In another small bowl, stir together the mayonnaise, ketchup, sriracha, and garlic. Season with salt and pepper.

4. In a medium bowl, combine the bear meat, curry powder, salt, and pepper. Use your hands to mix everything together. Form into 4 (6-inch) patties about 1-inch thick.

5. In a large, cast-iron skillet, heat the oil over medium-high heat until hot.

6. Add the patties and cook, flipping once, until the internal temperature of the patties reaches 160°F, for about 12 minutes per side. Remove from the heat.

7. While the patties are cooking, spread the butter on the cut sides of the baguette. Place the bread, cut-side up, on a sheet pan.

8. Put the sheet pan in the oven and bake until the baguette is lightly toasted, for about 5 minutes. Remove from the oven.

9. Spread the mayonnaise mixture on top of each baguette. Place a patty and some of the pickled carrots and jalapeño slices inside the baguette.

10. Garnish the burgers with cilantro sprigs. Close the burgers and serve immediately.

Russian-Inspired Bear Kotleti with Warm Cabbage Slaw

PREP TIME: 40 MINUTES / **COOK TIME:** 30 MINUTES / **YIELD:** 10 SERVINGS

OTHER GAME YOU CAN USE: ANY WILD GAME GROUND MEAT

Russian kotleti are similar to meatballs; they are just flavored and formed a bit differently. Apparently Russian kids eat kotleti the way American children consume chicken nuggets. But these are so delicious that it's perfectly okay to be an adult dish, too. Kotleti are a great use of bear meat and, with simple ingredients, they are a breeze to prepare.

3 slices sourdough bread, cut into small cubes

½ cup milk

3 pounds ground bear meat

2 tablespoons bacon fat

2 large eggs

1 tablespoon mayonnaise

½ medium onion, grated

1 teaspoon kosher salt

½ teaspoon freshly ground black pepper

Vegetable oil, for frying

4 ounces hickory-smoked bacon, diced

1 large onion, finely diced

2 tablespoons minced garlic

½ cup apple cider vinegar

1 tablespoon coarse-ground mustard

1 head cabbage, cored and shredded

1. In a medium bowl, soak the bread in the milk for about 10 minutes, then using a fork, mash the mixture up into pieces.

2. In a large bowl, combine the meat, bacon fat, eggs, mayonnaise, onion, salt, and pepper.

3. Add the bread and milk mixture and use your hands to combine. Form the meat into 10 patties.

4. In a large, cast-iron skillet, heat ¼ inch of oil over medium-high heat. Line a plate with paper towels.

5. Once hot, add 4 patties at a time and fry until cooked through, for 10 to 12 minutes, flipping halfway through. Remove from the heat.

6. In a medium, cast-iron skillet, cook the bacon over medium-high heat until crispy. Using a slotted spoon, transfer to the prepared plate.

7. Add the onion to the medium skillet and cook, stirring, until light golden brown, for 4 or 5 minutes.

8. Add the garlic and cook, stirring, for 2 minutes.

9. Add the vinegar, mustard, cabbage, and bacon. Toss to coat well, and cook, stirring, until the cabbage is warmed but not fully cooked, for about 3 minutes. Remove from the heat.

10. Transfer the cabbage to a serving plate, top with the bear patties, and serve immediately.

Coffee-Spiced Grilled Bear Tenderloin

PREP TIME: 10 MINUTES / **COOK TIME:** 25 MINUTES / **YIELD:** 4 TO 6 SERVINGS

OTHER GAME YOU CAN USE: VENISON

Bear meat pairs exceptionally well with my coffee rub—add the flavor of the grill and it's dynamite. When prepping your bear loin, make sure you trim the excess fat off because bear fat will ignite.

2 tablespoons Coffee Rub
   (page 246)

1 tablespoon vegetable oil

1 teaspoon kosher salt

1 teaspoon ground allspice

¾ teaspoon ground cinnamon

½ teaspoon ground nutmeg

1 pound bear tenderloin, trimmed
   of fat and silverskin

1. Preheat the grill to about 350°F, with an indirect setup (see page 3).

2. In a small bowl, combine the coffee rub, vegetable oil, salt, allspice, cinnamon, and nutmeg; mix well to make a paste.

3. Rub all sides of the tenderloin with the spiced paste.

4. Place the tenderloin on the grill away from the heat source and cook until the internal temperature of the tenderloin reaches 160°F, for 20 to 25 minutes. Remove from the grill. Transfer to a cutting board or serving platter. Let rest for 10 minutes before slicing and serving.

Chili-Lime Bear Jerky

PREP TIME: 45 MINUTES, PLUS 24 HOURS TO MARINATE / **COOK TIME:** 4 TO 5 HOURS

YIELD: 30 TO 40 PIECES

OTHER GAME YOU CAN USE: VENISON, ELK, WILD BOAR

Bear meat is not commonly made into jerky. It has been known to carry trichinosis; however, if you have fresh meat and dehydrate it at a high temperature, trichinosis becomes a non-issue. Bear meat is much leaner than venison, so the drying time is much longer.

2 tablespoons Worcestershire sauce

2 tablespoons soy sauce

2 tablespoons sambal oelek, sriracha, or Tabasco

1½ tablespoons freshly squeezed lime juice

1 teaspoon liquid smoke

½ teaspoon packed light or dark brown sugar

¼ teaspoon Prague Powder #1 (see page 5)

Grated zest of 1 lime

1 pound bear tenderloin, semi-frozen (see page 5), diagonally cut against the grain into ¼-inch-thick slices

1. In a large bowl, combine the Worcestershire sauce, soy sauce, sambal oelek, lime juice, liquid smoke, brown sugar, Prague Powder, and lime zest until well mixed.

2. Add the sliced bear and toss to fully coat. Cover and refrigerate for 24 hours.

3. Set the dehydrator to 165°F.

4. Lightly shake off any excess liquid and place the tenderloin slices on the dehydrator trays so they do not touch. Dehydrate for 4 to 5 hours. Your finished jerky should be pliable like leather and should fray and crack slightly at the point at which you bend it. Remove from the dehydrator.

STORAGE: Keep in an airtight container for up to 1 month.

WILD BOAR

Wild Boar Rillettes

PREP TIME: 30 MINUTES / **COOK TIME:** 3 HOURS, PLUS AT LEAST 2 HOURS TO CHILL
YIELD: 9 (4-OUNCE) MASON JARS

Oh, my love for rillettes is real. In Europe, rillettes are common appetizers, and I am totally there for it. You can make rillettes out of other meats, but my favorite is wild boar. Pair this rich appetizer with a mineral white wine, like a sauvignon blanc, and your summer nights on the porch just got a whole lot better. Serve chilled rillettes with toast, crackers, pickled vegetables, and whole-grain mustard.

2 pounds boneless wild boar shoulder, cut into 1½-inch chunks

1 teaspoon kosher salt, plus more as needed

1 cup rendered duck fat (see page 4), melted

6 sprigs thyme

5 medium cloves garlic, crushed

4 bay leaves

2 large shallots, coarsely chopped

⅛ teaspoon ground nutmeg

1. Set a rack in the lower position in the oven. Preheat the oven to 275°F. Put the boar in a 6-quart Dutch oven. Season with the salt. Pour the duck fat over the boar. Nestle the thyme, garlic, bay leaves, and shallots in with the boar.

2. Cover, put the pot in the oven, and bake until the meat is completely tender, for 3 hours. Remove from the oven.

3. Remove the thyme, garlic, bay leaves, and shallots. Set a strainer over a heatproof bowl and carefully pour the boar mixture into the strainer. Reserve the fat and juices.

4. Transfer the boar to a stand mixer fitted with the paddle attachment. Season with the nutmeg. Mix on low speed for 2 minutes.

5. Increase the speed to medium. Mix for 3 or 4 minutes, allowing the meat to break down and shred. Drizzle some of the reserved fat and juices back into the meat mixture, a couple tablespoons at a time, until the mixture is creamy. Season with salt, using more than to taste, because the boar will become bland as it chills.

6. Pack the meat tightly into glass jars, making sure not to get air bubbles trapped inside. Smooth the top of the meat, then pour a quarter inch of fat over it. Seal the jars with a lid and refrigerate.

7. Once the rillettes are completely chilled, they are ready to be served.

STORAGE: The rillettes can be frozen in plastic containers for 3 months; thaw in the refrigerator before serving.

Wild Boar Lard Chile Flake Crackers

PREP TIME: 45 MINUTES / **COOK TIME:** 30 MINUTES / **YIELD:** 40 CRACKERS
OTHER GAME YOU CAN USE: DUCK OR GOOSE FAT

Saving the fat from your harvest is essential in my book. Not only does meat taste better when it's cooked in its own fat, but that fat can also be used to make baked goods. I used to make these crackers every day in a restaurant I worked in years ago. The ones I used to make didn't have lard in them, and I'm sad my guests never got to try version 2.0, because the lard makes them even better than the originals. These crackers go great with my recipe for Wild Boar Rillettes on page 61.

2¾ cups all-purpose flour, preferably White Lily brand, plus more as needed

⅓ cup rendered wild boar lard (see page 4), melted

3 tablespoons chopped fresh chives

1 teaspoon red pepper flakes

½ teaspoon kosher salt

½ cup filtered water

Coarse sea salt, preferably Maldon, or coarse kosher salt

1. Set a rack in the middle position in the oven. Preheat the oven to 500°F. Place a pizza stone or a metal sheet pan on the rack. Let it heat up for at least 45 minutes prior to baking.

2. In a food processor, combine the flour, lard, chives, red pepper flakes, and salt. With the motor continuously running, drizzle in the water through the feed tube. The dough should come together in a large ball and feel soft but not sticky. If the dough is sticky, add 1 tablespoon of flour at a time and pulse to combine until the dough is tender and soft, but not sticky. Be careful not to make the dough too dense, either.

3. Divide the dough into 8 to 10 equal portions. Dust a work surface and rolling pin with flour. Roll out 1 portion at a time into an 8-inch round, thin enough that you can almost see through it. Sprinkle with some sea salt and lightly press the salt into the dough with your hand.

4. Lightly flour a sheet pan. Transfer the dough round to the back of the prepared sheet pan. Using a fork, gently prick holes all over it to keep it from puffing up as it bakes.

5. Carefully slide the dough round onto the hot pizza stone or place the sheet pan inside the oven. Bake for 2 or 3 minutes. Remove from the oven. Transfer to a wire rack to cool. (If some of the crackers are soft in the middle after they have cooled, put them in the oven until crisp, for 2 minutes.) Repeat the process with the remaining dough portions. Break the rounds into large pieces to serve.

Wild Boar Lard Flour Tortillas

PREP TIME: 15 MINUTES / **COOK TIME:** 20 MINUTES / **YIELD:** 16 TORTILLAS
OTHER GAME YOU CAN USE: DUCK OR GOOSE FAT

Once you go homemade, you may never go store-bought again. These tortillas are easy to make and highly addictive. Take a tortilla fresh off the stove, slather on a good butter, and sprinkle it with cinnamon and sugar—it's pure heaven.

3 cups all-purpose flour, plus more for rolling the dough

1 teaspoon baking powder

1 teaspoon kosher salt

⅓ cup rendered wild boar lard (see page 4), melted

1 cup warm water

1. In a stand mixer fitted with the dough hook, combine the flour, baking powder, and salt on medium speed.

2. With the machine running, add the lard, then slowly pour in the water. After about 1 minute, the mixture should come together into a ball; continue to mix until the ball is smooth.

3. Turn off the mixer. Dust a work surface and rolling pin with flour. Transfer the dough to the work surface and divide into 16 equal portions. Roll each portion in the flour very lightly, then use your hands to form into balls. Cover the balls with a clean kitchen towel and let rest for a few minutes; this helps relax the gluten, so you don't have tough tortillas.

4. Heat a large nonstick pan over medium heat. Roll each dough ball into a 7-inch round or use a tortilla press.

5. Once the pan is hot, put the dough round in the pan and cook until pale brown, for about 1 minute. Reduce the heat if it browns too quickly. Flip if needed and cook on the opposite side for 15 to 20 seconds. Transfer to a wire rack to cool. Repeat with the remaining dough rounds. Turn off the heat.

6. Store the tortillas in an airtight container in the refrigerator for up to 1 week.

STORAGE: To freeze, place a piece of parchment paper between each tortilla and store in a zip-top bag.

Slow Cooker Wild Boar Ragù

PREP TIME: 15 MINUTES / **COOK TIME:** 20 MINUTES, PLUS 8 HOURS ON LOW / **YIELD:** 12 SERVINGS
OTHER GAME YOU CAN USE: ANY BIG GAME

I first had wild boar ragù in Italy, and I can remember exactly how it tasted. It was perfection on a plate. This version lets the slow cooker do all the work. If you have some Italian venison sausage on hand, add it as well; about ½ pound of sausage will take this ragù to the next level.

2 pounds wild boar stew meat, cut into 2-inch pieces

1 large onion, finely diced

1 carrot, finely diced

4 cloves garlic, minced

1 cup red wine

1 (28-ounce) can crushed tomatoes

1 (28-ounce) can whole tomatoes, preferably San Marzano, drained and mashed

2 bay leaves

1 tablespoon chopped fresh thyme

1 tablespoon chopped fresh oregano

1 teaspoon kosher salt

½ teaspoon freshly ground black pepper

2 pounds fettuccine, preferably fresh

Grated Parmesan cheese, for garnish

1. In a slow cooker, combine the boar, onion, carrot, garlic, wine, crushed tomatoes, whole tomatoes, bay leaves, thyme, oregano, salt, and pepper; cover and cook on low for 8 hours.

2. Turn off the slow cooker. Transfer the mixture to a 5-quart Dutch oven. Cook over medium-high heat until the sauce has reduced slightly, for 15 minutes. As it cooks, using 2 forks, gently shred the boar into small pieces; the boar will be fork-tender, so this should be super easy.

3. While the ragù simmers, bring a large pot of salted water to a boil over high heat. Cook the fettuccine as the package directs. (If using fresh, cook for 3 minutes.) Remove from the heat. Drain.

4. Add the fettuccine to the ragù; toss to coat. Remove from the heat.

5. Serve the ragù immediately, sprinkled with Parmesan cheese.

Wild Boar Porchetta

PREP TIME: 20 MINUTES / **COOK TIME:** 3 HOURS 20 MINUTES / **YIELD:** 10 SERVINGS

When I was running a restaurant, I had many wild game options on the menu, and this was the most popular. It would sell out every night and for good reason; it's hands down the best thing ever. If you make just one recipe from this book, make this one! The belly is the piece they make bacon from, so you can imagine how flavor-packed this porchetta is. It's delicious served with roasted or mashed potatoes.

3 tablespoons kosher salt

3 tablespoons freshly ground black pepper

3 tablespoons chopped fresh rosemary

3 tablespoons chopped fresh sage

3 tablespoons minced garlic

1 tablespoon red pepper flakes

1 (3- to 4-pound) wild boar belly

1. Preheat the oven to 400°F.

2. In a small bowl, combine the salt, pepper, rosemary, sage, garlic, and red pepper flakes.

3. Using a paper towel, pat the belly dry. Place skin-side down on a work surface and rub with the seasoning. Roll up lengthwise to form a tight cylinder; use butcher's twine to tie the belly tightly at 2-inch intervals. Transfer to a roasting pan.

4. Put the roasting pan in the oven and roast for 1 hour.

5. Reduce the oven temperature to 300°F.

6. Roast until the skin is very crispy and the internal temperature in the center of the belly reaches 170°F, for about 2 hours 20 minutes.

7. Transfer the roll to a cutting board. Let rest for 20 minutes. Remove the twine and cut the porchetta into ½- to 1-inch-thick slices, using a serrated knife.

GAME TIP: You can give shoulder this porchetta treatment, though the flavor and texture will be different (the photo on page 48 shows it made with shoulder). Butterfly a 3- to 4-pound boneless shoulder roast, keeping the thickness as even as possible. Follow steps 2 and 3 above. Heat 2 tablespoons olive oil over high heat in a large, oven-proof skillet. Add the roll and sear on all sides until golden brown. Roast in the oven at 400°F until the internal temperature reaches 150°F at the thickest point, 30 to 40 minutes. Pick up with step 7.

Herb-Crusted Wild Boar Tenderloin

PREP TIME: 20 MINUTES / **COOK TIME:** 30 MINUTES / **YIELD:** 4 SERVINGS

OTHER GAME YOU CAN USE: ANY BIG GAME TENDERLOIN

Herbs can transform a dish, especially boar, which is milder than most wild game. I prefer fresh herbs to dried for this, but if you are in a pinch and need to use dried, add an extra tablespoon of olive oil to the mixture to help rehydrate the herbs.

½ cup grated Parmesan cheese

⅓ cup packed, fresh
   parsley leaves

1 medium shallot,
   coarsely chopped

1 large clove garlic, peeled

2 tablespoons minced
   fresh thyme

1 teaspoon minced fresh rosemary

1 teaspoon kosher salt

½ teaspoon freshly ground
   black pepper

¼ cup olive oil

½ cup panko bread crumbs

2 tablespoons Dijon mustard

1 pound wild boar tenderloin

1. Set a rack in the middle position in the oven. Preheat the oven to 350°F.

2. In a food processor, combine the Parmesan cheese, parsley, shallot, garlic, thyme, rosemary, salt, and pepper. Pulse about 10 times to break down the mixture.

3. Add the olive oil and bread crumbs; pulse 10 times to form a chunky paste.

4. Using a pastry brush, brush the mustard all over the tenderloin, then gently pack the herb paste on all sides. Transfer to a sheet pan.

5. Put the sheet pan in the oven and roast until the internal temperature in the center of the tenderloin reaches 150°F, for about 25 minutes. Remove from the oven. Transfer to a cutting board. Let rest for 20 minutes. Slice against the grain and serve immediately.

Slow Cooker Wild Boar Shoulder with Balsamic Glaze

PREP TIME: 10 MINUTES / **COOK TIME:** 5 HOURS ON HIGH / **YIELD:** 8 TO 10 SERVINGS
OTHER GAME YOU CAN USE: VENISON

Slow-cooking boar, which lets all the internal fat slowly melt, helps make it fork-tender and fantastic. Although you might be tempted to top this with your go-to BBQ sauce, please don't. Give the glaze a try; it's sweet and tangy and pairs so well with the boar.

1 (4-pound) bone-in wild boar shoulder

4 cups chicken broth

4 cloves garlic, minced

2 teaspoons chopped fresh sage

2 teaspoons kosher salt

¼ teaspoon freshly ground black pepper

2 sprigs rosemary

4 bay leaves

1 cup packed dark brown sugar

½ cup balsamic vinegar

¼ cup soy sauce

2 tablespoons whole-grain mustard

2 tablespoons cornstarch

1. In a slow cooker, combine the boar shoulder, broth, garlic, sage, salt, pepper, rosemary, and bay leaves; cover and cook on high for 4 hours.

2. To make the glaze, in a medium bowl, whisk together the brown sugar, vinegar, soy sauce, mustard, and cornstarch until smooth.

3. After the boar has cooked for 4 hours, pour the glaze over it, cover, and cook for 1 hour.

4. Turn off the slow cooker. Transfer the shoulder to a cutting board. Carve against the grain.

5. Serve the boar with the glaze spooned over the top.

Slow Cooker Wild Boar Ribs with Korean-Style BBQ Sauce

PREP TIME: 15 MINUTES / **COOK TIME:** 6 HOURS ON HIGH OR 9 HOURS ON LOW, PLUS 5 MINUTES TO MAKE THE SAUCE / **YIELD:** 6 SERVINGS

OTHER GAME YOU CAN USE: VENISON

Ribs made in the slow cooker might just change your life. They will literally be falling-off-the-bone tender. The cooking liquid gets transformed into a flavorful sauce to finish off the dish.

½ cup soy sauce

½ cup chicken broth

½ cup packed dark brown sugar

¼ cup freshly squeezed lime juice

4 cloves garlic, minced

2 tablespoons distilled
   white vinegar

2 tablespoons sesame oil

1 tablespoon rice vinegar

2 tablespoons minced
   fresh ginger

½ teaspoon liquid smoke

1 tablespoon gochujang or
   sriracha

5 pounds wild boar spareribs,
   each cut into 3 pieces

¼ cup cornstarch

¼ cup water

1 cup shredded carrots

4 scallions, green and white
   parts, thinly sliced

1 tablespoon toasted
   sesame seeds

1. In a small bowl, whisk together the soy sauce, broth, brown sugar, lime juice, garlic, white vinegar, sesame oil, rice vinegar, ginger, liquid smoke, and gochujang to combine.

2. Put the spareribs in a slow cooker and pour the sauce over them. Cover and cook until the meat is tender, on high for 6 hours or low for 9 hours.

3. Turn off the slow cooker. Transfer the spareribs to a platter. Transfer the cooking liquid to a large saucepan.

4. To make the sauce, in a small bowl, whisk together the cornstarch and water until smooth. Add to the pan. Bring to a boil over high heat. Cook, stirring constantly, until thickened, for 2 minutes.

5. Stir in the carrots. Remove from the heat.

6. Top the spareribs with the sauce and serve garnished with the scallions and sesame seeds.

Wild Boar and Venison Swedish Meatballs

PREP TIME: 30 MINUTES, PLUS 45 MINUTES TO CHILL / **COOK TIME:** 55 MINUTES / **YIELD:** 4 SERVINGS

OTHER GAME YOU CAN USE: ANY BIG GAME GROUND MEAT

We all know everyone goes to Ikea for the Swedish meatballs, not the furniture, right? Here is my wild take on that cult favorite. These are delicious spooned over mashed potatoes.

1 pound ground wild boar

8 ounces ground venison

1 onion, finely chopped

1 clove garlic, minced

½ cup panko bread crumbs

⅓ cup half-and-half

1 large egg, beaten

1 teaspoon kosher salt

½ teaspoon freshly ground
    black pepper

8 tablespoons (1 stick)
    unsalted butter

⅓ cup all-purpose flour

1¼ cups Venison Stock (page 264)
    or beef broth

¾ cup heavy cream

1 tablespoon Dijon mustard

2 teaspoons soy sauce

½ teaspoon Worcestershire sauce

1 tablespoon vegetable oil

1. In a large bowl, combine the boar, venison, onion, garlic, bread crumbs, half-and-half, egg, salt, and pepper. Use your hands to mix everything together.

2. Using a 2-ounce scoop, portion out the meat mixture. Using your hands, roll each portion to form a ball. Set on a sheet pan and refrigerate for 45 minutes.

3. Preheat the oven to 400°F.

4. Just before cooking the meatballs, to make the sauce, in a medium saucepan, melt the butter over medium heat.

5. Blend in the flour, whisking constantly for 1 minute.

6. Slowly whisk in the stock.

7. Add the cream, mustard, soy sauce, and Worcestershire sauce; whisk to combine.

8. Reduce the heat to very low. Simmer, stirring occasionally, while you cook the meatballs.

9. In a large, cast-iron skillet, heat the oil over medium-high heat. Working in small batches, add the meatballs, and cook, turning often, until browned on all sides, for about 8 minutes per batch. (If you crowd the skillet, they will steam instead of brown.) Remove from the heat. Transfer to a sheet pan.

10. Put the sheet pan in the oven and bake until the meatballs have cooked through, for about 30 minutes. Remove from the oven. Transfer to a serving dish.

11. Remove the sauce from the heat. Ladle over the meatballs and serve immediately.

Wild Boar, Jalapeño, and Cheddar Sausage

PREP TIME: 1 HOUR / **YIELD:** 5½ POUNDS SAUSAGE
OTHER GAME YOU CAN USE: ANY BIG GAME

This is hands down my absolute favorite sausage. It's utterly perfect when you get that bit of cheese oozing out. I like to stuff these sausages in casings, then freeze them so I always have them at the ready.

5 pounds wild boar butt, deboned and diced, chilled

1½ cups diced jalapeños

2 cups diced (¼-inch) Cheddar cheese

2 cups finely chopped onion

½ cup minced garlic

3 tablespoons paprika

3 tablespoons kosher salt

Hog casings, for stuffing (optional)

1. In a large bowl, combine the wild boar, jalapeños, and Cheddar cheese. Using the largest die, run the mixture through the grinder (see page 6).

2. Mix in the onion, garlic, paprika, and salt; using a medium die, run the mixture through the grinder again.

3. Stuff the sausage into casings (if using) or shape into patties.

STORAGE: Refrigerate the sausage in an airtight container for up to 6 days. Or vacuum-seal and freeze for up to 3 months.

Smoked Wild Boar Jerky

PREP TIME: 20 MINUTES, PLUS 24 HOURS TO MARINATE / **COOK TIME:** 4 TO 5 HOURS
YIELD: 40 TO 50 PIECES
OTHER GAME YOU CAN USE: ANY BIG GAME

Though I love my dehydrator for making jerky, a smoker develops flavors that liquid smoke just can't replicate; I like to use hickory wood for this. This jerky is marinated in beer and citrus; the acid cuts through the richness and saltiness for a flavorful and addictive result.

1 (14.9-ounce) bottle Guinness stout or dark beer of your choice

1 cup soy sauce

¼ cup pineapple juice

¼ cup freshly squeezed lime juice

¼ cup orange juice

¼ cup Worcestershire sauce

3 tablespoons packed light or dark brown sugar

1 tablespoon Morton Tender Quick Home Meat Cure (see page 5)

1 tablespoon garlic powder

1 tablespoon freshly ground black pepper

½ teaspoon cayenne pepper (optional but recommended)

2 pounds wild boar strip loin, tenderloin, or roast, trimmed of fat and connective tissue, semi-frozen (see page 5)

1. In a large bowl, combine the Guinness, soy sauce, pineapple juice, lime juice, orange juice, Worcestershire sauce, brown sugar, Morton Tender Quick, garlic powder, black pepper, and cayenne pepper (if using).

2. Slice the boar meat ¼ inch thick against the grain. Add to the bowl, tossing to fully coat. Cover and refrigerate for 24 hours.

3. Set an electric smoker to 180°F.

4. Remove the sliced boar from the marinade; discard the marinade. Lay the meat slices on the smoker grate without touching and smoke, for 4 to 5 hours. Your finished jerky should be pliable like leather and should fray and crack slightly at the point at which you bend it. Remove from the smoker.

STORAGE: Refrigerate in an airtight container for up to 3 months or store at room temperature for up to 1 month.

CHAPTER 4

Small Game

Small game—rabbit, hare, and squirrel—are fun to hunt and delicious to eat. Small game can easily be found where they like to eat—in clover fields, wheat fields, alfalfa, high grass, and in your backyard garden. If you are new to hunting or would like to get your children started with hunting, small game is a great introduction to the sport.

← Rabbit Sugo with Pappardelle, page 80

Rabbit and Hare

Rabbit is one of the healthiest meats you can eat, high in protein and very low in fat and calories compared to other meats, even chicken. And, yes, it does taste a little like chicken, but with a bit of earthiness. It takes to the same cooking preparations as chicken, so you can pan-sear, sauté, or braise it, depending on the dish.

One might think that hare would taste just like rabbit, but it's a bit different. Rabbit meat is fine in texture and almost all white, with a flavor and appearance similar to chicken. Hare meat is rather dark in color and much stronger in taste than rabbit, resembling that of dark-meat wild game.

Squirrel

Squirrel tastes like a subtler version of rabbit, with some saying the flavor resembles a cross between rabbit and chicken, with a hint of nuts. The meat is sweet, light in color, and finely textured. Squirrel pairs well with lots of flavors, from nuts and berries to bold tomato sauces and creamy dishes, making it extremely versatile.

Field-Dressing

When field-dressing small game, gut them right away because the meat sours pretty quickly (despite the European tradition of hanging hare for 7 days with the guts intact before preparing it). Although the hide will come off more easily prior to gutting the animal, the hide also helps protect the meat while in the field. For that reason, I recommend gutting in the field and skinning back at camp.

The Cuts

Small game can be broken up into five main pieces: the shoulder, saddle, loin, rib, and legs. The most prized pieces for small game like rabbit and hare are the legs because they carry most of the meat. When butchering rabbit, it's important to remove the silverskin and sinew, because they are chewy. Also remove as much fat as possible, because it is pungent and foul tasting.

The legs are particularly great for braising and frying. The saddle and loin are the most tender parts of the rabbit and are best sautéed, panfried, or grilled. The shoulder has lots of tendons, which makes them great for slow-cooking, long braises, and stews. There isn't much meat on the ribs, but they are a great flavor enhancer for stews, soups, and sauces.

Moroccan-Style Rabbit Tagine

PREP TIME: 1 HOUR, PLUS AT LEAST 2 HOURS TO MARINATE / **COOK TIME:** 1 HOUR 20 MINUTES
YIELD: 6 SERVINGS
OTHER GAME YOU CAN USE: HARE

A tagine is the pot traditionally used to cook this dish in Morocco. Its signature cone shape helps return the condensed steam back to the food, which results in a very moist product. Tagine recipes have layers of meat, vegetables, spice, and aromatics. If you don't have a tagine, a Dutch oven works fine.

¼ cup olive oil, plus
   2 tablespoons

2 cloves garlic, minced

1 bay leaf

2 teaspoons ground cinnamon

2 teaspoons ground cumin

1 teaspoon ground ginger

1 teaspoon ground turmeric

¼ teaspoon cayenne pepper

2 (2- to 3-pound) rabbits, each
   cut into 6 pieces

1 onion, finely diced

6 carrots, cut ¼-inch-thick
   on a bias

2 cups chicken broth

2 cups frozen peas

½ cup packed, fresh cilantro
   leaves, chopped

Kosher salt

Freshly ground black pepper

1. In a large bowl, whisk together ¼ cup of olive oil, the garlic, bay leaf, cinnamon, cumin, ginger, turmeric, and cayenne pepper.

2. Add the rabbits and turn over a couple times until fully coated. Cover and marinate in the refrigerator for at least 2 hours or up to 24 hours.

3. In a tagine or a large Dutch oven, heat the remaining 2 tablespoons of olive oil over medium-high heat.

4. Add the onion and carrots; cook, stirring occasionally, until the onion is translucent, for about 5 minutes.

5. Add the rabbits and spiced oil; stir to combine.

6. Add the broth and bring to a simmer.

7. Reduce the heat to medium-low. Cover and simmer until the rabbit is cooked through and tender, for about 1 hour.

8. Stir in the peas and cilantro. Season with salt and pepper.

9. Increase the heat to medium. Cook until the peas are heated through, for 5 to 7 minutes. Remove from the heat. Serve immediately.

Rabbit Cassoulet with Apples

PREP TIME: 20 MINUTES, PLUS 8 HOURS TO SOAK / **COOK TIME:** 1 HOUR 30 MINUTES
YIELD: 4 SERVINGS
OTHER GAME YOU CAN USE: HARE

Traditionally, a cassoulet is made with duck or goose, and sausage, but I have found that replacing the duck with rabbit is equal to if not better than the original. The apples bring a beautiful sweetness that is typically not seen in a cassoulet.

2 cups chicken broth

⅔ cup dried white beans, rinsed, soaked in water overnight, and drained

1 large onion, diced

1 tablespoon tomato paste

4 cloves garlic, minced

1 tablespoon chopped fresh thyme

1 tablespoon chopped fresh sage

1 bay leaf

2 red apples, cored, peeled, and diced

1 (14.5-ounce) can diced tomatoes, preferably San Marzano

5 tablespoons olive oil, divided

1 pound boneless rabbit saddle meat, cut into 2-inch chunks

8 ounces smoked sausage, cut into ½-inch pieces

Kosher salt

Freshly ground black pepper

1 cup plain bread crumbs

¼ cup grated Parmesan cheese

1 teaspoon garlic powder

2 tablespoons chopped fresh parsley

1. In a medium Dutch oven, stir together the broth, beans, onion, tomato paste, and garlic until the tomato paste dissolves. Add enough water to cover the beans by at least 2 inches. Bring to a boil over high heat. Add the thyme, sage, and bay leaf.

2. Reduce the heat to low. Cover, and simmer until the beans are tender, for 35 to 45 minutes.

3. Stir in the apples and tomatoes with their juices; simmer for 15 minutes.

4. While the beans are simmering, in a medium skillet, heat 2 tablespoons of olive oil over medium heat. Add the rabbit and cook, stirring, for 3 minutes. Add the sausage and cook, stirring occasionally, until the rabbit and sausage have slightly browned, for 5 to 7 minutes. Remove from the heat.

5. Transfer the rabbit and sausage to the bean mixture and stir to combine. Season with salt and pepper.

6. Preheat the oven to 350°F.

7. In a small bowl, combine the bread crumbs, Parmesan cheese, and garlic powder. Sprinkle evenly over the beans and rabbit.

8. Drizzle the remaining 3 tablespoons of olive oil over the bread crumbs.

9. Put the pot in the oven and bake until the bread crumbs are golden brown, for about 20 minutes. Remove from the oven.

10. Serve the cassoulet sprinkled with the parsley.

Slow Cooker Rabbit Provençal

PREP TIME: 20 MINUTES / **COOK TIME:** 8 HOURS ON LOW / **YIELD:** 6 SERVINGS

OTHER GAME YOU CAN USE: HARE

This simple dish has all the beautiful flavors of France. Preparing it in the slow cooker yields incredibly tender rabbit. I like to serve it ladled over couscous.

2 (2- to 3-pound) rabbits, each cut into 6 pieces

1 fennel bulb, stalks discarded, bulb thinly sliced (reserve a few fronds for garnish)

1 onion, finely diced

1 red bell pepper, cut into thin strips

1 yellow bell pepper, cut into thin strips

3 tablespoons minced garlic

Grated zest and juice of 1 orange

1 cup chicken broth

1 (14.5-ounce) can diced tomatoes, drained

½ cup chopped fresh parsley

½ cup pitted black olives

1. In a slow cooker, combine the rabbits, fennel, onion, red bell pepper, yellow bell pepper, garlic, orange zest and juice, broth, and tomatoes; cover and cook on low for 8 hours.

2. Turn off the slow cooker. Stir in the parsley and olives.

3. Serve the rabbit garnished with the reserved fennel fronds.

Rabbit in Red Wine with Potatoes and Mushrooms

PREP TIME: 20 MINUTES, PLUS OVERNIGHT TO MARINATE / **COOK TIME:** 1 HOUR 10 MINUTES
YIELD: 4 SERVINGS
OTHER GAME YOU CAN USE: HARE

This classic French stew, called *lapin à la cocotte*, is richly flavorful and the perfect comfort food on a cold winter's day.

¼ cup olive oil

1 teaspoon kosher salt

½ teaspoon freshly ground black pepper

1 (2- to 3-pound) rabbit, cut into 8 pieces

3 carrots, chopped

2 stalks celery, chopped

2 onions, diced

5 cloves garlic, minced

2 bay leaves

3 sprigs thyme

4 cups red wine, preferably cabernet sauvignon

2 potatoes, peeled and cut into large cubes

6 tablespoons (¾ stick) unsalted butter, cut into tablespoons

1 cup sliced mushrooms of your choice

¼ cup chopped fresh parsley

1. In a large bowl, combine the olive oil, salt, and pepper.

2. Add the rabbit, carrots, celery, onions, garlic, bay leaves, and thyme; toss until coated with the oil.

3. Pour in the wine, cover the bowl, and marinate in the refrigerator overnight.

4. Transfer the rabbit to a plate. Pour the marinade and vegetables into a 6-quart Dutch oven. Cover, bring to a boil over medium-high heat, and boil for 10 minutes.

5. Add the potatoes, cover, and cook just until the potatoes are tender, for about 12 minutes.

6. Add the rabbit, cover, and cook until cooked through and tender, for about 25 minutes.

7. Remove the lid. Reduce the heat to medium-low. Simmer to reduce the liquid, for about 10 minutes.

8. Add the butter and mushrooms; stir until the butter is melted and incorporated. Simmer for 10 minutes. Remove from the heat.

9. Serve the stew garnished with the parsley.

Portuguese-Style Rabbit

PREP TIME: 45 MINUTES / **COOK TIME:** 2 HOURS 5 MINUTES / **YIELD:** 4 SERVINGS

OTHER GAME YOU CAN USE: HARE

It's amazing how different spices and ingredients can transport you to a far-off place. This stew takes you right into the homes of Portugal, where every grandma is cooking this stew. You can substitute your choice of mushroom for the porcinis.

8 ounces hickory-smoked sliced bacon, cut into 1-inch pieces

1 (2-to 3-pound) rabbit, cut into 8 pieces

1 teaspoon kosher salt, plus more to taste

½ teaspoon freshly ground black pepper, plus more to taste

3 tablespoons vegetable oil (optional)

10 ounces fresh porcini mushrooms, sliced

1 onion, thinly sliced

2 bay leaves

2 tablespoons minced garlic

1 cup red wine

1 (28-ounce) can whole tomatoes, preferably San Marzano

1½ teaspoons dried oregano

½ teaspoon red pepper flakes

¼ cup chopped fresh parsley

1. Line a plate with paper towels.

2. In a large Dutch oven, cook the bacon over medium-high heat until crispy, for about 8 minutes. Using a slotted spoon, transfer to the prepared plate.

3. Season the rabbit with the salt and pepper. Add half of the rabbit to the bacon fat and cook, turning once, until golden brown on both sides, for 10 to 18 minutes. Transfer to a plate. Repeat with the remaining rabbit.

4. If you need more fat, add the oil. Add the mushrooms, onion, and bay leaves; cook, stirring frequently, until the mushrooms and onion are golden brown, for about 20 minutes.

5. Stir in the garlic and cook for 1 minute.

6. Add the wine, tomatoes with their juices, oregano, and red pepper flakes. Using a wooden spoon, slightly crush the tomatoes against the side of the pot.

7. Return the rabbit and any accumulated juices to the pot.

8. Reduce the heat to medium-low. Cover and simmer until the rabbit is cooked through and tender, for about 1 hour. Remove from the heat.

9. Remove the bay leaves. Season with salt and pepper if needed.

10. Garnish the rabbit with the bacon and parsley and serve.

Rabbit Sugo with Pappardelle

PREP TIME: 20 MINUTES / **COOK TIME:** 3 HOURS 20 MINUTES / **YIELD:** 6 SERVINGS

OTHER GAME YOU CAN USE: HARE

Sugo is similar to a ragù, just a bit less saucy. This beautiful pasta sauce is made with wine and broth instead of tomatoes, resulting in a lighter and brighter sauce, allowing the rabbit to bring the richness.

1 (3½-pound) rabbit, cut into 8 pieces

1 teaspoon kosher salt, plus more to taste

½ teaspoon freshly ground black pepper, plus more to taste

3 tablespoons olive oil

4 tablespoons (½ stick) unsalted butter

1 cup shiitake or cremini mushrooms, stemmed (if using shiitakes) and sliced

1 small onion, finely diced

1 cup chopped celery

½ cup finely diced carrots

3 cloves garlic, minced

3 bay leaves

1½ cups white wine

2 cups chicken broth

1 pound pappardelle

Shaved Pecorino Romano cheese, for serving

1. Season the rabbit with salt and pepper.

2. In a large Dutch oven, heat the olive oil over medium-high heat until hot.

3. Add half of the rabbit and cook, turning once, until golden brown on both sides, for about 10 minutes. Transfer to a plate. Repeat with the remaining rabbit.

4. Add the butter to the pot and melt.

5. Add the mushrooms and onion; cook, stirring a few times, until lightly browned, for 5 to 7 minutes.

6. Stir in the celery and carrots; cook until softened, for 7 or 8 minutes.

7. Stir in the garlic and cook for 2 minutes.

8. Return the rabbit and any accumulated juices to the pot.

9. Stir in the salt, pepper, and bay leaves; cook for about 5 minutes.

10. Add the wine and, using a wooden spoon, scrape up any browned bits from the bottom of the pot. Cook until the wine reduces by half, for 6 to 8 minutes.

11. Add the broth.

12. Reduce the heat to low. Cover and simmer until the rabbit is so tender it falls off the bone, for 1½ to 2 hours.

13. Remove the rabbit and put it on a platter. Using 2 forks, shred the meat and discard the bones.

14. Skim off any fat that may have risen to the top of the sauce, then stir the rabbit meat back in. Cook until the sauce thickens, for 20 to 30 minutes. Season with salt and pepper if needed. Remove from the heat.

15. Remove the bay leaves. Cover the pot and keep warm.

16. Bring a large pot of salted water to a boil over high heat. Cook the pappardelle as the package directs. Remove from the heat. Drain, then toss with the sugo.

17. Serve the pasta topped with shavings of Pecorino Romano cheese.

Garlicky Rabbit with White Wine and Fresh Herbs

PREP TIME: 20 MINUTES / **COOK TIME:** 1 HOUR 25 MINUTES / **YIELD:** 2 SERVINGS
OTHER GAME YOU CAN USE: HARE

This recipe originates from Ischia, a volcanic island off the coast of Naples, Italy. It is known for its mineral-rich thermal waters, fresh seafood, and rabbit. You'll find this traditional dish served over roasted potatoes in many of the island's restaurants.

1 (2- to 3-pound) rabbit, cut into
   serving pieces

Kosher salt

Freshly ground black pepper

¼ cup all-purpose flour

3 to 4 tablespoons vegetable oil

1 cup diced onion

2 tablespoons minced garlic

½ teaspoon red pepper flakes

2 cups dry white wine

2 cups chicken broth

1 cup large-diced tomatoes

Grated zest of 1 lemon

2 bay leaves

2 tablespoons chopped
   fresh parsley

2 tablespoons chopped fresh basil

1. Season the rabbit pieces with salt and pepper, then lightly dust with the flour.

2. In a large skillet, heat 3 tablespoons of vegetable oil over high heat.

3. Add half of the rabbit and cook, turning once, until golden brown on both sides, for 6 to 8 minutes. Transfer to a plate. Repeat with the remaining rabbit.

4. Add the remaining 1 tablespoon oil, if needed, to the skillet. Add the onion and cook, stirring, until slightly browned, for about 5 minutes.

5. Stir in the garlic and red pepper flakes; cook for 2 minutes.

6. Add the wine and, using a wooden spoon, scrape up any browned bits from the bottom of the skillet. Cook for about 5 minutes.

7. Return the rabbit and any accumulated juices to the skillet.

8. Add the broth, tomatoes, lemon zest, and bay leaves.

9. Reduce the heat to medium. Cook for about 45 minutes.

10. Stir in the parsley and basil.

11. Increase the heat to high. Cook until the sauce has thickened, for 10 to 15 minutes. Season with salt and pepper. Remove from the heat.

Rabbit Roulade

PREP TIME: 30 MINUTES, PLUS 3 HOURS TO CHILL / **COOK TIME:** 50 MINUTES / **YIELD:** 2 SERVINGS
OTHER GAME YOU CAN USE: HARE

If you want a recipe that will completely "wow" your guests, this is it! A roulade is simply a roll-up; in this case deboned rabbit wrapped around pork sausage and then entirely encased in strips of bacon. It needs to be firmed up before cooking, so be sure to include plenty of time to chill it sufficiently.

1 (2- to 3-pound) rabbit

8 ounces pork sausage, removed from its casings

6 strips bacon, preferably hickory-smoked

2 tablespoons olive oil

1. Debone the rabbit legs and remove any connective tissue or silver skin. Remove the 2 rabbit saddles, keeping them in one piece as much as possible.

2. Lay a 15-inch sheet of plastic wrap on a work surface. Arrange the strips of bacon horizontally in the middle of the plastic wrap, overlapping each other by ¼ inch; there should not be any space between the strips of bacon.

3. Arrange the rabbit saddles vertically, close to the right end of the strips of bacon. Place the saddles so that they reach almost to the top and bottom of the bacon. Fill in with the deboned leg meat. Crumble the sausage in the middle of the rabbit meat vertically.

4. Roll up the roulade. To do this, gently lift the right side of the plastic wrap and wrap the bacon around the saddle meat. Continue to roll the roulade until the saddles are completely wrapped in bacon and you have a little log. Compress the roulade by wrapping both ends of the plastic wrap tightly so they are securely held and sealed. Use kitchen twine to secure the ends. The bundle needs to be watertight. Refrigerate the roulade for at least 3 hours.

5. To cook the roulade, bring a large pot of water to a simmer over medium heat. Place the roulade (still in its plastic wrap) in the water and simmer gently for 40 minutes. You don't want to cook it at a hard boil.

CONTINUED >

6. Remove the roulade from the water and transfer it to a cutting board. Let cool for about 10 minutes, then remove the plastic wrap.

7. In a large skillet, heat the olive oil over medium-high heat until hot.

8. Add the roulade and sear on all sides until well browned, for about 10 minutes. Remove from the heat. Transfer to a cutting board, cut into 1-inch-thick slices, and serve.

Peruvian-Style Grilled Rabbit

PREP TIME: 20 MINUTES, PLUS 24 HOURS TO MARINATE / **COOK TIME:** 1 HOUR / **YIELD:** 4 SERVINGS
OTHER GAME YOU CAN USE: HARE

It's time to up your BBQ game and think beyond steaks and tomatoey sauces. Rabbit is wonderful on the grill, and here we serve it in the style found in Peruvian restaurants. The bright, herb-infused sauce pairs well with the delicious charred bits we all love. I like to serve this with baked sweet potatoes.

3 tablespoons olive oil

2 tablespoons white-wine vinegar

2 tablespoons minced garlic

1 teaspoon dried thyme

1 teaspoon dried oregano

1 teaspoon chopped fresh
  rosemary

½ teaspoon ground cumin

1 (2- to 3-pound) rabbit

Kosher salt

Freshly ground black pepper

1 cup red-wine vinegar

3 tablespoons chopped fresh
  cilantro

3 tablespoons chopped fresh
  tarragon

3 tablespoons chopped fresh mint

3 tablespoons chopped
  fresh parsley

1. To make the marinade, in a large bowl, whisk together the olive oil, white-wine vinegar, garlic, thyme, oregano, rosemary, and cumin.

2. Season the rabbit with salt and pepper. Add to the marinade. Toss to fully coat. Cover and refrigerate for 24 hours.

3. Preheat the grill to 375°F to 400°F, with an indirect setup (see page 3).

4. Place the rabbit on the grill away from the heat source, close the lid, and cook until the internal temperature of the rabbit reaches 160°F, for about 1 hour. Baste and turn about every 20 minutes. Remove from the grill.

5. While the rabbit is grilling, to make the herb sauce, in a blender combine the red-wine vinegar, cilantro, tarragon, mint, and parsley. Blend until smooth.

6. Serve the rabbit whole or cut into pieces, drizzled with the herb sauce.

Hare Biryani

PREP TIME: 15 MINUTES, PLUS 2 HOURS TO MARINATE / **COOK TIME:** 55 MINUTES / **YIELD:** 4 SERVINGS
OTHER GAME YOU CAN USE: RABBIT

This recipe is a simplified version of the classic Indian dish, made with ingredients you can find in the supermarket. Serve ladled over basmati rice.

3 tablespoons plain yogurt

1 tablespoon freshly squeezed lemon juice

1 teaspoon minced garlic

1 teaspoon minced, peeled, fresh ginger

½ teaspoon kosher salt

¼ teaspoon ground turmeric

1 pound hare saddles, cut into 1-inch cubes

2 tablespoons unsalted butter

1 onion, diced

3 cups coconut milk

¼ cup chopped fresh mint

1 teaspoon garam masala

1. To make the marinade, in a large bowl, whisk together the yogurt, lemon juice, garlic, ginger, salt, and turmeric.

2. Add the hare and stir until coated. Cover and refrigerate for 2 hours.

3. In a medium, cast-iron Dutch oven, melt the butter over medium-high heat.

4. Add the onion and cook, stirring occasionally, until slightly browned, for 7 or 8 minutes.

5. Add the hare meat and marinade. Cook, stirring occasionally, until almost all the marinade has evaporated.

6. Stir in the coconut milk, mint, and garam masala.

7. Reduce the heat to medium-low. Cover and simmer until the hare is tender, for 30 to 45 minutes. Remove from the heat and serve.

Grilled Lemony Hare Skewers with Quick Feta Dip

PREP TIME: 20 MINUTES, PLUS 4 TO 8 HOURS TO MARINATE / **COOK TIME:** 20 MINUTES / **YIELD:** 4 SERVINGS

OTHER GAME YOU CAN USE: RABBIT

Lemon makes everything delicious! And if you have access to Meyer lemons, definitely use them—they have a floral sweetness that pairs beautifully with wild hare. This recipe is inspired by bright flavors of the Mediterranean. The feta dip will be a recipe you keep coming back for! I like to serve this with warm pita bread.

2 to 3 pounds hare saddles, cut into chunks, and legs

1 recipe Herb-Lemon Marinade (page 237)

1 (8-ounce) block feta cheese

½ cup sour cream

½ cup mayonnaise

Grated zest of 1 lemon

1 small clove garlic, peeled

¼ teaspoon dried dill

¼ teaspoon dried thyme

¼ teaspoon freshly ground black pepper

1 teaspoon ground sumac (optional)

⅛ teaspoon kosher salt

1. In a large bowl, combine the hare and marinade, turning to fully coat. Cover and refrigerate for 4 to 8 hours.

2. To make the dip, in a food processor, combine the feta cheese, sour cream, mayonnaise, lemon zest, garlic, dill, thyme, pepper, sumac (if using), and salt; process until smooth and creamy. Transfer to a large bowl, cover, and refrigerate until ready to serve.

3. Preheat the grill to 375°F to 400°F.

4. Remove the hare from the marinade. Thread the saddle meat onto skewers. Place the skewers and legs on the grill directly over the fire. Close the lid and cook for 10 minutes.

5. Baste the hare with the marinade, then flip and baste again. Close the lid and cook, until the hare is cooked through, for about 10 minutes. Remove from the heat.

6. Serve the hare immediately with the dip on the side.

Pan-Seared Hare Loins with Rosemary Butter and Pickled Spiced Cranberries

PREP TIME: 20 MINUTES / **COOK TIME:** 30 MINUTES, PLUS SEVERAL HOURS TO COOL / **YIELD:** 4 SERVINGS
OTHER GAME YOU CAN USE: RABBIT

Pickles and hare? Say what? Well, I say, "Heck yeah!" Hare naturally has a slight sweetness to it, and the sweet-tart pickled cranberries are a perfect pairing.

2 cups apple cider vinegar

2 cups packed light or dark brown sugar

1 tablespoon kosher salt

1 teaspoon allspice berries

1 teaspoon pink peppercorns

¼ teaspoon whole cloves

6 star anise pods

2 shallots, chopped

1 (12-ounce) bag fresh or frozen cranberries

4 cinnamon sticks

2 strips orange zest

4 hare loins

Kosher salt

Freshly ground black pepper

5 tablespoons unsalted butter

2 sprigs rosemary

1. To make the brine, in a medium saucepan, combine the vinegar, brown sugar, and salt. Bring to a rolling boil over high heat.

2. Meanwhile, tie up the allspice berries, peppercorns, cloves, star anise, and shallots in a small cheesecloth bag or put them in a tea ball infuser.

3. Once the brine is boiling, add the cranberries, cinnamon sticks, and cheesecloth bag. Return to a boil and boil for 10 minutes. Remove from the heat.

4. Stir in the orange zest. Let the mixture cool to room temperature, then remove the cheesecloth bag, but leave in the cranberries, cinnamon sticks, and zest. If not serving right away, transfer to an airtight container and refrigerate for up to 5 days. Bring back to room temperature before serving.

5. Using a paper towel, pat the hare loins dry. Season well with salt and pepper.

6. In a large, cast-iron skillet, heat the butter and rosemary over medium heat.

7. Once the butter coats the bottom of the skillet, increase the heat to high. Heat the skillet for 1 or 2 minutes.

8. Add the loins and cook until golden brown on both sides and the center has an internal temperature of 160°F, for 8 to 10 minutes. Remove from the heat.

9. Slice the loins, transfer to a serving platter, and drizzle with the rosemary-scented butter from the skillet. Serve with the cranberries on the side.

Brunswick Stew

PREP TIME: 30 MINUTES / **COOK TIME:** 1 HOUR 40 MINUTES / **YIELD:** 4 SERVINGS
OTHER GAME YOU CAN USE: RABBIT

Virginia and the city of Brunswick, Georgia, both lay claim to the creation of Brunswick stew. I am fully on the side of my home state, Georgia, but I love my own version of this traditional stew best.

2 or 3 squirrels, cleaned

3 cups chicken broth

4 tablespoons (½ stick) unsalted butter

2 onions, thinly sliced

2 tablespoons minced garlic

½ cup port or Madeira wine

1 (14.5-ounce) can whole tomatoes

1 cup drained canned lima beans

1 cup frozen corn kernels

2 tablespoons Worcestershire sauce

1½ teaspoons kosher salt

1 teaspoon freshly ground black pepper

½ teaspoon chopped fresh rosemary

2 bay leaves

Chopped fresh chives, for garnish

Chopped fresh parsley, for garnish

1. In a large, cast-iron Dutch oven, combine the squirrels and broth. Bring to a boil over high heat.

2. Reduce the heat to medium-low. Cover and simmer until the squirrels are tender, for about 30 minutes. Remove from the heat.

3. Transfer the squirrels to a plate. Pour the broth into a large heat-proof bowl and wash and dry the pot.

4. Once the squirrels are cool enough to handle, remove and discard the bones, and shred the meat.

5. In the same Dutch oven, melt the butter over medium-high heat.

6. Add the onions and cook, stirring occasionally, until golden brown, for about 5 minutes.

7. Stir in the garlic and cook for 2 minutes.

8. Add the squirrel and reserved broth. Using a wooden spoon, scrape up any browned bits from the bottom of the pot.

9. Stir in the port, tomatoes, lima beans, corn, Worcestershire sauce, salt, pepper, rosemary, and bay leaves. Cover and simmer over low heat to let the flavors develop, for 45 to 60 minutes. Remove from the heat.

10. Serve the stew with a sprinkling of chives and parsley.

Easy Squirrel Stroganoff

PREP TIME: 15 MINUTES / **COOK TIME:** 40 MINUTES / **YIELD:** 4 OR 5 SERVINGS

OTHER GAME YOU CAN USE: RABBIT, HARE

Stroganoff is warm, hearty, creamy, and rich—exactly what you want to eat after a long day of hunting. This one is incredibly easy, with the egg noodles cooking right in the sauce.

3 tablespoons unsalted butter

12 ounces cremini mushrooms, sliced

1 onion, diced

1 pound squirrel meat, cut into 1-inch chunks

1 tablespoon minced garlic

½ teaspoon minced fresh thyme

3 tablespoons all-purpose flour

¼ cup dry white wine

4 cups beef broth

2 tablespoons Worcestershire sauce

1 tablespoon Dijon mustard

8 ounces egg noodles

Kosher salt

Freshly ground black pepper

½ cup sour cream

2 tablespoons chopped fresh parsley

1. In a large skillet, melt the butter over medium heat.

2. Add the mushrooms and onion; cook, stirring occasionally, until the mushrooms and onion have browned, for 7 or 8 minutes.

3. Add the squirrel meat and garlic; cook for 5 to 8 minutes.

4. Stir in the thyme, then the flour, until fully incorporated; mash any lumps.

5. Add the wine and, using a wooden spoon, scrape up any browned bits from the bottom of the skillet.

6. Stir in the broth, Worcestershire sauce, mustard, and egg noodles. Season with salt and pepper. Bring to a boil.

7. Reduce the heat to medium-low. Cover and simmer until the noodles are fully cooked, for 10 to 12 minutes.

8. Stir in the sour cream and simmer for 2 or 3 minutes. Remove from the heat.

9. Serve the stroganoff sprinkled with the parsley.

Sweet-and-Sour Squirrel

PREP TIME: 20 MINUTES / **COOK TIME:** 50 MINUTES / **YIELD:** 4 SERVINGS

OTHER GAME YOU CAN USE: RABBIT, HARE

Who doesn't love sweet-and-sour pork, especially at 1 a.m. on a Friday night? Well, this version with squirrel will have you thinking twice about takeout! Serve over freshly cooked rice.

8 ounces squirrel meat, cut into bite-size pieces

1 large egg, beaten

2 teaspoons kosher salt, divided

1 teaspoon cornstarch, plus ½ cup

3 cups peanut oil

½ cup all-purpose flour

½ teaspoon freshly ground black pepper

½ teaspoon garlic powder

2 tablespoons vegetable oil

1 tablespoon minced garlic

1 red bell pepper, chopped

1 cup diced pineapple

¼ cup sugar

¼ cup rice vinegar

2 tablespoons ketchup

½ teaspoon red pepper flakes (optional)

Sesame seeds or chopped scallions, white and green parts, for garnish

1. In a medium bowl, combine the squirrel meat, egg, 1 teaspoon of salt, and 1 teaspoon of cornstarch; stir until the meat is fully coated. Cover with plastic wrap and refrigerate for 10 minutes.

2. In a medium, cast-iron Dutch oven, heat the peanut oil to 350°F. Line a plate with paper towels.

3. In a medium bowl, whisk together the flour, remaining ½ cup of cornstarch, 1 teaspoon of salt, the pepper, and garlic powder.

4. Add the squirrel meat to the bowl and toss to fully coat.

5. Deep-fry the squirrel meat in the hot oil, 5 to 8 pieces at a time, until golden, for 8 to 10 minutes. Using a slotted spoon, transfer to the prepared plate. Turn off the heat.

6. In a medium skillet, heat the vegetable oil over medium-high heat until hot.

7. Add the garlic and cook, stirring, for 2 minutes.

8. Add the bell pepper and cook, stirring, until slightly softened, for about 5 minutes.

9. Add the pineapple and cook until slightly caramelized, for about 5 minutes.

10. Stir in the sugar, vinegar, ketchup, and red pepper flakes (if using); simmer until thickened, for about 10 minutes.

11. Add the fried squirrel and toss gently until fully coated. Remove from the heat.

12. Sprinkle the squirrel with sesame seeds and serve.

CHAPTER 5

Ducks and Geese

Duck, Duck, Goose is a game we are still playing as adults, but this time it ends with a delicious meal! I love early mornings in a layout blind, watching the sun slowly come up. Or keeping my hands warm wrapped around a cup of coffee in a sit-down blind while chatting with friends about how epic our last goose hunt was and how you hope this one will be just as good. Then, after a day of shotguns in the air, everyone crowds around a tailgate to enjoy the harvest as quickly as possible. Good food and good friends are why I love duck and goose hunting.

← Chipotle Duck-Confit Tacos with Grilled Pineapple Salsa, page 104

Ducks

The most popular duck to hunt in North America is the mallard, but there are also teal ducks, canvasbacks, pintails, and buffleheads; all yielding a delicious harvest. Duck has distinctive dark red meat that is sweet and somewhat earthy.

Geese

North America has four distinct classes of geese: dark geese, light geese, gray geese, and Brant. Dark geese are the most popular and include Canada geese. Light geese include the popular Ross's geese and their cousins, the snow geese. Specklebelly geese are the most common gray geese and are considered to be the best tasting of all geese. Brant are smaller geese with two varieties: Atlantic and Pacific.

Field-Dressing

It's best to dress ducks and geese within 2 to 3 hours of harvest. Waiting longer increases the chance of rigor mortis, which affects the quality of the meat. If you are planning on a long hunt, have a cooler in which to keep whole birds chilled until you can field-dress them. Place the birds in clean plastic bags and store on ice in the cooler for transportation.

The Cuts

Duck and geese have the same butchery cuts; however, a goose will be slightly larger. The breast meat should always be butchered with the skin left on so that the skin can get crispy and the underlying fat can render during cooking. It's best to score the skin with a sharp knife to let the fat render and to pan-sear the breast, skin-side down, over medium-high heat. You can also supreme a breast, which means to cut the breast so that the wing is still attached. This cut is perfect for slow-cooking or braising.

The legs and thighs are best cooked bone-in for braising, roasting, or making confit. The tender and sweet tenderloin is a slim cut that sits underneath the breast meat and is best quickly sautéed or cooked over direct heat. The livers are particularly delicious and can be made into pâté or simply panfried.

A beautiful way to cook a duck or goose is to roast it whole. Leaving the bird intact will keep the natural juices and fats inside and produce a tender outcome. Plus, roasting or smoking a bird whole will yield a delicious crisp skin. You can treat it the same way you do a Thanksgiving turkey and stuff it as well, with good results.

DUCK

Duck Lollipops with Plum Sauce

PREP TIME: 20 MINUTES / **COOK TIME:** 45 MINUTES / **YIELD:** 5 SERVINGS

Who doesn't automatically love a recipe with the word *lollipop* in it? It just screams fun! And these duck lollipops certainly are fun. The drumettes of ducks often get overlooked, but they can be treated the same as chicken drumettes.

10 duck drumettes, skin attached, patted dry

1 (16-ounce) jar plum jam

3 tablespoons grated onion

2 tablespoons apple cider vinegar

1 tablespoon packed light or dark brown sugar

1 tablespoon grated fresh ginger

1 teaspoon red pepper flakes

1 clove garlic, minced

1. Using a pair of kitchen shears, cut the skin and tendons around the base of each drumette to the bone. Peel, scrape, and push the skin and meat towards the thick end to make a lollipop shape.

2. Preheat the oven to 350°F. Set a wire rack over a sheet pan.

3. Arrange the duck lollipops in a single layer on the wire rack.

4. Put the sheet pan in the oven and bake until the lollipops are browned and the internal temperature reaches 165°F, for 30 to 45 minutes. Remove from the oven.

5. Meanwhile, to make the plum sauce, in a medium saucepan, whisk together the jam, onion, vinegar, sugar, ginger, red pepper flakes, and garlic; bring to a boil over medium-high heat. Boil for 3 to 5 minutes. Remove from the heat. Keep warm.

6. Once the duck lollipops are cooked, put ¼ cup of the plum sauce in a large bowl and add about 4 lollipops to it. Toss the lollipops in the sauce to coat, then transfer to a platter. Repeat with the remaining lollipops and sauce. Serve with extra sauce if desired.

Duck Confit

PREP TIME: 15 MINUTES, PLUS 12 TO 24 HOURS TO CURE / **COOK TIME:** 2 TO 3 HOURS

YIELD: 4 SERVINGS

OTHER GAME YOU CAN USE: GOOSE

Duck confit takes me back to my time in France. If you can master only one French recipe, it has to be this one! You can also confit goose the same way.

½ cup kosher salt

2 tablespoons sugar

4 large duck legs, thighs attached (about 3 pounds)

4 cloves garlic, crushed

8 sprigs thyme

1 shallot, sliced

1 teaspoon black peppercorns

½ teaspoon whole juniper berries

4 cups rendered duck fat (see page 4)

1. In a medium bowl, stir together the salt and sugar.

2. Rub half of the mixture all over the legs, into the skin and meat.

3. Add the garlic, thyme, shallot, peppercorns, and juniper berries to the remaining mixture; stir until well distributed.

4. Sprinkle half of the remaining salt-sugar-herb mixture on the bottom of a large bowl. Pack the legs into the mixture, pressing them down. Top with the remaining salt-sugar-herb mixture. Cover with plastic wrap and refrigerate for 12 to 24 hours.

5. Preheat the oven to 225°F.

6. In a small saucepan, melt the duck fat over medium heat.

7. Brush the salt and seasonings off the duck legs. Arrange them in a single yet snug layer in a small Dutch oven.

8. Pour the melted duck fat over the duck pieces. The duck should be completely submerged in fat.

9. Put the pot in the oven and bake until the duck meat can be easily pulled from the bone, for 2 to 3 hours. Remove from the oven.

10. Cool and store the duck legs in the fat. Duck confit will keep in the refrigerator for several weeks when covered in fat.

GAME TIP: This can be made with goose breast and leg meat. Prepare the recipe the same as you would the duck, with these adjustments: Use 5 cups rendered goose fat, making sure all the meat is covered with it. Increase the cook time to 3 to 4 hours.

Duck-Confit Salade Landaise

PREP TIME: 15 MINUTES / **COOK TIME:** 15 MINUTES / **YIELD:** 2 SERVINGS

OTHER GAME YOU CAN USE: GOOSE

This recipe is a perfect way to take a super-rich ingredient like duck confit and lighten it up a bit. This salad is one you will keep going back to. And the salad dressing is wonderful over cooked meats.

3 ounces baguette, cut into
   1-inch cubes

7 tablespoons olive oil, divided

Dash kosher salt, plus
   ½ teaspoon

2 tablespoons finely diced shallot

2 tablespoons red-wine vinegar

1 tablespoon honey

1 teaspoon Dijon mustard

¼ teaspoon freshly ground
   black pepper

1 cup baby arugula

1 cup mixed greens

1 cup frisée

2 ounces walnuts, chopped

½ cup cherry tomatoes, halved

6 ounces duck confit meat
   (page 97), shredded

1. Preheat the oven to 325°F.

2. To make the croutons, put the baguette cubes on a sheet pan and drizzle with 3 tablespoons of olive oil. Toss to fully coat. Sprinkle with a dash of salt.

3. Put the sheet pan in the oven and bake until the baguette cubes are golden brown and crunchy, for 10 to 12 minutes. Remove from the oven.

4. To make the dressing, in a small bowl, whisk together the shallot, vinegar, honey, mustard, pepper, and the remaining 4 tablespoons of olive oil and ½ teaspoon of salt.

5. In a large salad bowl, combine the arugula, mixed greens, and frisée.

6. Add the walnuts and tomatoes. Toss, then drizzle with enough of the dressing to lightly coat. Top with the croutons and duck confit.

Classic British Duck-Hunt Stew

PREP TIME: 30 MINUTES / **COOK TIME:** 1 HOUR 20 MINUTES / **YIELD:** 6 TO 8 SERVINGS

OTHER GAME YOU CAN USE: GOOSE

A classic stew never goes out of style. And it doesn't get any more classic than this one. According to tradition, this stew is served after a day spent in the field waterfowl shooting. Although my recipe takes a few liberties with the original, I think the British would still approve!

6 strips bacon, diced

3 tablespoons unsalted butter

1 onion, finely chopped

4 boneless, skinless duck
   breasts, diced

5 cloves garlic, minced

3 tablespoons tomato paste

1 cup red wine

3 cups beef broth

10 allspice berries

2 bay leaves

1 cinnamon stick

3 Yukon Gold potatoes, peeled
   and diced

1 (14-ounce) can crushed
   tomatoes

1 pound mushrooms, quartered

2 teaspoons dried oregano

Chopped fresh parsley,
   for garnish

1. Line a plate with paper towels.

2. In a Dutch oven, cook the bacon over medium-high heat until just crispy, for 5 minutes. Using a slotted spoon, transfer to the prepared plate.

3. Add the butter to the bacon fat and melt.

4. Add the onion and cook until golden brown, for 5 minutes.

5. Working in batches if needed, add the duck and cook until browned on all sides, for 3 to 4 minutes.

6. Add the garlic and cook for 2 minutes.

7. Stir in the tomato paste and cook until slightly darkened.

8. Add the wine and, using a wooden spoon, scrape up any browned bits from the bottom of the pot.

9. Add the broth.

10. Using a piece of cheesecloth, make a sachet. Put the allspice, bay leaves, and cinnamon stick in the cloth and tie with kitchen twine. Add to the pot.

11. Stir in the potatoes, crushed tomatoes, mushrooms, and oregano. Bring to a simmer.

12. Reduce the heat to medium-low. Cover and simmer for about 1 hour to let the flavors meld. Remove from the heat.

13. Sprinkle the stew with parsley and serve immediately.

Butter Duck

PREP TIME: 10 MINUTES / **COOK TIME:** 35 MINUTES / **YIELD:** 4 SERVINGS

OTHER GAME YOU CAN USE: TURKEY

Butter chicken is one of my favorite Indian dishes, but it's even better with duck. It's creamy, filled with spices, and rich in flavor.

1 tablespoon vegetable oil

1 tablespoon unsalted butter

1 onion, diced

3 cloves garlic, minced

1 teaspoon grated or minced fresh ginger

1½ pounds boneless, skinless duck breasts, cut into ½-inch dice

1 (6-ounce) can tomato paste

1 tablespoon garam masala

1½ teaspoons kosher salt

1 teaspoon paprika

1 teaspoon chili powder

1 teaspoon ground cumin

1 teaspoon ground cinnamon

½ teaspoon freshly ground black pepper

1 cup heavy cream

Hot cooked basmati rice, for serving

1. In a large skillet, heat the oil and butter over medium-high heat until the butter has melted.

2. Add the onion and cook until golden brown, for about 5 minutes.

3. Stir in the garlic and ginger; cook for 2 minutes.

4. Stir in the duck, tomato paste, garam masala, salt, paprika, chili powder, cumin, cinnamon, and pepper. Cook until the duck has cooked through, for 10 to 12 minutes.

5. Stir in the cream.

6. Reduce the heat to medium-low. Cover and simmer, stirring occasionally, until the flavors meld, for 10 to 15 minutes. Remove from the heat.

7. Serve the duck with the gravy ladled over rice.

SLOW COOKER BUTTER DUCK: If you would like to "set it and forget it," this is a great recipe in the slow cooker. Just add all the ingredients except the cream to the slow cooker, and cook on low for 8 hours. Then stir in the cream, let it heat through, and serve.

Indian-Spiced Duck Breasts with Puy Lentils

PREP TIME: 20 MINUTES / **COOK TIME:** 1 HOUR / **YIELD:** 6 SERVINGS
OTHER GAME YOU CAN USE: GOOSE

Last time I was in London, I ate at a Michelin-starred Indian restaurant and it blew my mind. This recipe is completely inspired by my dinner that night, except my version is probably much less time-consuming.

2 tablespoons olive oil

1 teaspoon yellow mustard seeds

1 teaspoon cumin seeds

1 small onion, finely chopped

1 clove garlic, minced

1 tablespoon grated or minced fresh ginger

1 teaspoon garam masala (optional)

2 cups chicken broth

1 teaspoon kosher salt

½ teaspoon freshly ground black pepper

1 cup Puy lentils, picked over and rinsed

4 skin-on boneless duck breasts

¼ cup Indian-Style Spice Rub (page 248)

4 tablespoons (½ stick) unsalted butter

1. In a large Dutch oven, heat the oil over medium-high heat until hot.

2. Add the mustard seeds and cumin seeds; cook until they start to pop, for about 2 minutes.

3. Add the onion and cook, stirring, until slightly golden brown, for 4 minutes.

4. Stir in the garlic, ginger, and garam masala (if using); cook for 2 minutes.

5. Add the broth, salt, pepper, and lentils; bring to a boil.

6. Reduce the heat to medium-low. Cover and simmer, stirring occasionally, until most of the liquid is absorbed and the lentils are tender, for 30 to 40 minutes. Remove from the heat.

7. While the lentils are cooking, preheat the oven to 325°F.

8. Pat the duck breasts dry and rub both sides with the spice rub.

9. In a large, cast-iron skillet, heat the butter over medium-high heat until melted and hot.

10. Add 2 of the duck breasts, skin-side down. Allow the fat to render and the skin to crisp, then flip and cook for about 3 minutes. Transfer to a plate. Repeat with the remaining 2 breasts.

11. Return the breasts to the skillet, skin-side up. Turn off the heat.

12. Put the skillet in the oven, and bake until the breasts reach an internal temperature of 135°F, for 6 to 8 minutes. Remove from the oven.

13. Slice the duck breasts and serve immediately on top of the lentils.

Five-Spice Crispy Duck Breasts with Cranberry Mostarda

PREP TIME: 25 MINUTES / **COOK TIME:** 35 MINUTES / **YIELD:** 4 SERVINGS
OTHER GAME YOU CAN USE: GOOSE

I first created this recipe on a whim one night at a restaurant where I was working. It's simple to make, yet complex in flavor. Try the mostarda with venison as well, though it's spectacular on just about all wild game!

FOR THE MOSTARDA:

1 (12-ounce) package fresh or frozen cranberries

1 cup sugar

1 cup water

¾ cup freshly squeezed orange juice

2 bay leaves

¼ cup white wine

2 tablespoons coarse-ground mustard

1 teaspoon chopped fresh thyme

1 teaspoon ground cinnamon

¼ teaspoon ground allspice

FOR THE DUCK:

4 skin-on boneless duck breasts

2 tablespoons Chinese five-spice powder

3 tablespoons unsalted butter

1. **To make the mostarda:** In a medium saucepan, combine the cranberries, sugar, water, orange juice, and bay leaves; bring to a boil over high heat.

2. Reduce the heat to low. Simmer, stirring often, until the cranberries soften and the liquid has reduced by half, for 20 to 25 minutes.

3. Stir in the wine, mustard, thyme, cinnamon, and allspice; simmer for 5 minutes. Remove from the heat.

4. **To make the duck:** Preheat the oven to 325°F.

5. Using a paper towel, pat the duck breasts dry. Score the skin all over—the more scoring, the better! Season with the five-spice powder on both sides.

6. In a large, cast-iron skillet, melt the butter over medium-high heat until hot.

7. Working in batches if needed, add the duck breasts, skin-side down. Cook until the skin is golden brown and slightly crisp, for 6 to 10 minutes. (Try not to move the duck breasts while searing; they will easily lift from the skillet when ready to be flipped.) Turn off the heat.

8. Flip the duck breasts. Put the skillet in the oven and cook until the internal temperature of the duck reaches 135°F, for 5 to 8 minutes. Remove from the oven.

9. Slice the duck breasts and serve with the mostarda.

Smoked Whole Duck with Aïoli

PREP TIME: 10 MINUTES, PLUS 8 HOURS TO MARINATE / **COOK TIME:** 4 HOURS / **YIELD:** 4 SERVINGS
OTHER GAME YOU CAN USE: GOOSE

Trust me when I say smoking a whole duck is much better than smoking pieces of duck. The most important step for a good result is drying the duck in the refrigerator. This process forms a film on the skin, called a pellicle, which allows the smoke to adhere to the surface of the meat during smoking.

1 (3- to 4-pound) duck, cleaned

1 onion, quartered

¼ cup honey

¼ cup rice vinegar

3 tablespoons soy sauce

2 tablespoons freshly squeezed
    lemon juice

2 tablespoons freshly squeezed
    orange juice

Kosher salt

1 recipe Aïoli (page 257)

1. Using paper towels, pat the duck dry.

2. Put the onion in the cavity and set the duck on a platter. Refrigerate, uncovered, for at least 8 hours or overnight.

3. In a small bowl, whisk together the honey, vinegar, soy sauce, lemon juice, and orange juice.

4. Set an electric smoker to 200°F to 225°F.

5. Rub the duck well with salt, inside and out.

6. Put the duck in the smoker and smoke using applewood (see page 4), basting with the honey mixture every hour, until the internal temperature of the duck reaches 165°F, for about 4 hours. Remove from the smoker. Transfer to a cutting board and let rest until the internal temperature reaches 170°F, for about 10 minutes.

7. Carve the duck into pieces and serve with the Aïoli on the side.

Chipotle Duck-Confit Tacos with Grilled Pineapple Salsa

PREP TIME: 20 MINUTES / **COOK TIME:** 30 MINUTES / **YIELD:** 4 SERVINGS

OTHER GAME YOU CAN USE: GOOSE

The one dish chefs are great at making is tacos! Why? Because of family meal, which is when the kitchen staff of a restaurant eats together before customers arrive. Got left-over duck confit? Make a taco! That's exactly how this recipe came about. I made it for family meal and my coworkers kept asking for it.

4 confit duck legs (page 97)

½ cup chicken broth

3 tablespoons soy sauce

1 teaspoon chipotle powder

½ teaspoon ground cumin

Extra-virgin olive oil, for brushing the grill

1 pineapple, peeled, cored, and cut into thick rounds

1 ripe mango, peeled, pitted, and finely diced

1 jalapeño, seeded and minced

½ red onion, chopped

Grated zest and juice of 1 lime

2 tablespoons chopped fresh cilantro

Kosher salt

8 corn tortillas, warmed

1. On a microwave-safe plate, microwave the legs for 1 minute. Remove the skin and shred the meat.

2. In a medium skillet, combine the broth, soy sauce, chipotle powder, and cumin; bring to a simmer over medium-high heat.

3. Add the duck.

4. Reduce the heat to low. Simmer until the liquid has reduced by half, for about 20 minutes. Remove from the heat.

5. Meanwhile, brush the grill with olive oil. Preheat the grill to 400°F to 450°F.

6. Place the pineapple on the grill directly over the fire. Cook for about 10 minutes on each side. Remove from the heat. Transfer to a plate to cool. Cut into ¼- to ½-inch pieces.

7. To make the salsa, in a medium bowl, combine the pineapple, mango, jalapeño (add it to taste), onion, lime zest and juice, and cilantro. Season with salt.

8. Serve the duck confit on top of the tortillas with the salsa.

Duck Bacon

PREP TIME: 15 MINUTES, PLUS 12 HOURS TO BRINE AND DRY /
COOK TIME: 2 HOURS, PLUS 30 MINUTES TO COOL / **YIELD:** 8 SERVINGS

You know that saying "good things take time"? Well, this recipe is the epitome of that saying. Yes, it takes some time to make, but if you love regular bacon, this will be well worth the effort.

4 cups cold water

1 cup freshly squeezed orange juice

1 cup strong brewed coffee

1 cup kosher salt

½ cup packed light or brown sugar

¼ cup maple syrup

2½ tablespoons Morton Tender Quick Home Meat Cure (see page 5)

5 cinnamon sticks

5 star anise pods

5 cloves

4 cups ice cubes

6 skin-on boneless duck breasts

1. To make the brine, in a 9-inch square glass baking dish, whisk together the water, orange juice, coffee, kosher salt, brown sugar, maple syrup, and Morton's Tender Quick until the salt and sugar have dissolved.

2. Stir in the cinnamon sticks, star anise, cloves, and ice.

3. Add the duck breasts and weigh them down using a large plate that fits inside the container to keep them completely submerged. Refrigerate for at least 8 hours.

4. Remove the duck breasts from the brine; discard the brine. Rinse the duck well under cold running water. Pat very dry and set on a clean plate. Refrigerate until a thin skin (called the pellicle) forms, for 4 hours.

5. Set an electric smoker to 225°F.

6. Put the duck in the smoker and smoke using applewood or cherry wood (see page 4) until the internal temperature of the duck reaches 165°F, for 2 hours. Remove from the smoker. Transfer to a cutting board to cool to room temperature, for about 30 minutes. If not using immediately, refrigerate in an airtight container for up to 5 days.

7. To prepare, thinly slice the breast meat and fry in a cast-iron skillet over medium-high heat, just as you would bacon. Cook the duck slices on each side until nice and crispy. Remove from the heat.

Duck and Pork Sausage

PREP TIME: 45 MINUTES / **COOK TIME:** 15 MINUTES / **YIELD:** 4½ POUNDS

OTHER GAME YOU CAN USE: GOOSE, WILD BOAR

Duck is an understated ingredient to use in sausage. It brings a beautiful richness to sausage that pork just can't. Please note that having chilled plates makes all the difference because room-temperature plates will actually begin to melt the fat. It's important to keep the fat as cold as possible during the grinding process.

3 pounds boneless duck meat, diced and chilled

1½ pounds pork belly, diced and chilled

1½ tablespoons kosher salt

1 tablespoon chopped fresh sage

1 tablespoon freshly ground black pepper

1 teaspoon ground allspice

½ cup white wine

Hog casings, for stuffing (optional)

1. Grind the duck and pork belly together (see page 6).

2. In a large bowl, combine the ground meat, salt, sage, pepper, allspice, and wine. Use your hands to mix everything together, working fast so that the meat does not heat up.

3. Stuff the sausage mixture into casings (see page 6) or hand-roll the ground meat into individual sausage shapes.

4. To cook the sausages, grill over medium-high heat for 10 to 15 minutes, turning occasionally. Remove from the heat.

GAME TIP: When preparing this dish with wild boar, use meat from the shoulder or butt.

STORAGE: Refrigerate for up to 5 days or vacuum-seal in 1-pound portions and freeze for up to 3 months.

Creamy Duck-Fat Polenta

PREP TIME: 10 MINUTES / **COOK TIME:** 55 MINUTES / **YIELD:** 6 SERVINGS

OTHER GAME YOU CAN USE: GOOSE FAT

Polenta is totally the underdog of grains. Chefs use it all the time in restaurants to add an unbelievably creamy texture to a dish. But it pairs well with anything you would eat mashed potatoes with. Making a pot roast? Try pairing it with this!

1 cup coarse-ground cornmeal

5 cups chicken broth

2 teaspoons kosher salt, plus more to taste

½ teaspoon freshly ground black pepper

½ cup grated Parmesan cheese

¼ teaspoon ground nutmeg

2 ounces rendered duck fat (see page 4), melted

3 tablespoons chopped fresh chives

1. In a medium saucepan, whisk together the cornmeal and broth. Add the salt and pepper. Cook over low heat, stirring occasionally, until the mixture comes to a low simmer; you do not want it to boil. Cover and cook for 40 to 45 minutes, stirring occasionally, until the mixture is thick and creamy. Remove from the heat.

2. Stir in the Parmesan cheese, nutmeg, and duck fat. Season with salt and pepper if needed.

3. Serve the polenta immediately, sprinkled with the chives.

Duck-Fat French Fries

PREP TIME: 10 MINUTES / **COOK TIME:** 40 MINUTES / **YIELD:** 6 SERVINGS

OTHER GAME YOU CAN USE: GOOSE FAT

I remember sitting at a café in France watching people walk by and eating my first ever duck-fat French fries—I was in complete heaven! Because I want the world to be as happy as I was sitting at that café, I developed this recipe to make it as simple as possible, using store-bought fries. These are delicious served with Aïoli (page 257).

Nonstick cooking spray, for greasing

2 pounds frozen French fries

2 cups rendered duck fat (see page 4)

Kosher salt or truffle salt

1. Preheat the oven to 400°F. Line 2 sheet pans with aluminum foil. Grease the foil with nonstick cooking spray.

2. Divide the French fries between the sheet pans and arrange in a single layer.

3. Put the sheet pans in the oven and bake for 10 minutes. Remove from the oven.

4. While the French fries are baking, in a cast-iron Dutch oven, heat the duck fat to 375°F. Line a plate with paper towels.

5. Carefully add about one-quarter of the fries and fry until golden brown and slightly crispy, for 5 or 6 minutes. Transfer to the prepared plate. Immediately season with salt. Repeat with the remaining fries. Turn off the heat.

PRO TIP: For the best texture, be sure to work in small batches when frying; you don't want the temperature of the duck fat to fall below 375°F.

Duck-Fat, Cheddar, and Scallion Biscuits

PREP TIME: 10 MINUTES / **COOK TIME:** 20 MINUTES / **YIELD:** 10 BISCUITS

OTHER GAME YOU CAN USE: GOOSE FAT

I once spent two weeks baking every type of biscuit possible. I made angel biscuits, yeast biscuits, cream biscuits; you name it, I made it. These are my favorite. I like to add a dab of butter to a warm biscuit and drizzle hot honey over it. Delicious!

2 cups all-purpose flour, preferably White Lily brand, plus more for rolling the dough

1 tablespoon baking powder

½ teaspoon kosher salt

½ cup rendered duck fat (see page 4), frozen

½ cup shredded sharp Cheddar cheese

¼ cup thinly sliced scallions, green and white parts

¾ cup buttermilk

1 large egg

1. Preheat the oven to 400°F. Line a sheet pan with parchment paper.

2. In a large bowl, whisk together the flour, baking powder, and salt.

3. Add the duck fat, Cheddar cheese, and scallions; using a pastry cutter, cut the duck fat into the flour until the dough is about the size of peas.

4. Add the buttermilk and gently stir until the dough just comes together. You don't want to overwork the dough, or you will have tough biscuits.

5. Dust a clean work surface and rolling pin with flour and put the dough on top. Pat down with your hands, then roll out to about 1-inch thickness.

6. Using a 3-inch cookie cutter or biscuit cutter, cut the dough into circles. Place on the prepared sheet pan so they are slightly touching. (Biscuits rise more when they touch.)

7. In a small bowl, whisk the egg with a splash of water. Brush on top of the biscuits.

8. Put the sheet pan in the oven and bake until golden brown on top, for 15 to 20 minutes. Remove from the oven.

Duck-Fat Shortbread Cookies with Coffee Glaze

PREP TIME: 10 MINUTES, PLUS 1 HOUR TO CHILL / **COOK TIME:** 20 MINUTES / **YIELD:** 12 COOKIES
OTHER GAME YOU CAN USE: GOOSE FAT

Duck fat is a little miracle worker. When used in baking, it brings a richness that you just can't get from anything else. Whether you are making cookies or biscuits, the fat must always be cold.

4 tablespoons (½ stick) unsalted butter, divided, plus more for greasing

¾ cup granulated sugar

5 tablespoons cold rendered duck fat (see page 4)

1 teaspoon kosher salt

1 large egg

1 large egg yolk

2½ cups all-purpose flour

½ teaspoon ground cinnamon

¼ teaspoon ground cardamom (optional)

¾ cup powdered sugar

2 tablespoons strong coffee or espresso, chilled

1. Lightly grease a 10-inch springform pan.

2. In a stand mixer fitted with the paddle attachment, beat the granulated sugar, duck fat, butter, and salt on medium speed until pale and fluffy, for 1 to 2 minutes. Add the egg and egg yolk; continue beating until combined.

3. Turn off the mixer. Add the flour, cinnamon, and cardamom (if using); pulse on low speed just until the mixture comes together as a dough.

4. Scrape the dough into the prepared pan and spread into an even layer. Using a sharp, thin knife, lightly score the surface into 12 wedges, then gently poke small holes on the top, but be careful not to go all the way through. Refrigerate until chilled solid, for about 1 hour.

5. Preheat the oven to 325°F.

6. Put the pan in the oven and bake until the shortbread is set and just barely browned at the edges, for 16 to 18 minutes. Remove from the oven.

7. While the shortbread is still hot, remove the side of the spring-form pan and, using a thin knife, neatly slice into triangles. Let cool completely before removing from the pan.

8. To make the glaze, in a small bowl, whisk together the powdered sugar and coffee.

9. Once the shortbread is completely cool, using a fork, drizzle the glaze over the cookies.

Duck-Fat Salted Bourbon Caramels with Smoked Salt

PREP TIME: 15 MINUTES / **COOK TIME:** 45 MINUTES, PLUS 2 HOURS 15 MINUTES TO COOL

YIELD: 45 CANDIES

OTHER GAME YOU CAN USE: GOOSE FAT

Living in the South has given me a deep appreciation of smoked meats, hunting, and Bourbon; they all go hand in hand. And this gem of a recipe combines them all in a perfect little treat! Don't skip on the smoked salt at the end; it ties everything together. You need a candy thermometer for this recipe.

Nonstick cooking spray, for greasing

1 cup heavy cream

8 tablespoons (1 stick) unsalted butter

5 tablespoons rendered duck fat (see page 4)

1½ cups sugar

¼ cup corn syrup

2 tablespoons water

2 teaspoons Bourbon

1 teaspoon vanilla extract

⅛ teaspoon kosher salt

Smoked sea salt, for topping

1. Line a 9-inch square baking dish with parchment paper. Grease with nonstick cooking spray.

2. In a small saucepan, heat the cream, butter, and duck fat over medium heat until the butter and duck fat have melted. Stir until combined. Remove from the heat.

3. In a medium saucepan, combine the sugar, corn syrup, and water; bring to a boil. Cook, without stirring, until the mixture reaches 320°F on a candy thermometer.

4. Once the mixture reaches 320°F, remove it from the heat. Slowly pour in the cream mixture, whisking to combine.

5. Return the pan to the heat and cook to 250°F for soft caramels or 260°F for firmer caramels.

6. Once the desired temperature has been reached, quickly whisk in the Bourbon, vanilla, and salt. Immediately pour into the prepared baking dish. Let cool for 10 to 15 minutes, then sprinkle with the smoked sea salt.

7. Let the caramel cool for at least 2 hours. Then, spray a knife with nonstick cooking spray; this will prevent the caramel from sticking to your knife and make cutting easier. Cut the caramel into individual squares.

8. Wrap individual caramels in wax paper and store in an airtight container at room temperature for up to 2 weeks.

GEESE

Smoked Goose Gumbo

PREP TIME: 15 MINUTES / **COOK TIME:** 2 HOURS 15 MINUTES, PLUS 2 TO 4 HOURS
TO SMOKE THE GOOSE / **YIELD:** 6 TO 8 SERVINGS
OTHER GAME YOU CAN USE: DUCK, VENISON

Whenever gumbo is brought up, everyone will chime in with what they think makes a great gumbo, so if you are partial to a particular roux color or spice blend, go ahead and make those swaps, but please try it with goose fat instead of butter for the roux. It's quite possibly a gumbo game changer.

12 ounces boneless, skinless goose breasts

1 cup rendered goose fat, duck fat (page 4), or unsalted butter

1 cup all-purpose flour

5 cloves garlic, minced

3 stalks celery, minced

1 green bell pepper, minced

1 large onion, minced

1 pound white button mushrooms, sliced

2 teaspoons kosher salt, plus more to taste

1 teaspoon Cajun seasoning

½ teaspoon freshly ground black pepper

2 bay leaves

10 cups beef broth

8 ounces andouille sausage, cut into thin rounds

1 teaspoon hot sauce, such as sriracha

1 teaspoon Worcestershire sauce

Hot cooked white rice, for serving

1. Pat the goose breasts dry, set on a plate, and refrigerate for 45 minutes.

2. Set the smoker to 220°F. If your smoker does not have a drip pan, cover a sheet pan with aluminum foil and place under the grates, beneath where the goose will sit, to catch any rendered fat and drippings.

3. Put the goose in the smoker and smoke goose using hickory wood (see page 4) until the internal temperature of the goose reaches 150°F, for 2 to 4 hours. Remove from the smoker.

4. In a large Dutch oven, melt the fat over high heat. Sprinkle in the flour and whisk until smooth. Reduce the heat to medium-low. Cook, whisking constantly until the roux is the color of peanut butter, for 20 to 25 minutes.

5. Add the garlic, celery, bell pepper, and onion; cook until all the vegetables are soft, for 10 to 15 minutes. Add the mushrooms, salt, Cajun seasoning, pepper, and bay leaves; cook, stirring, for 5 minutes.

6. Whisk in the broth and bring to a boil. Reduce the heat to medium. Cover and simmer until the gumbo has thickened, for about 1 hour. Skim off fat as needed during cooking.

7. Chop the smoked goose meat and add it with the sausage, hot sauce, and Worcestershire sauce to the gumbo. Cook for 15 to 20 minutes. Remove from the heat.

8. To serve the gumbo, ladle into bowls over cooked white rice.

Goose Pastrami Sandwiches

PREP TIME: 1 HOUR, PLUS 3 DAYS TO CURE THE GOOSE / **COOK TIME:** 4 HOURS / **YIELD:** 6 SERVINGS
OTHER GAME YOU CAN USE: VENISON

This recipe cures for 3 days, so be sure to plan ahead. It is totally worth all the effort, and I promise it will be the best pastrami you have ever had!

FOR CURING THE GOOSE BREASTS:

¼ cup Morton Tender Quick Home Meat Cure (see page 5)

¼ cup packed light or dark brown sugar

¼ cup freshly ground black pepper

2 tablespoons garlic powder

1 tablespoon onion powder

2 teaspoons dried rosemary

2 teaspoons dried thyme

1 teaspoon ground coriander

2 (1-pound) skinless goose breasts

1 cup ice cubes

FOR THE PASTRAMI RUB:

¼ cup freshly ground black pepper

2 tablespoons ground coriander

1 tablespoon packed light or dark brown sugar

1 tablespoon paprika

2 teaspoons garlic powder

2 teaspoons onion powder

1 teaspoon dry mustard

¼ teaspoon red pepper flakes

1. **To cure the goose breasts:** In a medium bowl, whisk together the Morton Tender Quick, brown sugar, pepper, garlic powder, onion powder, rosemary, thyme, and coriander.

2. Season the goose breasts liberally with the cure. Be sure that all the meat is fully covered in a thick coating.

3. Put the breasts in a large zip-top bag. Pour any remaining cure into the bag. Press out as much air as possible. (If you have a chamber vacuum or a vacuum sealer, use it.)

4. Refrigerate the breasts for 3 days. Flip the bag twice a day to keep the cure rotating.

5. After 3 days, rinse the goose breasts well under cold water.

6. In a large bowl, soak the breasts in cold water with the ice cubes for 30 minutes to remove the cure.

7. Remove the breasts and pat dry using a clean towel or paper towel.

8. **To make the pastrami rub:** In a small bowl, combine the pepper, coriander, brown sugar, paprika, garlic powder, onion powder, dry mustard, and red pepper flakes.

9. Season the breasts on all sides with the rub.

10. Set an electric smoker to 220°F.

FOR THE RUSSIAN DRESSING:

½ cup mayonnaise

2 tablespoons ketchup

½ tablespoon horseradish sauce (optional)

½ teaspoon hot sauce

½ teaspoon Worcestershire sauce

¼ teaspoon onion powder

¼ teaspoon freshly ground black pepper

¼ teaspoon smoked paprika

⅛ teaspoon kosher salt

FOR THE SANDWICHES:

1 cup shredded coleslaw mix

12 slices rye bread

6 slices Swiss cheese

11. Put the breasts in the smoker and smoke using hickory wood or applewood (see page 4) until the internal temperature of the goose reaches 150°F, for 2 to 4 hours. Remove from the smoker. Transfer to a cutting board and let rest for 15 minutes. Cut against the grain into thin slices.

12. **To make the Russian dressing:** In a small bowl, whisk together the mayonnaise, ketchup, horseradish sauce (if using), hot sauce, Worcestershire sauce, onion powder, pepper, paprika, and salt.

13. **To make the sandwiches:** In a medium bowl, toss the coleslaw mix with 1 to 3 tablespoons of the Russian dressing.

14. Spread about ½ tablespoon of the dressing on 1 slice of bread. Add a layer of sliced goose pastrami, then some of the dressed coleslaw.

15. Top with a slice of Swiss cheese and another slice of rye bread. Repeat to make the remaining sandwiches. Cut each in half and serve.

GAME TIP: To make this with venison, use a tenderloin. Timing for the smoking will be the same.

Goose Bulgogi Tacos with Quick Pickled Daikon

PREP TIME: 20 MINUTES / **COOK TIME:** 1 HOUR 30 MINUTES / **YIELD:** 5 SERVINGS

Bulgogi is a traditional South Korean meat preparation. Once you master this recipe, you will be able to make it anytime on a whim. You can take all these same flavorings and apply it to any meat.

1 cup distilled white vinegar

¼ cup sugar

1 tablespoon kosher salt

1 cup daikon radish matchsticks

5 cloves garlic, peeled

1 onion, cut into large pieces

1½ cups soy sauce

¼ cup sesame oil

1 pear, cored and cut into large pieces

2 (1-pound) boneless, skinless goose breasts

¼ cup mayonnaise

2 tablespoons sriracha

10 corn tortillas, warmed

3 tablespoons chopped fresh cilantro

Sesame seeds, for garnish

1. In a small saucepan, combine the vinegar, sugar, and salt; bring to a boil over high heat. Remove from the heat. Let cool for 10 minutes.

2. Stir in the daikon and let sit to pickle, for 30 to 60 minutes.

3. In a blender, combine the garlic, onion, soy sauce, sesame oil, and pear; blend until smooth. Transfer to a large, cast-iron Dutch oven.

4. Add the goose breasts and bring to a simmer over medium-high heat.

5. Reduce the heat to medium-low. Cover and simmer for about 1 hour. Remove from the heat. Transfer the breasts to a cutting board. Using 2 forks, shred the meat.

6. Return the meat to the pot, and cook over medium heat for 5 minutes. Remove from the heat.

7. In a small bowl, whisk together the mayonnaise and sriracha.

8. To assemble the tacos, fill each tortilla with about ¼ cup of the shredded meat, then top with a dollop of the sriracha mayonnaise and a sprinkle of cilantro. Garnish with sesame seeds and top with 4 or 5 pickled daikon matchsticks.

GAME TIP: To make with venison, use tenderloin or backstrap cut into 1/4-inch pieces. Add at step 4 and simmer for 20 minutes in step 5. There is no need to shred the meat.

BBQ Pulled-Goose Sliders with Slightly Pickled Red Cabbage Slaw

PREP TIME: 10 MINUTES / **COOK TIME:** 6 TO 8 HOURS ON LOW, PLUS 15 MINUTES / **YIELD:** 6 SERVINGS
OTHER GAME YOU CAN USE: DUCK

Your next football game is calling for these. If you want to get a jump start on cooking—so you don't miss the game—make the meat the day before, refrigerate, and reheat in a Dutch oven over medium heat for 20 minutes.

FOR THE SLAW:

1 small red cabbage (about 1½ pounds), cored and finely shredded

2 medium Granny Smith apples, cored and cut into matchsticks

1 large carrot, shredded

⅔ cup cider vinegar

1 tablespoon honey

1 tablespoon olive oil

1 teaspoon kosher salt

½ teaspoon black pepper

FOR THE GOOSE:

4 cups chicken broth

¼ cup Worcestershire sauce

4 tablespoons (½ stick) unsalted butter, divided

1 onion, chopped

2 tablespoons chopped garlic

2 to 3 pounds boneless, skinless goose breasts

1 (8-ounce) bottle barbecue sauce of your choice

1 (12-roll) package Hawaiian rolls

1. **To make the slaw:** In a large bowl, toss the cabbage, apples, and carrots together until well combined.

2. In a small bowl, whisk the vinegar, honey, olive oil, salt, and pepper together, then drizzle over the cabbage mixture. Toss until fully coated. Cover and refrigerate while you prepare the goose.

3. **To prepare the goose:** In a slow cooker, combine the broth, Worcestershire sauce, 2 tablespoons of butter, the onion, and garlic. Top with the goose breasts. Cover and cook on low for 6 to 8 hours.

4. Turn off the slow cooker. Transfer the breasts to a cutting board. Using 2 forks, shred the meat.

5. In a cast-iron skillet, melt the remaining 2 tablespoons of butter over medium-high heat.

6. Add the shredded meat and barbecue sauce; cook, stirring occasionally, until heated through, for 10 to 15 minutes. Remove from the heat.

7. Fill each of the rolls with about ¼ cup of the goose. Toss the slaw together one more time; top each of the sliders with some of the slaw, and serve.

Goose Casserole with Brie

PREP TIME: 30 MINUTES / **COOK TIME:** 1 HOUR / **YIELD:** 12 SERVINGS

OTHER GAME YOU CAN USE: DUCK

Casseroles are simple and easy to make; they comfort and instantly warm you up. This is my stepped-up version of a casserole that still has all those warm and fuzzy feels. Brie is the secret ingredient.

Nonstick cooking spray, for greasing

3 pounds boneless, skinless goose meat, diced

8 ounces Brie cheese, cut into pieces

3 cups cooked wild rice

½ cup chopped cremini mushrooms

½ cup chopped celery

½ cup heavy cream

3 tablespoons unsalted butter, melted

2 shallots, finely chopped

1 tablespoon minced garlic

1 teaspoon chopped fresh thyme

1 teaspoon chopped fresh sage

1 teaspoon kosher salt

½ teaspoon freshly ground black pepper

¼ cup grated Parmesan cheese

1. Preheat the oven to 350°F. Grease a 9-by-13-inch baking dish with nonstick cooking spray.

2. In a large bowl, gently stir together the goose, Brie cheese, rice, mushrooms, celery, cream, butter, shallots, garlic, thyme, sage, salt, and pepper. Spread into the prepared dish.

3. Sprinkle evenly with the Parmesan cheese.

4. Put the baking dish in the oven and bake until the casserole is hot and bubbling in the center, for about 1 hour. Remove from the oven.

Crispy-Skinned Goose with Balsamic-Blackberry Sauce

PREP TIME: 10 MINUTES / **COOK TIME:** 45 MINUTES / **YIELD:** 4 SERVINGS
OTHER GAME YOU CAN USE: DUCK

Berries play really well with wild game. This sauce is also lovely with grilled, roasted, or pan-seared venison, elk, bear, or pheasant.

3 tablespoons unsalted butter

1 shallot, minced

1 cup blackberries

1 tablespoon packed light or dark brown sugar

1 tablespoon honey

2 bay leaves

½ cup balsamic vinegar

Grated zest of 1 orange

¼ cup freshly squeezed orange juice

2 tablespoons chopped fresh mint

1 teaspoon chopped fresh thyme

4 confit goose legs (page 120)

3 cloves garlic, peeled

1 small bunch fresh thyme

1. Preheat the oven to 350°F.

2. In a medium saucepan, melt the butter over medium-high heat.

3. Add the shallot and cook for about 3 minutes.

4. Stir in the blackberries, brown sugar, honey, and bay leaves. Using a wooden spoon, gently crush the blackberries.

5. Stir in the vinegar, orange zest, orange juice, mint, and thyme leaves.

6. Reduce the heat to medium. Cook until the sauce has slightly thickened, for 12 to 15 minutes. Remove from the heat. Keep warm.

7. Heat a large, cast-iron skillet over high heat until hot.

8. Add the goose legs, skin-side down, garlic, and thyme. (You don't need to add any fat to the skillet; the confit will have plenty around it to crisp the skin.) Cook until the skin is golden brown and crispy, for about 10 minutes. Turn off the heat.

9. Turn the legs. Put the skillet in the oven and bake until heated through, for 15 minutes. Remove from the oven.

10. Serve the goose immediately, topped with the sauce.

GAME TIP: If you make this dish with duck, use 6 confit legs.

Braised Goose Legs with Spiced Orange Sauce

PREP TIME: 10 MINUTES / **COOK TIME:** 2 HOURS 30 MINUTES / **YIELD:** 4 SERVINGS
OTHER GAME YOU CAN USE: DUCK

If you want to create a showstopping dish to impress your guests, this is it! Don't worry, it's super simple to make—it's a one-pot wonder, made in a Dutch oven. If you can find them, this dish is fantastic with blood oranges.

4 goose legs

Kosher salt

3 tablespoons vegetable oil

2 teaspoons freshly ground black pepper, plus more to taste

2 teaspoons ground coriander

1 teaspoon chopped fresh rosemary

1½ cups chicken broth

Juice of 3 oranges

2 teaspoons packed light or dark brown sugar

¼ cup orange marmalade

6 tablespoons water

2 teaspoons cornstarch

1. Preheat the oven to 300°F.

2. Using paper towels, pat the goose legs dry. Season with salt.

3. In a large, cast-iron Dutch oven, heat the vegetable oil over medium-high heat.

4. Add the goose legs and sear until browned on all sides, for 10 to 15 minutes. Transfer to a plate.

5. Add the pepper, coriander, and rosemary to the pot; stir until combined and fragrant, for 30 to 45 seconds.

6. Add the broth and, using a wooden spoon, scrape up any browned bits from the bottom of the pot.

7. Stir in the orange juice and brown sugar.

8. Return the goose legs and any accumulated juices to the pot.

9. Cover, put the pot in the oven, and roast for 2 hours. Remove from the oven.

10. Remove the goose legs to a clean plate. Place the pot over medium-high heat. Stir in the marmalade.

11. In a small bowl, whisk together the water and cornstarch until smooth. Whisk into the liquid in the pot and cook, stirring frequently, until the sauce thickens, for about 10 minutes. Season with salt and pepper.

12. Return the goose legs to the pot and spoon the sauce over the legs. Remove from the heat. Serve immediately.

Goose Schnitzel with Jaeger Sauce

PREP TIME: 20 MINUTES / **COOK TIME:** 30 MINUTES / **YIELD:** 4 SERVINGS

OTHER GAME YOU CAN USE: WILD BOAR, VENISON

This is the very first dish I had when I was in Germany and, boy, did it give me warm feelings.

FOR THE SCHNITZEL:

2 boneless, skinless goose breasts, cut in half horizontally

1 cup all-purpose flour

2 teaspoons paprika

1 teaspoon kosher salt, plus more to taste

1 teaspoon freshly ground black pepper

2 large eggs

1 cup panko bread crumbs

¼ cup vegetable oil

FOR THE SAUCE:

1 tablespoon unsalted butter

1 large shallot, chopped

8 ounces cremini mushrooms, sliced

½ cup white wine

½ cup beef broth

½ cup heavy cream

2 tablespoons unsalted butter, softened

2 tablespoons all-purpose flour

½ teaspoon kosher salt

¼ teaspoon freshly ground black pepper

2 tablespoons chopped fresh parsley

1. **To make the schnitzel:** Place each breast cutlet between 2 pieces of wax paper. Using a meat mallet, pound to ¼-inch thickness.

2. Set out 3 large bowls. In one bowl, whisk together the flour, paprika, salt, and pepper; in another bowl, whisk together the eggs; and put the bread crumbs in the remaining bowl.

3. In a large, cast-iron skillet, heat the oil over medium-high heat until hot.

4. Dredge each breast cutlet in the flour mixture, dip in the egg wash, then dredge in the bread crumbs, pressing lightly to get an even coating on both sides.

5. Working in batches, add the cutlets to the skillet and cook, flipping once, until golden brown, for about 4 minutes per batch. Transfer to a platter. Season immediately with salt. Turn off the heat.

6. **To make the sauce:** In a clean skillet, melt the butter over medium heat.

7. Add the shallot and cook, stirring, until translucent, for 2 minutes.

8. Add the mushrooms and cook, stirring, until browned, for about 5 minutes.

9. Add the wine and broth; using a wooden spoon, scrape up any browned bits from the bottom of the skillet. Let the liquid reduce for about 3 minutes.

CONTINUED >

10. Add the cream and bring to a boil.

11. Reduce the heat to medium-low.

12. In a small bowl, mix together the butter and flour to form a paste. Add to the skillet, stirring until fully incorporated.

13. Return the sauce to a boil, stirring often, until thickened. Remove from the heat. Stir in the salt and pepper.

14. Top the breasts with the sauce and garnish with the parsley. Serve immediately.

GAME TIP: To prepare with venison, use 2 (1-inch-thick) steaks, cut in half horizontally. To prepare with boar, use 2 (1-inch-thick) boneless chops, cut in half horizontally.

Spiced Roast Goose with Figs

PREP TIME: 45 MINUTES / **COOK TIME:** 4 HOURS / **YIELD:** 8 SERVINGS

OTHER GAME YOU CAN USE: DUCK

This dish screams the holidays. If you are thinking of trying something new for Thanksgiving, this is what you have been looking for. Roasted goose never tastes better than when it is slathered in warm spices and served with sweet figs. If you have pink peppercorns, substitute them for the black peppercorns, upping the amount to 2 teaspoons.

FOR THE GOOSE:

1 (12-pound) goose, wing tips removed

¼ cup vegetable oil

Kosher salt

Freshly ground black pepper

2 large onions, quartered

1 tablespoon allspice berries

1 teaspoon black peppercorns

3 green cardamom pods (optional)

1. **To make the goose:** Set a rack in the middle position in the oven. Preheat the oven to 425°F.

2. Make sure the goose doesn't have any quills still attached to the skin. Place the goose on a rack in a roasting pan. Using a paring knife, gently cut slits in the skin all over, making sure not to pierce the meat. This helps the rendered fat escape.

3. Brush the vegetable oil all over the goose skin. Season with salt and pepper.

4. Stuff the onions into the cavity.

5. Using a spice grinder or coffee grinder, grind the allspice, peppercorns, and cardamom (if using), until finely ground. Sprinkle over the goose.

6. Put the roasting pan in the oven and roast for 30 minutes.

7. Reduce the oven temperature to 325°F.

8. Roast the goose for 2 hours.

9. Reduce the oven temperature again to 275°F.

10. Continue to roast until the internal temperature of the goose reaches 165°F at the center of the breast, for 35 to 45 minutes. Remove from the oven. Let rest for 20 to 30 minutes before carving.

CONTINUED >

FOR THE SAUCE:

4 tablespoons (½ stick)
   unsalted butter

2 large shallots,
   finely chopped

1 pound dried figs

8 ounces dried apricots

2 cups beef broth

⅓ cup brandy

2 tablespoons orange
   marmalade

11. **To make the sauce:** While the goose rests, in a medium saucepan, melt the butter over medium-high heat.

12. Add the shallots and cook, stirring, until soft, for about 4 minutes.

13. Add the figs, apricots, broth, brandy, and marmalade; bring to a simmer.

14. Reduce the heat to medium-low. Cook, stirring occasionally, until the liquid has reduced by half, for about 30 minutes. Remove from the heat.

15. Carve the goose and serve with the fig sauce.

GAME TIP: If making with duck, cook to the same internal temperature; it will take 30 to 45 minutes less time to cook than goose.

Hawaiian-Style Goose Jerky

PREP TIME: 20 MINUTES, PLUS 24 HOURS TO MARINATE / **COOK TIME:** 6 TO 8 HOURS
YIELD: 2 DOZEN PIECES
OTHER GAME YOU CAN USE: VENISON

Move over BBQ jerky; this Hawaiian-flavored jerky is taking over! I love the flavors of Hawaiian BBQ. The sweet tropical fruits paired with a salty, spicy kick are outstanding.

3 pounds boneless, skinless goose breasts

1 cup soy sauce

¼ cup pineapple juice

3 tablespoons packed light or dark brown sugar

2 tablespoons kosher salt

1 tablespoon Worcestershire sauce

1 tablespoon grated or minced fresh ginger

1 tablespoon minced garlic

½ teaspoon red pepper flakes

1. Cut the goose breasts into 1- to 1½-inch-by-¼-inch-thick strips.

2. To make the marinade, in a large bowl, whisk together the soy sauce, pineapple juice, brown sugar, salt, Worcestershire sauce, ginger, garlic, and red pepper flakes until the sugar and salt dissolve.

3. Add the goose strips to the marinade. Cover and refrigerate for at least 24 hours.

4. Set the dehydrator to 140°F.

5. Lift the goose strips from the marinade and let drain slightly. Place on the dehydrator trays so they do not touch. Dehydrate for 6 to 8 hours. Your finished jerky should be pliable like leather and should fray and crack slightly at the point at which you bend it. Remove from the dehydrator.

STORAGE: Keep in an airtight container at room temperature for up to 1 month.

CHAPTER 6

Upland Game Birds

Coffee in one hand, shotgun in the other, and a dog by your side—it's the perfect way to start a great day. Upland hunting—pheasant, quail, grouse, dove, and turkey—has taken my heart, not because of the beautiful birds, but because of my dog, Remi. I've been training her to bird-hunt since she was six months old. And every time we hit the field, it brings joy not only to me but also to Remi. Sitting down at the table and sharing a meal with my family that Remi and I worked together to harvest is the perfect way to end the day.

Pheasant 130
Quail 140
Grouse 151
Dove 157
Turkey 162

← Pan-Seared Citrus-Marinated Quail with Sesame-Ginger Slaw, page 142

Pheasant

Pheasants are my favorite birds to hunt. Wild pheasant is very lean and if not cooked with care, will end up being very dry. Pheasant is similar to chicken but with a slightly stronger smell and flavor. The key to pheasant is to cook it covered, between 250°F to 325°F with moisture. I think you get the best flavor cooking it on the bone, and it also benefits from brining.

Quail

Quail are very small birds that belong to the same family as pheasant and partridge. Though they are ground dwellers, they can fly 40 to 50 miles per hour, which makes them extremely fun to hunt with dogs. Quail are best cooked quickly over high heat or slowly over low heat. Just like pheasant, they can get tough if even slightly overcooked, so it's best to brine them prior to cooking.

Grouse

If you have ever hunted grouse, you know their low, deep belly calls. Grouse are little plump birds that look similar to quail and have extremely lean meat. They should be brined prior to cooking for the best results.

Dove

Doves are dark-meat birds with hardly any fat on them. Since they are a darker meat, dove breasts don't overcook as easily as quail or pheasant do. Although most hunters use the breasts to make poppers, there are even more delicious ways to cook dove, and I hope these recipes will inspire you.

Turkey

Wild turkey is not at all like store-bought birds. The best thing you can do once you harvest a turkey is to immediately pluck the feathers because once their skin gets tough, it becomes more difficult to pluck. Turkeys are best eaten the day they are harvested. The two best tips I can give you when cooking wild turkey is to brine it and then to baste it as much as possible!

Field-Dressing

You should field-dress the bird right after it's shot. You can do this by laying the bird on its back and gently pulling off the feathers that are just below the breastbone. This will clear a path for making the first cut. You want to make the cut from just below the breastbone all the way down to the anal opening. Please make sure not to puncture the intestines because that will spoil the meat. Then, gently reach in and take out the viscera by pulling downward. Lastly, you will want to remove the crop and windpipe. If you are hunting in warm weather, blood can be an issue and any left over after gutting can spoil the meat. I usually stuff a large handful of dry grass into the cavity to absorb any blood that may leak in. If you are hunting in cold weather, leave the cleaned cavity open, which will help cool the bird down faster.

If you want to keep the skin on your game bird, it's best to pluck the feathers right after it has been shot because the feathers will pull out much more easily while the body is still warm. If you decide to pluck the feathers later, you need to chill the bird down completely, then dip it in a water bath of 180°F—any hotter or colder and the skin will tear.

Wild vs. Farmed Game Birds

Wild game birds aren't like farmed birds at all. Pen-raised birds are much fatter, and their bones are much softer in comparison to wild ones. Farm-raised bird meat will cook faster, is less dense, and is not as filling as wild-game bird meat. As a bird lives in the wild, it gets strong, which makes the meat grow denser. This is not the same thing as toughness, although the sinews in a wild bird do get extremely tough. The major difference is the flavor, thanks to diet. If you are expecting a game bird from the frozen section of your market to be the same as a wild bird that's been eating bugs, plants, and insects, you are sadly mistaken. Farmed birds are raised eating grains, which helps give them more flavor and more fat. So, when cooking wild game birds, it is best to impart fat in as many ways as possible.

PHEASANT

Grilled Pheasant Salad with Candied Pine Nuts and Sherry Vinaigrette

PREP TIME: 30 MINUTES / **COOK TIME:** 30 MINUTES / **YIELD:** 4 SERVINGS
OTHER GAME YOU CAN USE: QUAIL, VENISON

This is my favorite salad. It's sweet, salty, and citrusy, and the sugared pine nuts take it over the top. You just might find yourself making a large batch of the nuts simply for snacking!

1 pheasant, cut into 8 pieces

1 tablespoon kosher salt, plus more to taste

1 teaspoon freshly ground black pepper, plus more to taste

½ cup extra-virgin olive oil, plus more for brushing

2½ tablespoons packed light or dark brown sugar

2 tablespoons salted butter

2 ounces pine nuts

3 tablespoons sherry vinegar

1 tablespoon freshly squeezed lemon juice

2 teaspoons Dijon mustard

1 shallot, minced

3 cups baby arugula

3 cups baby kale

½ cup finely shredded red cabbage

5 scallions, green and white parts, chopped

2 oranges, peeled and segmented

1. Preheat the grill to 300°F to 350°F.

2. Season the pheasant with the salt and pepper.

3. Brush the grill grates with olive oil to prevent sticking.

4. Place the pheasant on the grill, skin-side down, directly over the fire. Cook, turning once, until the internal temperature of the pheasant reaches 165°F, for 20 to 24 minutes. Remove from the heat. Transfer to a clean plate. Let cool.

5. In a small saucepan, combine the brown sugar and butter. Cook, stirring, over medium heat, until the butter melts.

6. Add the pine nuts and cook, stirring, until coated with the mixture and golden brown, for about 5 minutes. Remove from the heat. Pour onto a sheet of wax paper to cool. Once cooled, crumble the pine nuts.

7. To make the vinaigrette, in a small bowl, whisk together the olive oil, vinegar, lemon juice, mustard, and shallot. Season with salt and pepper.

8. Remove the pheasant meat from the bones and shred into pieces.

9. In a large salad bowl, combine the arugula, kale, and cabbage. Toss with 2 to 3 tablespoons of the vinaigrette until coated.

10. Top with the pheasant, scallions, oranges, and pine nuts; serve.

GAME TIP: To prepare this dish with quail, decrease the grilling time to 10 to 12 minutes. To prepare with venison, use a 1-inch-thick steak, preferably cut from the backstrap. Grill for 4 or 5 minutes per side, then cut into 1/4-inch-thick slices against the grain to serve.

Pheasant Samosas with
Mango-Tamarind Chutney

PREP TIME: 45 MINUTES / **COOK TIME:** 30 MINUTES / **YIELD:** 4 TO 6 SERVINGS

OTHER GAME YOU CAN USE: DUCK, GOOSE

These are my take on my favorite New York City street food. If I were you, I would double the recipe, assemble the samosas, bake one batch, and freeze the other; stored in a plastic freezer bag, they will keep for about 3 months.

FOR THE SAMOSAS:

1½ pounds boneless, skinless pheasant breasts, cut into ½-inch pieces

2 tablespoons Indian-Style Spice Rub (page 248)

¼ cup olive oil

½ cup chopped onion

1 (10-ounce) package frozen mixed vegetables

Kosher salt

Freshly ground black pepper

1 (17.3-ounce) box frozen puff pastry, thawed

1 large egg, beaten

1. **To make the samosas:** Preheat the oven to 400°F. Line a sheet pan with parchment paper.

2. Sprinkle the pheasant with the spice rub on all sides; be sure to use all of it.

3. In a large sauté pan, heat the olive oil over medium heat until hot.

4. Add the onion and cook, stirring, until translucent, for 5 minutes.

5. Add the pheasant and cook, turning, until lightly browned on all sides, for about 6 minutes.

6. Stir in the frozen mixed vegetables. Season with salt and pepper. Remove from the heat.

7. Lay 1 sheet at a time of the puff pastry on a work surface. Using a 3-inch round cookie cutter, cut as many circles out of the dough as you can. Put the circles on the prepared sheet pan. Add 1 tablespoon of the pheasant filling to the center of the rounds. Using a pastry brush, brush half of each round with the egg wash. Fold 1 side over the filling and press down with your fingers to seal. Poke a small hole in one of the sides. Repeat with the remaining puff pastry.

8. Put the sheet pan in the oven and bake for 15 minutes, or until the samosas are golden brown. Remove from the oven.

FOR THE CHUTNEY:

1 ripe medium mango, peeled, seeded, and chopped

10 dates, pitted

½ cup packed light or dark brown sugar

¼ cup tamarind paste or freshly squeezed lime juice

1 tablespoon minced garlic

1 tablespoon grated or minced fresh ginger

1 tablespoon apple cider vinegar

1 tablespoon ketchup

1 teaspoon red pepper flakes

9. **To make the chutney:** While the samosas are baking, in a food processor, combine the mango, dates, brown sugar, tamarind paste, garlic, ginger, vinegar, ketchup, and red pepper flakes. Pulse until semi-smooth with some chunky pieces. Serve in a bowl alongside the samosas.

Fettuccine with Pheasant and Morel Sauce

PREP TIME: 10 MINUTES / **COOK TIME:** 40 MINUTES / **YIELD:** 6 SERVINGS
OTHER GAME YOU CAN USE: DUCK, GOOSE

If you love morels and pasta, or just love pasta, this dish is for you. I love foraging for morels, especially after an evening rainfall.

4 ounces bacon, finely diced

12 ounces pheasant breast meat, cut into 1-inch pieces

6 ounces fresh morels, porcini, or other mushrooms, chopped

2 tablespoons unsalted butter

2 shallots, minced

¼ cup brandy

1 cup heavy cream

½ cup grated Parmesan cheese

Kosher salt

1 pound fettuccine

Freshly ground black pepper

Shaved Parmesan cheese, for serving

1. Line a plate with paper towels.

2. In a large skillet, cook the bacon over medium-high heat until just crispy, for 5 minutes. Transfer to the prepared plate, reserving the fat in the skillet.

3. Add the pheasant and cook, turning, until browned on all sides and cooked through, for 5 minutes. Transfer to a clean plate.

4. To make the sauce, add the morels to the pan and cook until they release their water; continue to cook until the liquid evaporates, for about 4 minutes.

5. Add the butter and shallots; cook until the shallots are translucent and soft, for about 3 minutes.

6. Stir in the brandy and cook for 1 minute.

7. Bring a large pot of salted water to a boil over high heat.

8. Stir the cream and Parmesan cheese into the skillet; cook until the sauce has slightly thickened, for about 10 minutes.

9. Return the pheasant and bacon to the skillet.

10. Cover the skillet. Reduce the heat to low to keep warm.

11. Cook the fettuccine as the package directs. Remove from the heat. Drain and add to the skillet. Toss to fully coat with the sauce. Season with salt and pepper. Remove from the heat.

12. Serve the pasta topped with Parmesan cheese.

Pulled-Pheasant Pasta Bake

PREP TIME: 15 MINUTES / **COOK TIME:** 50 MINUTES / **YIELD:** 4 SERVINGS
OTHER GAME YOU CAN USE: TURKEY, WILD BOAR, VENISON

When I prepare pheasant, I always cook or smoke more than one at a time, allowing me to have cooked meat at the ready, especially for this dish.

1 teaspoon kosher salt, plus more for cooking the rigatoni

1 pound rigatoni

2 tablespoons olive oil

1 yellow onion, finely chopped

3 cloves garlic, minced

1½ cups shredded, cooked pheasant meat

1 (28-ounce) can crushed tomatoes, preferably San Marzano

½ cup heavy cream

½ teaspoon freshly ground black pepper

½ teaspoon Italian seasoning

1 cup shredded mozzarella cheese

½ cup grated Parmesan cheese

2 tablespoons chopped fresh basil

1. Preheat the oven to 350°F.

2. Bring a large pot of salted water to a boil over high heat. Cook the rigatoni as the package directs. Remove from the heat. Drain.

3. While the rigatoni cooks, in a large skillet, heat the olive oil over medium-high heat.

4. Add the onion and cook, stirring, until tender, for about 5 minutes.

5. Add the garlic and cook for 2 minutes.

6. Add the pheasant, tomatoes, cream, salt, pepper, and Italian seasoning. Bring to a simmer.

7. Reduce the heat to low. Simmer for 15 minutes.

8. Add the rigatoni to the sauce and stir to coat. Transfer to a 9-by-13-inch baking dish.

9. Sprinkle with the mozzarella and Parmesan.

10. Put the baking dish in the oven and bake until bubbly, for 25 minutes. Remove from the oven.

11. Garnish the pasta with the basil and serve.

Stir-Fried Pheasant with Garlic Noodles

PREP TIME: 20 MINUTES / **COOK TIME:** 15 MINUTES / **YIELD:** 4 SERVINGS

OTHER GAME YOU CAN USE: DUCK, QUAIL, TURKEY, VENISON

If your family loves Chinese takeout, I guarantee this dish will quickly become a favorite. It's simple to make and a great use of whatever you have on hand. Get creative and try it with other wild game or veggies!

4 (5-ounce) packages ramen noodles

½ cup olive oil

1½ pounds boneless, skinless pheasant breasts, thinly sliced

5 cloves garlic, minced

1 tablespoon grated or minced fresh ginger

½ cup shredded carrots

½ cup sugar snap peas

1 bunch scallions, green and white parts, thinly sliced

¼ cup soy sauce

2 tablespoons rice vinegar

1 teaspoon sesame oil

1 teaspoon freshly ground black pepper

½ teaspoon sugar

Chopped fresh cilantro, for serving

Sesame seeds, for serving

1. Bring a large pot of water to a boil over high heat. Cook the ramen noodles as the package directs. Remove from the heat. Drain.

2. While the noodles are cooking, heat a wok or large skillet over high heat until it is hot.

3. Put the olive oil and pheasant in the wok. Cook, turning, until browned on all sides and cooked through, for 5 minutes.

4. Add the garlic and ginger; cook for 2 minutes.

5. Add the carrots, sugar snap peas, scallions, soy sauce, vinegar, and sesame oil; cook, stirring, until the carrots are crisp-tender, for about 5 minutes.

6. Stir in the pepper and sugar.

7. Reduce the heat to low. Stir in the ramen noodles. Remove from the heat.

8. Serve the stir-fry sprinkled with cilantro and sesame seeds.

GAME TIP: To prepare with venison, use 1 1/2 pounds venison backstrap cut into 1/4-inch-thick strips.

Fried Pheasant with Sriracha Aïoli

PREP TIME: 15 MINUTES / **COOK TIME:** 45 MINUTES / **YIELD:** 4 TO 6 SERVINGS
OTHER GAME YOU CAN USE: TURKEY

Crunchy fried pheasant with spicy aïoli—all you need is a pint of beer and you're set for a good time. The key to tasty fried pheasant is adding the seasoning to the batter: not only salt and pepper, but also herbs and spices. Try this recipe with fresh herbs as well.

2 cups all-purpose flour

2 tablespoons cornstarch

2 tablespoons kosher salt, plus more to taste

1 tablespoon freshly ground black pepper

1 tablespoon smoked paprika

1 tablespoon garlic powder

1 tablespoon ground ginger

2 teaspoons dried thyme

3 large eggs

2 cups panko bread crumbs

1 quart peanut oil

1 pheasant, cut into 8 pieces

Honey, for serving

1 recipe Sriracha Aïoli (page 257), for serving

1. In a large bowl, whisk together the flour, cornstarch, salt, pepper, paprika, garlic powder, ginger, and thyme.

2. In a large shallow bowl, beat the eggs.

3. Put the bread crumbs in a medium bowl.

4. In a large Dutch oven, heat the oil to 350°F. Set a wire rack over a sheet pan. Set another rack over paper towels.

5. Working with one piece at a time, dredge the pheasant in the flour mixture, making sure it's evenly covered. Then dip into the egg mixture to coat. Dredge in the bread crumbs. Place on the rack set over the sheet pan.

6. Once the oil is up to temperature, fry 3 pieces of pheasant in the oil at a time (if you add more, the temperature of the oil will drop and the pheasant will not fry as well), turning once, for 10 to 12 minutes. Place on the rack set over paper towels. Immediately season with salt. Turn off the heat.

7. Serve the pheasant immediately with a drizzle of honey and the aïoli alongside.

GAME TIP: To prepare with turkey, use breast meat cut into 1-inch-thick strips and increase the frying time to 12 to 14 minutes.

Guinness-Braised Pheasant

PREP TIME: 10 MINUTES / **COOK TIME:** 1 HOUR 40 MINUTES / **YIELD:** 4 SERVINGS
OTHER GAME YOU CAN USE: QUAIL

Pheasant and beer; a good ending to a day of hunting. Beer is a beautiful liquid to braise with; it adds depth of flavor and, when reduced, it brings a slight sweetness. Braising long and slow helps develop even more flavor and turns tougher meat cuts into fork-tender goodness. This dish is delicious with roasted vegetables, mashed potatoes, or Creamy Duck-Fat Polenta (page 107).

8 skin-on pheasant pieces
  (4 breasts and 4 legs)
1 (10-ounce) bottle
  Guinness stout
3 tablespoons balsamic vinegar
4 sprigs thyme
2 shallots, minced
1 bay leaf
4 tablespoons (½ stick)
  unsalted butter
1 onion, chopped
1 clove garlic, minced
1 tablespoon all-purpose flour
½ cup chopped walnuts
¼ cup dried currants or raisins

1. In a large bowl, toss together the pheasant, Guinness, vinegar, thyme, shallots, and bay leaf to fully coat. Cover and refrigerate overnight.

2. Remove the pheasant pieces from the marinade; reserve the marinade. Pat dry using a paper towel.

3. In a large Dutch oven, melt the butter over medium-high heat.

4. Working in batches, add the pheasant, skin-side down, and sear, turning once, until golden brown on all sides, for 7 or 8 minutes per batch. Transfer to a plate.

5. Add the onion to the pot and cook until translucent, for 5 minutes.

6. Stir in the garlic and cook for 2 minutes.

7. Sprinkle in the flour and stir to combine.

8. Whisk in the reserved marinade and bring to a boil.

9. Return the pheasant and any accumulated juices to the pot.

10. Reduce the heat to medium-low. Cover and simmer until tender, for 1 hour.

11. Reduce the heat to medium. Stir in the walnuts and currants; cook until thickened, for 10 minutes. Remove from the heat. Serve immediately.

Grilled Pheasant with Chimichurri

PREP TIME: 20 MINUTES / **COOK TIME:** 35 MINUTES / **YIELD:** 4 SERVINGS

OTHER GAME YOU CAN USE: QUAIL, VENISON

This is one of my favorite outdoor dishes! Fresh chimichurri and grilled pheasant are a perfect pairing. Serve with a chilled glass of sauvignon blanc, and you have a superb meal for a summer night. Pheasant is a lean meat like chicken and grilling it is easy.

FOR THE CHIMICHURRI:

1 cup packed fresh flat-leaf parsley leaves

⅓ cup extra-virgin olive oil

3 tablespoons red-wine vinegar

3 cloves garlic, peeled

2 teaspoons dried oregano

½ teaspoon red pepper flakes

½ teaspoon kosher salt

¼ teaspoon freshly ground black pepper

FOR THE PHEASANT:

1 pheasant, cut into 8 pieces

1½ teaspoons kosher salt

1 teaspoon freshly ground black pepper

1 teaspoon paprika

4 tablespoons (½ stick) butter

1 clove garlic, minced

1. **To make the chimichurri:** Put the parsley, olive oil, vinegar, garlic, oregano, red pepper flakes, salt, and pepper in a food processor. Pulse until combined but with a slightly chunky texture; you don't want a smooth paste. Transfer to a serving bowl.

2. Preheat the grill to 350°F to 425°F.

3. **To make the pheasant:** Season both sides of the pheasant pieces with the salt, pepper, and paprika.

4. In a small saucepan, melt the butter over medium heat.

5. Add the garlic and cook until fragrant, for about 2 minutes. Remove from the heat.

6. Brush the pheasant with the garlic butter. Place the pheasant on the grill, skin-side down, directly over the fire. Cook, turning occasionally and basting with the butter, until browned, for 15 to 18 minutes.

7. Reduce the heat to 300°F. Continue to cook until the internal temperature of the pheasant reaches 160°F, for about 10 minutes. Remove from the heat. Transfer to a plate, cover with aluminum foil, and let rest for 5 minutes.

8. Serve the pheasant with the chimichurri.

GAME TIP: To prepare with venison, use flank steak and grill for 3 or 4 minutes per side.

QUAIL

Roasted Quail with Warm Red Lentil Salad

PREP TIME: 25 MINUTES / **COOK TIME:** 40 MINUTES / **YIELD:** 4 SERVINGS
OTHER GAME YOU CAN USE: GROUSE, DOVE

Sometimes you crave a healthy dish, and when I do, I turn to this dish every time. I will double the batch of lentils and eat it all week with some roasted veggies added to it. Healthy never tasted so good!

4 quail

3 tablespoons olive oil

Kosher salt

Freshly ground black pepper

2 tablespoons unsalted butter

2 stalks celery, finely diced

2 carrots, finely diced

1 onion, finely diced

1 cup red lentils, rinsed and
　picked over

3 cups water

2 cups chicken broth

¼ cup chopped fresh chives

2 tablespoons extra-virgin
　olive oil

2 tablespoons red-wine vinegar

1 tablespoon Dijon mustard

1 clove garlic, minced

1. Preheat the oven to 400°F.

2. Using a paper towel, pat the quail dry and place in a single layer in a large, cast-iron skillet. Drizzle with the olive oil to fully coat. Season with salt and pepper.

3. Put the skillet in the oven and roast until the internal temperature of the quail reaches 165°F, for about 20 minutes. Remove from the oven.

4. While the quail roasts, in a large saucepan, melt the butter over medium-high heat.

5. Add the celery, carrots, and onion; cook until softened, for 5 to 7 minutes.

6. Stir in the lentils, water, and broth; bring to a boil.

7. Reduce the heat to medium-low. Cover and simmer until the liquid has been absorbed, for about 25 minutes. Remove from the heat.

8. In a medium bowl, whisk together the chives, extra-virgin olive oil, vinegar, mustard, and garlic. Season with salt and pepper.

9. Add the lentils and toss to coat. Serve with the quail.

Pan-Seared Citrus-Marinated Quail with Sesame-Ginger Slaw

PREP TIME: 45 MINUTES, PLUS AT LEAST 6 HOURS TO MARINATE / **COOK TIME:** 25 MINUTES
YIELD: 6 SERVINGS
OTHER GAME YOU CAN USE: GROUSE, DOVE

I was born and raised in California, and my cooking often reflects it. California is a fusion of different cuisines with fresh, healthy ingredients, and this dish is a perfect example of that. It's bright with flavors from citrus and refreshing, thanks to the slaw.

FOR THE QUAIL:

½ cup extra-virgin olive oil

Juice of 3 oranges

Juice of 3 limes

1 (1-inch) piece fresh
  ginger, minced

4 cloves garlic, minced

8 boneless quail breasts

3 tablespoons unsalted butter

1. **To make the quail:** In a large bowl, whisk together the olive oil, orange juice, lime juice, ginger, and garlic.

2. Add the quail and toss until fully coated. Cover and refrigerate for 6 to 8 hours.

3. In a large skillet, melt the butter over medium-high heat.

4. Remove the quail breasts from the marinade; reserve the marinade. Gently lay the quail breasts in the skillet and sear, turning once, until golden brown, for about 10 minutes.

5. Add the reserved marinade and bring to a simmer.

6. Reduce the heat to medium-low. Cover and simmer, turning occasionally, until the internal temperature of the quail reaches 145°F, for 8 to 10 minutes. Remove from the heat. Transfer to a cutting board.

FOR THE SLAW:

1 (14- to 16-ounce) bag
  coleslaw mix
1 cup shredded carrots
1 yellow bell pepper, cut into
  thin strips
½ cup chopped fresh cilantro
¼ cup sliced scallions, green
  and white parts
2 oranges, peeled and
  segmented

FOR THE VINAIGRETTE:

2 tablespoons extra-virgin
  olive oil
1 tablespoon soy sauce
1 tablespoon rice vinegar
1 tablespoon packed light or
  dark brown sugar
1 tablespoon toasted
  sesame oil
½ teaspoon minced
  fresh ginger
1 tablespoon chili-garlic paste
  (optional)
Kosher salt
Freshly ground black pepper

7. **To make the slaw:** In another large bowl, combine the coleslaw mix, carrots, bell pepper, cilantro, scallions, and oranges.

8. **To make the vinaigrette:** In a small bowl, whisk together the olive oil, soy sauce, vinegar, brown sugar, sesame oil, ginger, and chili-garlic paste (if using). Season with salt and pepper if needed.

9. Add ¼ cup of the vinaigrette to the slaw mix and toss until fully coated.

10. Gently slice the quail breasts and serve on the slaw, with a ladle of the pan sauce on top.

Korean-Style Fried Quail

PREP TIME: 15 MINUTES / **COOK TIME:** 30 MINUTES / **YIELD:** 4 SERVINGS

OTHER GAME YOU CAN USE: PHEASANT, TURKEY

This is my most popular dish, and for good reason—it's amazing! It's inspired by my time in South Korea. Here, gochujang, a chili paste made with fermented soybeans, provides salty, spicy, and sweet flavors all at once. It is key to the dish. Look for it in the international section of your grocery store.

1 tablespoon vegetable oil or grapeseed oil

1 tablespoon minced garlic

⅓ cup ketchup

⅓ cup sugar

¼ cup gochujang (Korean red pepper paste) or sriracha

1 tablespoon distilled white vinegar

1 tablespoon toasted sesame seeds

½ cup cornstarch

⅓ cup all-purpose flour

½ teaspoon kosher salt, plus more to taste

½ teaspoon freshly ground black pepper

½ teaspoon garlic powder

½ teaspoon ground ginger

½ teaspoon baking soda

4 quail, each cut into 4 pieces

1 large egg, beaten

4 cups peanut oil

1. In a small saucepan, heat the oil over low heat.

2. Add the garlic and cook until fragrant, for about 2 minutes.

3. Whisk in the ketchup, sugar, gochujang, vinegar, and sesame seeds; simmer until hot, for 3 minutes. Remove from the heat. Keep warm.

4. In a medium bowl, whisk together the cornstarch, flour, salt, pepper, garlic powder, ginger, and baking soda.

5. In a large bowl, combine the quail pieces and egg, tossing to fully coat.

6. In a large, cast-iron Dutch oven, heat the peanut oil to 350°F. Line a plate with paper towels.

7. Dredge the quail in the cornstarch mixture to fully coat. Fry half of the quail until the internal temperature reaches 145°F, for 4 or 5 minutes. Using a slotted spoon, transfer the quail to the prepared plate. Immediately season with salt. Repeat with the remaining quail. Turn off the heat. Transfer to a large bowl.

8. Pour the warm sauce over the quail and turn to fully coat. Serve immediately.

GAME TIP: To prepare with pheasant, increase the frying time to 8 minutes or until the internal temperature reaches 165°F.

Brown Butter–Braised Quail with Mustard-Caper Sauce

PREP TIME: 15 MINUTES / **COOK TIME:** 35 MINUTES / **YIELD:** 4 SERVINGS
OTHER GAME YOU CAN USE: GROUSE, DOVE

Is there anything better than something being braised in butter? Absolutely not! This mustard-caper sauce came to me one night when I wanted a sauce for roasted cauliflower. I ended up loving it so much, I started using it with proteins as well. It's basically amazing on everything.

4 quail

Kosher salt

Freshly ground black pepper

8 tablespoons (1 stick)
   unsalted butter

2 shallots, finely chopped

2 cloves garlic, minced

1 tablespoon all-purpose flour

1 cup white wine

½ cup chicken broth

2 tablespoons coarse-
   grain mustard

2 tablespoons capers, drained

2 tablespoons chopped
   fresh parsley

1. Season the quail with salt and pepper.

2. In a large Dutch oven, melt the butter over medium-high heat.

3. Add the quail, and cook until browned on both sides, for about 4 minutes. Transfer to a plate.

4. Add the shallots and garlic to the pot; cook, stirring, for 2 minutes.

5. Whisk in the flour until fully incorporated.

6. Whisking constantly, add the wine in a slow stream.

7. Add the broth. Bring to a simmer.

8. Return the quail to the pot.

9. Reduce the heat to medium-low. Cover and simmer until the internal temperature of the quail reaches 145°F, for about 20 minutes. Transfer the quail to a serving plate.

10. To finish the sauce, whisk the mustard, capers, and parsley into the liquid in the pot. Simmer for 1 minute. Remove from the heat.

11. Pour the sauce over the quail and serve immediately.

Riesling-Braised Quail

PREP TIME: 20 MINUTES / **COOK TIME:** 55 MINUTES / **YIELD:** 4 SERVINGS

OTHER GAME YOU CAN USE: GROUSE

During my travels in Germany, I grew to love riesling wines because, quite frankly, you can't escape them. Riesling is definitely Germany's favorite grape. I prefer to cook this with an off-dry, or kabinett, riesling. The delicate flavors of riesling highlight the quail in a beautiful way.

4 quail

Kosher salt

Freshly ground black pepper

1 tablespoon olive oil

2 tablespoons unsalted butter

2 shallots, finely diced

1 leek, white part only, thoroughly rinsed and thinly sliced

1 teaspoon minced garlic

2 cups riesling

1 tablespoon white-wine vinegar

1 tablespoon packed light or dark brown sugar

1 sprig thyme

1 sprig rosemary

½ cup heavy cream

2 tablespoons unsalted butter

1. Preheat the oven to 425°F.

2. Place a quail, breast-side down, on a cutting board. Using a chef's knife or poultry shears, cut down each side of the backbone to remove it. Turn the quail over and press down on the breastbone using the heel of your hand to gently flatten it. Season on both sides with salt and pepper. Repeat with the remaining quail.

3. In a large, cast-iron skillet, heat the olive oil over high heat until hot.

4. Add the quail, skin-side down, and sear until golden brown, for 5 to 7 minutes. Transfer to a plate.

5. Reduce the heat to medium-high. Add the butter, shallots, and leek to the skillet; cook until softened, for 8 to 10 minutes.

6. Add the garlic and cook for 2 minutes.

7. Stir in the riesling, vinegar, brown sugar, thyme, and rosemary.

8. Return the quail to the skillet, skin-side up. Turn off the heat.

9. Put the skillet in the oven and roast until the internal temperature of the quail reaches 145°F, for 20 to 25 minutes. Remove from the oven. Transfer the quail to a serving plate.

10. Return the skillet to the stove over high heat and let the liquid reduce for 10 minutes.

11. Reduce the heat to low. Stir in the cream.

12. To finish the sauce, add the butter and whisk until melted and the sauce is velvety in texture. Season with salt and pepper. Remove from the heat.

13. Pour the sauce over the quail and serve.

Milk Tea–Poached Quail with Roasted Grapes

PREP TIME: 15 MINUTES / **COOK TIME:** 50 MINUTES / **YIELD:** 6 SERVINGS

OTHER GAME YOU CAN USE: GROUSE, DOVE

Milk is an underestimated tenderizer. And tea is an underestimated flavor enhancer. And grapes, well, they are definitely underestimated in savory dishes. When I was traveling through China, I ate a lot of dishes flavored with tea. The milk tea dishes were delicate in flavor and always made me ask what was in it. Adding roasted grapes gives amazing depth. You'll ask yourself why you've never tried it before!

2 cups chicken broth

1 cup whole milk

1 tablespoon loose jasmine tea

1 tablespoon kosher salt

¼ teaspoon freshly ground white pepper

6 quail

5 cups seedless grapes

2 tablespoons olive oil

½ cup white wine

1 tablespoon unsalted butter

1 teaspoon chopped fresh sage

1 shallot, minced

1. Preheat the oven to 450°F.

2. In a large Dutch oven, whisk together the broth, milk, tea, salt, and pepper over medium-high heat.

3. Add the quail. Bring to a boil.

4. Reduce the heat to medium-low. Cover and simmer until the quail has cooked through, for about 30 minutes.

5. Meanwhile, put the grapes on a sheet pan and drizzle with the olive oil. Gently roll the grapes in the oil to coat.

6. Put the sheet pan in the oven and roast until the grapes burst and soften, for about 30 minutes. Remove from the oven.

7. Transfer the quail to a plate. Increase the heat to high. To finish the sauce, add the wine, butter, sage, and shallot. Cook until the liquid has reduced by a quarter, for about 10 minutes.

8. Reduce the heat to low. Return the quail to the pot, turning them over in the sauce. Simmer until heated through, for 3 to 5 minutes. Remove from the heat.

9. Serve the quail with the sauce alongside the roasted grapes.

Bacon-Wrapped Sausage-Stuffed Quail with Pesto Cream Sauce

PREP TIME: 20 MINUTES / **COOK TIME:** 45 MINUTES / **YIELD:** 4 TO 8 SERVINGS
OTHER GAME YOU CAN USE: GROUSE, DOVE

Quail hardly have any fat on them, so it's best to add some when cooking them. Here, bacon helps create a moist quail that would otherwise come out dry on a grill. I added sausage to stuff the quail at first solely to add fat to the cavity, but it makes this dish tasty as well!

8 ounces Italian sausage,
  removed from casings

8 quail

8 strips bacon

¾ cup heavy cream

¼ cup whole milk

¼ cup prepared pesto

2 tablespoons unsalted butter

¼ teaspoon kosher salt

¼ teaspoon freshly ground
  black pepper

½ cup grated Parmesan cheese

1. Preheat the grill to 350°F to 400°F.

2. Divide the sausage among the quail, taking a piece and placing it inside each cavity.

3. Using a toothpick, secure a strip of bacon at the neck area, and wrap it around the quail; finish by wrapping the 2 quail legs together with it. Secure with another toothpick. Repeat with the remaining bacon and quail.

4. Place the quail on the grill directly over the fire. Cook, turning occasionally, for 20 minutes, then move to a cooler spot or a top rack until the internal temperature in the cavity of the quail registers 145°F, for 25 more minutes. Remove from the heat.

5. Meanwhile, to make the sauce, in a small saucepan, heat the cream and milk over medium heat until hot but not boiling.

6. Stir in the pesto, butter, salt, and pepper.

7. Reduce the heat to low. Simmer for 5 minutes.

8. Stir in the Parmesan cheese until melted. Remove from the heat.

9. Serve the quail topped with the sauce.

Grilled Quail with BBQ Sauce and Texas Toast

PREP TIME: 40 MINUTES / **COOK TIME:** 15 MINUTES / **YIELD:** 8 SERVINGS
OTHER GAME YOU CAN USE: GROUSE, DOVE

Spatchcocking is a great technique to cook poultry faster and more evenly. Cut out the backbone with a large chef knife or poultry shears and open the bird up like a book. It's best to brine the quail an hour before cooking; doing so will keep the meat moist.

FOR THE QUAIL:

8 quail

16 bamboo skewers (optional)

1 tablespoon kosher salt

1 teaspoon freshly ground black pepper

1½ cups BBQ sauce of your choice

FOR THE TEXAS TOAST:

8 tablespoons (1 stick) unsalted butter, melted

2 tablespoons olive oil

5 cloves garlic, minced

½ teaspoon dried parsley

¼ teaspoon kosher salt

¼ cup freshly ground black pepper

1 loaf soft white bread or Texas toast bread

1. **To make the quail:** Place a quail, breast-side down, on a cutting board. Using a chef's knife or poultry shears, cut down either side of the backbone to cut it out. Turn the quail over and press down on the breastbone with the heel of your hand to gently flatten it. (Optional: Tuck the legs in slightly and, taking 1 skewer, pierce 1 leg at a diagonal angle through to the opposite wing. Repeat with the other side so that the quail is spread with 2 diagonal skewers. This helps the bird keep its shape.) Repeat with the remaining quail. Season the quail on both sides with the salt and pepper.

2. Preheat the grill to 350°F to 400°F. Place the quail on the grill directly over the fire. Cook, basting with the BBQ sauce and turning occasionally, until the internal temperature of the quail registers 145°F, for 12 to 14 minutes. Remove from the heat.

3. **To make the Texas toast:** While the grill is preheating, set a rack in the middle position in the oven. Place a sheet pan on it. Preheat the oven to 375°F.

4. In a bowl, whisk together the butter, olive oil, garlic, parsley, salt, and pepper. Brush both sides of the bread with the mixture.

5. Remove the heated sheet pan from the oven. Arrange the bread slices in a single layer on it. Put the sheet pan back in the oven and bake until the bread is golden brown, turning once, for 10 to 12 minutes. Remove from the oven.

6. To serve, remove the skewers from the quail (if using) and place the quail on top of the Texas toast.

GROUSE

Thai-Style Sheet Pan Pizza with Peanut Sauce and Grouse

PREP TIME: 30 MINUTES / **COOK TIME:** 15 MINUTES / **YIELD:** 6 SERVINGS
OTHER GAME YOU CAN USE: QUAIL, DOVE, PHEASANT, TURKEY

We all love pizza! This one is delicious and super fun to make with kids. My daughter loves this pizza, but she loves rolling out the dough and making her own pie even more. Don't worry about making perfect circles; this pizza comes together on a sheet pan, which eliminates all the work for you.

All-purpose flour, for rolling the dough

1 pound pizza dough

½ cup Thai-Inspired Peanut Sauce (page 260)

2 cups shredded mozzarella cheese

1 cup shredded, cooked grouse meat

1 cup shredded carrots

1 cup bean sprouts

2 scallions, green and white parts, sliced

2 tablespoons chopped fresh cilantro

2 limes, cut into wedges

1. Preheat the oven to 450°F.

2. Dust a work surface and rolling pin with flour.

3. Roll out the pizza dough to the size of a medium sheet pan. Transfer the dough to the pan and use your hands to gently press it out to all the edges and into the corners.

4. Spread the peanut sauce all over the dough.

5. Sprinkle evenly with the mozzarella cheese and top with the grouse meat.

6. Put the sheet pan in the oven and bake until the cheese melts and the crust is firm and browned, for 12 to 15 minutes. Remove from the oven.

7. Top the pizza with the carrots, bean sprouts, scallions, and cilantro.

8. Cut the pizza into pieces and serve with the lime wedges to squeeze on top.

Coconut-Lime Grouse over Ginger Rice

PREP TIME: 15 MINUTES / **COOK TIME:** 30 MINUTES / **YIELD:** 4 SERVINGS
OTHER GAME YOU CAN USE: QUAIL, DOVE, PHEASANT, TURKEY

I'm a big meal prepper and eat healthy about 85 percent of the time. I created this dish originally because I wanted something flavorful without having to resort to frying or long cooking times. This dish has been a staple in my house ever since. When I want carbs, I make a large batch of this rice. But when I want to reduce carbs, I replace the rice with cauliflower rice. You would never know the difference.

2 tablespoons olive oil

½ medium red onion, chopped

¼ teaspoon kosher salt

¼ teaspoon freshly ground black pepper

1 Anaheim chile, thinly sliced

1 pound grouse breast meat, cut into 1-inch chunks

1 cup chicken broth

3 tablespoons freshly squeezed lime juice

1 tablespoon chopped fresh cilantro

½ teaspoon red pepper flakes (optional)

¼ teaspoon ground turmeric

½ cup full-fat coconut cream

2 cups hot cooked white rice

1 tablespoon grated or minced fresh ginger

1. In a large skillet, heat the olive oil over medium-high heat.

2. Add the onion. Season with the salt and pepper. Cook until softened, for about 5 minutes.

3. Add the chile and cook for 2 minutes.

4. Add the grouse meat and cook, stirring, until browned on all sides, for about 3 minutes.

5. Stir in the broth, lime juice, cilantro, red pepper flakes (if using), and turmeric. Bring to a simmer.

6. Reduce the heat to medium-low. Simmer for 8 to 10 minutes to let the liquid reduce.

7. Stir in the coconut cream and simmer for 5 minutes. Remove from the heat.

8. Use 2 forks to fluff the rice. Stir the ginger into the rice.

9. Serve the grouse mixture over the rice.

Braised Grouse Breast in Tarragon–White Wine Sauce

PREP TIME: 15 MINUTES / **COOK TIME:** 45 MINUTES / **YIELD:** 6 SERVINGS
OTHER GAME YOU CAN USE: PHEASANT, QUAIL

Tarragon is an herb that doesn't get enough love. It has a sweet, almost anise-like flavor and is absolutely delicious paired with game birds, chicken, and fish.

2 tablespoons unsalted butter

2 shallots, finely diced

2 cloves garlic, minced

2 teaspoons chopped fresh
tarragon

6 boneless, skinless grouse
breast halves

1 cup chicken broth

½ cup dry white wine

½ cup crème fraîche or
sour cream

½ teaspoon grated lemon zest

Kosher salt

Freshly ground black pepper

3 tablespoons chopped
fresh chives

1. Preheat the oven to 350°F.

2. In a large Dutch oven, melt the butter over medium heat.

3. Add the shallots and cook, stirring, until lightly browned, for about 5 minutes.

4. Add the garlic and tarragon; cook for 1 minute.

5. Arrange the grouse breasts in a single layer in the pot.

6. Pour in the broth and wine.

7. Cover, put the pot in the oven, and bake until the grouse is tender, for 30 minutes. Remove from the oven. Gently transfer the grouse breasts to a serving plate.

8. Return the pot to the stove over medium-high heat. Stir in the crème fraîche and lemon zest; simmer until the sauce has slightly thickened, for about 5 minutes. Season with salt and pepper if needed. Remove from the heat.

9. To serve, spoon the thickened sauce over the grouse and garnish with the chives.

GAME TIP: Cook time will be the same if you use quail; if using pheasant, increase it by 5 minutes.

Panfried Grouse with Mint Pesto

PREP TIME: 20 MINUTES / **COOK TIME:** 30 MINUTES / **YIELD:** 2 SERVINGS
OTHER GAME YOU CAN USE: QUAIL, DOVE

I adore pesto; it's always an amazing way to flavor dishes. Traditionally pesto is made with basil, but I love changing up the herbs to create new versions, which is how this came to be. The mint pesto is beautiful in this dish, but try it with venison, bear, or duck as well.

2 large or 4 small grouse, cut into quarters

1 teaspoon kosher salt, plus more to taste

Freshly ground black pepper

¼ cup peanut oil

¼ cup dry red wine

¾ cup packed fresh mint leaves

¼ cup fresh flat-leaf parsley leaves

2 scallions, green and white parts, thickly sliced

2 medium cloves garlic, peeled

Grated zest of 1 small lemon

2 tablespoons extra-virgin olive oil

1 tablespoon red-wine vinegar

1. Season the grouse with the salt and pepper.

2. In a large skillet, heat the peanut oil over high heat.

3. Add the grouse, skin-side down, and fry until the skin is golden brown, for 4 or 5 minutes; flip and cook for 5 to 7 minutes.

4. Reduce the heat to medium-low. Add the wine, cover, and cook until the internal temperature of the grouse reaches 145°F, for about 10 minutes. Remove from the heat.

5. To make the pesto, in a food processor, combine the mint, parsley, scallions, garlic, and lemon zest; pulse until chopped.

6. With the machine running, add the olive oil in a thin stream through the feed tube, then add the vinegar. Process until smooth. Season with salt.

7. Drizzle the grouse with the pesto. Serve immediately.

Prosciutto-Wrapped Grouse with Balsamic-Glazed Beets

PREP TIME: 20 MINUTES / **COOK TIME:** 45 MINUTES / **YIELD:** 4 SERVINGS
OTHER GAME YOU CAN USE: QUAIL

The beautiful thing about this dish is it's all cooked in the oven at the same time. The prosciutto brings a crispy component that also keeps the grouse moist. The beets are transformed by the balsamic vinegar and maple syrup into something sinful.

4 grouse

2 teaspoons kosher salt, plus
    more to taste

Freshly ground black pepper

4 sprigs thyme

4 thin slices prosciutto

6 medium beets, peeled and cut
    into 1½-inch chunks

2 tablespoons olive oil

⅓ cup balsamic vinegar

1 tablespoon maple syrup

1. Preheat the oven to 400°F.

2. Season the cavity of each grouse with salt and pepper.

3. Put a sprig of thyme inside each grouse.

4. Wrap a slice of prosciutto around each grouse, starting from the head, then going in between the legs and under the belly. Set on a plate.

5. On a sheet pan, toss the beets with the olive oil. Season with the salt.

6. Nestle the grouse around the beets.

7. Put the sheet pan in the oven and roast until the internal temperature of the grouse reaches 145°F, for 35 to 40 minutes. Remove from the oven. Transfer the grouse to a serving platter.

8. Meanwhile, to make the balsamic glaze, in a small saucepan, combine the vinegar and maple syrup. Simmer over medium heat until the liquid has slightly thickened and coats the back of a metal spoon, for 3 or 4 minutes. Remove from the heat.

9. Pour the balsamic glaze over the beets on the sheet pan and gently toss to coat.

10. Serve the beets alongside the grouse.

DOVE

The Ultimate Dove Poppers

PREP TIME: 20 MINUTES, PLUS AT LEAST 30 MINUTES TO CHILL / **COOK TIME:** 25 MINUTES
YIELD: 12 SERVINGS
OTHER GAME YOU CAN USE: GROUSE, QUAIL, VENISON

When I first started blogging about wild game, it was my mission to show everyone there was more to wild game than making a popper. Those dang poppers just ran rampant on Instagram. So, I decided that if everyone wanted a popper, I might as well make the best ones possible. After many attempts, these were the crowd favorite. So please, if you're going to make a popper, make these!

6 large jalapeños

¼ cup softened cream cheese

¼ cup crumbled feta cheese

12 boneless dove breasts

6 to 12 strips bacon

2 large eggs

1 cup panko bread crumbs

1 quart peanut oil (optional)

1. Cut the jalapeños in half horizontally and scrape out all the seeds and membrane (the membrane carries a lot of the chile's heat).

2. In a small bowl, cream together the cream cheese and feta.

3. To assemble the poppers, take a half jalapeño and fill the middle with the cheese mixture.

4. Place a dove breast on top of it, then take a strip of bacon and wrap it around the jalapeño. (If the jalapeño is small, cut the bacon in half.) Secure the bacon with a toothpick if needed. Repeat with the remaining jalapeño halves, cheese mixture, and bacon.

5. Put the eggs in a shallow bowl and beat using a fork. Put the bread crumbs in another shallow bowl.

6. Dip the jalapeños in the eggs, making sure to fully coat them. Then dredge in the bread crumbs, rolling to fully coat. To help the coating stick, refrigerate the panko-crusted poppers for 30 to 60 minutes.

7. To cook, you can fry or grill the poppers. To fry, heat the peanut oil to 375°F, then fry in small batches for 5 or 6 minutes per batch. To grill, preheat the grill to 350°F to 400°F, with an indirect setup (see page 3). Place the jalapeños on the grill away from the fire. Cover and cook until the dove and bacon are cooked and the coating is crisp and golden, for about 15 minutes. Remove from the grill.

Shortcut Dove Empanadas

PREP TIME: 1 HOUR / **COOK TIME:** 35 MINUTES / **YIELD:** 8 SERVINGS
OTHER GAME YOU CAN USE: PHEASANT, QUAIL, GROUSE, TURKEY, VENISON

Nothing transports me back to childhood faster than Mexican food, especially empanadas. My mom made a savory version and a sweet version. Weekend mornings were about filling empanadas with jam for breakfast. But no matter what version we were making, they were always a hit. Now I make them with my little one. This recipe is my favorite; try doubling the batch and freezing the extras.

3 tablespoons olive oil

1 small yellow onion, minced

1 small red bell pepper,
   finely diced

½ teaspoon red pepper flakes

1 teaspoon kosher salt

½ teaspoon freshly ground
   black pepper

½ teaspoon ground cumin

1 pound boneless dove
   meat, minced

1 small russet potato, cooked,
   peeled, and finely diced

3 scallions, green and white
   parts, chopped

1 (14.1-ounce) box frozen
   piecrusts, thawed

½ cup shredded Monterey
   Jack cheese

1 large egg, beaten

1. Preheat the oven to 400°F. Line a sheet pan with parchment paper.

2. In a large skillet, heat the olive oil over medium heat.

3. Add the onion, bell pepper, red pepper flakes, salt, black pepper, and cumin; cook until the vegetables have softened, for about 5 minutes.

4. Add the dove meat and cook, stirring, until cooked through, for 5 minutes.

5. Stir in the potato and scallions. Remove from the heat.

6. Using a 5-inch round pastry cutter, cut out 4 circles from each piecrust sheet.

7. Place 2 tablespoons of the filling in the center of each circle and top with 1 tablespoon of cheese.

8. Using a pastry brush, brush the rim of the circle with the egg. Fold over the dough and press the edges firmly together. Using a fork, crimp the edges to seal. Put the empanadas on the prepared sheet pan.

9. Put the sheet pan in the oven and bake until the empanadas are golden brown, for 20 minutes. Remove from the oven. Serve immediately.

Dove Nuggets with Yum Yum Sauce

PREP TIME: 15 MINUTES, PLUS AT LEAST 30 MINUTES TO MARINATE / **COOK TIME:** 35 MINUTES
YIELD: 4 TO 6 SERVINGS
OTHER GAME YOU CAN USE: GROUSE, QUAIL

Nuggets never tasted so good! Let's be honest, we all love chicken nuggets, no matter what age we are. Don't worry, your kids will love this adult version, too. Once you try the yum yum sauce, you'll know exactly how it got its name.

2 large eggs

1 cup milk

2 tablespoons
   Worcestershire sauce

20 boneless dove breasts

1 cup all-purpose flour

½ cup bread crumbs

2 teaspoons kosher salt, plus
   more to taste

1 teaspoon garlic powder

½ teaspoon freshly ground
   black pepper

½ teaspoon onion powder

½ teaspoon chili powder

3 cups peanut oil or canola oil

1 recipe Yum Yum Sauce
   (page 261)

1. In a medium bowl, whisk together the eggs, milk, and Worcestershire sauce.

2. Put the dove breasts in the milk mixture, cover, and refrigerate for 30 minutes to 12 hours.

3. In another medium bowl, whisk together the flour, bread crumbs, salt, garlic powder, pepper, onion powder, and chili powder.

4. In a large, cast-iron Dutch oven, heat the peanut oil to 300°F (be careful not to let it get higher than that). Set a wire rack over paper towels.

5. Working in batches of 5 or 6 dove breasts, dredge in the flour mixture, making sure to coat well, and fry in the hot oil for 3 to 5 minutes per batch. Using a slotted spoon, transfer the dove nuggets to the rack. Immediately season with salt. Repeat with the remaining dove breasts. Turn off the heat.

6. Serve the nuggets with the sauce for dipping.

Port-Glazed Grilled Dove

PREP TIME: 15 MINUTES / **COOK TIME:** 30 MINUTES / **YIELD:** 4 TO 8 SERVINGS
OTHER GAME YOU CAN USE: GROUSE, QUAIL

Your grilling game just got kicked up a notch with this recipe. Wine is such a beautiful ingredient to cook with, but port, my goodness; port is even better. This quick sauce showcases the beauty and complexity of port. Try it on venison as well; it's equally amazing.

8 doves

8 sprigs thyme

8 sprigs rosemary

Kosher salt

Freshly ground black pepper

1 cup tawny port

½ cup red-wine vinegar

1 teaspoon Dijon mustard

2 teaspoons olive oil

½ teaspoon grated lemon zest

1. Preheat the grill to 275°F to 300°F.

2. Using paper towels, pat the doves dry. Place a sprig of thyme and a sprig of rosemary in each cavity. Season the outside of the doves with salt and pepper.

3. To make the port glaze, in a medium saucepan, combine the port, vinegar, mustard, olive oil, and lemon zest. Bring to a simmer over medium heat. Cook until the mixture starts to reduce and thicken, for 8 to 10 minutes. Remove from the heat.

4. Place the doves on the grill directly over the fire. Close the grill and cook for about 2 minutes.

5. Using a pastry brush, brush the port glaze onto the doves. Repeat every 2 minutes until the internal temperature of the doves reaches 160°F, for 20 to 25 minutes. Remove from the heat. Serve immediately.

TURKEY

Turkey, Kale, and Lemon Soup

PREP TIME: 15 MINUTES / **COOK TIME:** 25 MINUTES / **YIELD:** 4 SERVINGS

OTHER GAME YOU CAN USE: PHEASANT, QUAIL

This soup comes together in no time at all. And it's even more wonderful the next day. But wait, it gets better. Do you have leftover wild game meat in the refrigerator? Perfect! Make this soup and substitute your wild game meat for the wild turkey. Just make sure it's cut into pieces.

2 tablespoons olive oil

½ medium onion, diced

3 medium carrots, diced

3 stalks celery, diced

3 cloves garlic, minced

5 cups chicken broth

1 teaspoon Worcestershire sauce

1 bay leaf

2 sprigs thyme

½ teaspoon Dijon mustard

1½ cups shredded smoked wild turkey breast (see page 175)

1 bunch kale, stemmed, leaves cut into 1-inch pieces

1 (12-ounce) package egg noodles

1 tablespoon grated lemon zest

3 tablespoons freshly squeezed lemon juice

Kosher salt

Freshly ground black pepper

Grated Parmesan cheese, for garnish

1. In a stockpot, heat the olive oil over medium-high heat.

2. Add the onion, carrots, and celery; cook, stirring, until translucent, for about 5 minutes.

3. Add the garlic and cook for 2 minutes.

4. Stir in the broth, Worcestershire sauce, bay leaf, thyme, mustard, and turkey. Bring to a gentle boil.

5. Reduce the heat to medium-low. Stir in the kale, noodles, and lemon zest; simmer for 10 minutes.

6. Stir in the lemon juice. Season with salt and pepper. Remove from the heat.

7. Serve the soup immediately, garnished with Parmesan cheese.

Fontina Turkey Burgers with Sun-Dried Tomato Aïoli

PREP TIME: 15 MINUTES / **COOK TIME:** 15 MINUTES / **YIELD:** 4 SERVINGS

OTHER GAME YOU CAN USE: ANY GROUND WILD GAME MEAT

Look no further; the best turkey burger is here! The wave of dry turkey burgers is gone, my friends. These are moist and bursting with flavor, and the addition of feta gives a little surprise pop of salty goodness. Then, topped with melted Fontina cheese, it's a turkey burger dream come true. I like to pan-sauté these patties, but you can also grill them; just put a sheet of aluminum foil on the grill, spray with cooking spray, and place the patties on the foil to cook.

1 recipe Classic Aïoli (page 257)

2 tablespoons minced, sun-dried tomatoes

1 pound ground wild turkey meat

2 cloves garlic, minced

1 large egg, beaten

¼ cup crumbled feta cheese

2 tablespoons chopped fresh parsley

1 tablespoon milk

1 tablespoon Worcestershire sauce

1 teaspoon kosher salt

¼ teaspoon freshly ground black pepper

3 tablespoons vegetable oil

8 slices Fontina cheese

4 brioche hamburger buns

4 to 8 iceberg lettuce leaves

Sliced tomatoes, for serving

1. In a bowl, stir together the aïoli and sun-dried tomatoes. Cover and refrigerate until ready to serve.

2. In a large bowl, mix together the turkey, garlic, egg, feta cheese, parsley, milk, Worcestershire sauce, salt, and pepper. Form into 4 burger patties.

3. In a medium skillet, heat the vegetable oil over medium heat.

4. Add the patties and cook, flipping once, until the internal temperature reaches 165°F, for about 10 minutes.

5. Right before the patties have finished cooking, place 2 slices of Fontina cheese on each patty, cover, and cook until melted, for 1 minute. Remove from the heat.

6. To assemble the burgers, spread the aïoli mixture on the bottom of the top buns. Place the patties on the bottom buns and cover with the lettuce, tomato, and the top bun; serve.

Wild Turkey Larb in Cabbage Cups

PREP TIME: 20 MINUTES / **COOK TIME:** 10 MINUTES / **YIELD:** 4 SERVINGS

OTHER GAME YOU CAN USE: ANY GROUND WILD GAME MEAT

Larb is a delicious Laotian dish; essentially a salad of cooked ground meat mixed with fresh herbs and wrapped in a cabbage or lettuce leaf. It's simple to make, packed with flavor, and extremely healthy. If you want to make this dish Paleo, substitute coconut aminos for the soy sauce and cauliflower rice for the rice; also leave out the sugar.

3 tablespoons olive oil

1 pound ground wild turkey

1 tablespoon minced garlic

1 tablespoon grated or minced fresh ginger

3 small shallots, finely diced

1½ teaspoons soy sauce

¼ teaspoon sugar

Juice of 2 limes

2 tablespoons chopped fresh cilantro

2 tablespoons chopped fresh mint

3 scallions, green and white parts, thinly sliced

1 red chile, thinly sliced (optional)

Hot cooked rice, for serving

1 head cabbage, quartered, cored, and separated into leaves

1. In a medium, cast-iron skillet, heat the olive oil over medium-high heat.

2. Add the turkey and, using a wooden spoon, break up any clumps. Cook, stirring, until just starting to brown, for about 4 minutes.

3. Stir in the garlic, ginger, shallots, soy sauce, sugar, and lime juice. Cook, stirring, until the turkey is no longer pink, for about 5 minutes. Remove from the heat.

4. Stir in the cilantro, mint, scallions, and chile (if using).

5. To serve, add a little rice topped with some turkey mixture to each cabbage leaf and roll up to eat.

Fried Turkey Sandwich with Not-So-Secret Sauce

PREP TIME: 40 MINUTES, PLUS 12 HOURS TO MARINATE / **COOK TIME:** 20 MINUTES / **YIELD:** 4 SERVINGS

OTHER GAME YOU CAN USE: VENISON, WILD BOAR

Do you crave Chick-Fil-A on Sundays when they aren't open? You're not alone. But now you can enjoy a turkey version any day you like. The key is the pickle brine.

FOR THE SAUCE:

½ cup mayonnaise

2 tablespoons ketchup

1 tablespoon Dijon mustard or whole-grain mustard

1 tablespoon minced dill pickles

1 teaspoon dill pickle juice

1 teaspoon garlic powder

½ teaspoon onion powder

¼ teaspoon paprika

⅛ teaspoon cayenne pepper

FOR THE SANDWICHES:

1 (2-pound) boneless wild turkey breast

3 cups dill pickle juice

1 cup water

¼ cup apple cider vinegar

1 tablespoon plus 2 teaspoons kosher salt, divided, plus more to taste

1 quart whole milk

3 large eggs

1¾ cups all-purpose flour

½ cup milk powder

¼ cup instant mashed potato powder

2 teaspoons garlic powder

1. **To make the sauce:** In a small bowl, whisk together the mayonnaise, ketchup, mustard, dill pickles, pickle juice, garlic powder, onion powder, paprika, and cayenne pepper until well blended. Cover and refrigerate until ready to use.

2. **To make the sandwiches:** Cut the turkey breast crosswise into 4 pieces, then cut each in half. Pound each piece out into a ½-inch-thick cutlet.

3. Put the cutlets in a large bowl and pour the dill pickle juice, water, vinegar, and 1 tablespoon of salt over them. Cover and refrigerate for 12 hours.

4. In a large bowl, whisk together the milk and eggs.

5. In a shallow pan, whisk together the flour, milk powder, potato powder, remaining 2 teaspoons of salt, the garlic powder, onion powder, black pepper, cayenne pepper, dry mustard, and baking soda.

6. In a large Dutch oven or a large, high-sided skillet, heat the peanut oil to 350°F. Set a wire rack over paper towels.

7. Remove the turkey cutlets from the bowl and pat dry. Dip each cutlet in the egg mixture, then dredge in the flour mixture to coat fully.

2 teaspoons onion powder

1 teaspoon freshly ground
  black pepper

1 teaspoon cayenne pepper

1 teaspoon dry mustard

1 teaspoon baking soda

4 cups peanut oil

4 hamburger buns

Dill pickles, for serving

8. Working in batches, fry the cutlets in the hot oil, turning, until golden brown, for 3 or 4 minutes per batch. Using tongs, transfer to the wire rack. Immediately season with salt. Turn off the heat.

9. To assemble the sandwiches, smear some of the sauce on the buns. Place a cutlet on the bottom bun; cover with pickles and the top bun. Serve immediately.

GAME TIP: If you want to substitute, use venison or wild boar cutlets of the same weight. Cook time will be the same.

Grilled Wild Turkey Kebabs with Tzatziki

PREP TIME: 25 MINUTES, PLUS 2 OR 3 HOURS TO MARINATE / **COOK TIME:** 15 MINUTES / **YIELD:** 6 SERVINGS
OTHER GAME YOU CAN USE: VENISON

I love grilling! It gets me out of the kitchen and outdoors with nature. And usually I'm never alone, either in the company of a cocktail, a friend, or both. So why not catch up with your friends while grilling the best turkey kebabs ever? These are super easy and always come out perfectly, even if you accidentally overcook them. Serve with warm pita bread.

FOR THE TURKEY:
½ cup freshly squeezed
   lemon juice
3 tablespoons olive oil
2 cloves garlic, minced
1 teaspoon kosher salt
1 teaspoon dried oregano
½ teaspoon freshly ground
   black pepper
½ teaspoon ground cinnamon
½ teaspoon paprika
2 pounds boneless turkey breast,
   cut into ¾-inch chunks

FOR THE TZATZIKI:
1 cup plain, whole-milk
   Greek yogurt
½ cup grated cucumber
2 tablespoons extra-virgin
   olive oil
1 tablespoon chopped fresh dill
1 tablespoon chopped fresh mint
1 tablespoon freshly squeezed
   lemon juice
1 medium clove garlic, minced
½ teaspoon kosher salt

¼ teaspoon freshly ground
   black pepper

FOR THE SKEWERS:
1 red onion, cut into large pieces
2 bell peppers, cut into
   large pieces
2 zucchini, cut into ½-inch-
   thick slices

1. **To make the turkey:** In a large bowl, whisk together the lemon juice, olive oil, garlic, salt, oregano, pepper, cinnamon, and paprika.

2. Add the turkey and toss to coat. Cover and refrigerate for 2 to 3 hours.

3. **To make the tzatziki:** In a medium bowl, whisk together the yogurt, cucumber, olive oil, dill, mint, lemon juice, garlic, salt, and pepper. (Tzatziki can be made 1 day in advance and stored, covered, in the refrigerator.)

4. **To make the skewers:** When ready to grill, thread the turkey, onion, bell peppers, and zucchini onto 6 metal skewers or 6 wooden skewers that have been soaked in water for at least 10 minutes.

5. Preheat the grill to 275°F to 300°F.

6. Place the skewers on the grill directly over the fire. Cook, turning, until the turkey has cooked through, for 10 to 12 minutes. Remove from the heat.

7. Serve the kebabs alongside the tzatziki.

Curried Turkey with Potatoes

PREP TIME: 20 MINUTES / **COOK TIME:** 45 MINUTES / **YIELD:** 4 SERVINGS

OTHER GAME YOU CAN USE: PHEASANT, VENISON

I love a good curry; it's warm, spicy, oh so satisfying, and even better the next day. This turkey curry can be made with cooked ground meat or shredded meat as well, which makes it perfect for using up leftover meat.

¼ cup vegetable oil

1 pound turkey breast, cut into 1-inch cubes

1 medium onion, chopped

2 cloves garlic, minced

1 tablespoon grated or minced fresh ginger

1 teaspoon kosher salt, plus more to taste

1 tablespoon curry powder

1 teaspoon ground turmeric

1 teaspoon ground cumin

1 teaspoon ground coriander

½ cup chicken broth

2 large Yukon Gold potatoes, peeled and cut into 1-inch chunks

4 roma tomatoes, diced

1 cup frozen peas

Freshly ground black pepper

1 tablespoon chopped fresh cilantro

Hot cooked basmati rice, for serving

1. In a large Dutch oven, heat the vegetable oil over medium-high heat.

2. Add the turkey and cook, turning, until lightly browned on all sides, for 5 to 7 minutes.

3. Add the onion and cook, stirring, until golden brown, for 4 or 5 minutes.

4. Stir in the garlic, ginger, and salt; cook for 2 minutes.

5. Stir in the curry powder, turmeric, cumin, coriander, broth, and potatoes. Bring to a simmer.

6. Reduce the heat to medium-low. Cover, and simmer until the potatoes are tender, for 20 to 25 minutes.

7. Stir in the tomatoes and peas; cover and simmer for 5 minutes. Season with salt and pepper.

8. Stir in the cilantro. Remove from the heat.

9. Serve the curry on top of the rice.

Slow Cooker Wild Turkey Pozole Rojo

PREP TIME: 15 MINUTES / **COOK TIME:** 4 HOURS ON HIGH OR 8 HOURS ON LOW / **YIELD:** 8 SERVINGS
OTHER GAME YOU CAN USE: PHEASANT, WILD BOAR, VENISON

Pozole was a childhood staple for me, and I have fond memories of my family packed into the kitchen eating pozole, drinking beer, and laughing. This dish is a one-pot wonder. If you have any leftover shredded smoked or cooked meats, feel free to substitute them for the raw meat; just add the cooked meat to the pot in the last hour of cooking.

FOR THE POZOLE:

3 tablespoons olive oil

1 large onion, diced

3 cloves garlic, minced

1 (1½- to 2-pound) boneless wild turkey breast, cut into 1½-inch pieces

1 (29-ounce) can crushed tomatoes

1 (29-ounce) can tomato sauce

1 (29-ounce) can hominy, drained

1 (8-ounce) can diced green chiles

1½ cups crushed pineapple

4 cups chicken broth

2 cups shredded carrots

3 tablespoons Worcestershire sauce

1 teaspoon kosher salt

¼ teaspoon freshly ground black pepper

3 tablespoons chopped fresh cilantro, for serving

Radishes, for serving

Lime wedges, for serving

FOR THE SLAW:

2 cups shredded cabbage

2 tablespoons distilled white vinegar

1 tablespoon olive oil

½ teaspoon kosher salt

½ teaspoon freshly ground black pepper

1. **To make the pozole:** In a slow cooker, combine the olive oil, onion, garlic, turkey, crushed tomatoes, tomato sauce, hominy, green chiles, pineapple, broth, carrots, Worcestershire sauce, salt, and pepper; cover and cook on high for 4 hours or low for 8 hours.

2. **To make the slaw:** In a large bowl, combine the cabbage, vinegar, olive oil, salt, and pepper. Toss to coat well.

3. Turn off the slow cooker. To serve, top a bowl of the soup with some of the cabbage slaw and the cilantro, radishes, and lime wedges.

Slow Cooker Turkey Tinga Taquitos with Avocado Crema

PREP TIME: 20 MINUTES / **COOK TIME:** 20 MINUTES, PLUS 8 ½ HOURS ON LOW / **YIELD:** 8 SERVINGS
OTHER GAME YOU CAN USE: PHEASANT

You are going to love these! The turkey is made in the slow cooker and the taquitos baked to crunchy perfection in the oven. And the avocado crema will become your next favorite dipping sauce—I love it with veggies or crackers or smeared on toast with roasted tomatoes.

FOR THE TAQUITOS:
1 (2-pound) boneless
   turkey breast
4 cups red enchilada sauce
1 large onion, coarsely chopped
3 canned chipotle chiles in adobo
   sauce, finely chopped
1 teaspoon kosher salt
½ teaspoon dried oregano
¼ teaspoon freshly ground
   black pepper

Olive oil, for greasing
16 tortillas, warmed
2 cups shredded Mexican cheese
Shredded lettuce, for serving
Sour cream, for serving

FOR THE CREMA:
2 ripe avocados, seeded
   and peeled
1 cup sour cream
½ cup chopped fresh cilantro

½ teaspoon kosher salt
¼ teaspoon freshly ground
   black pepper
¼ teaspoon ground cumin
2 tablespoons freshly squeezed
   lime juice
Grated zest of 2 limes

1. **To make the taquitos:** In a slow cooker, combine the turkey, enchilada sauce, onion, chiles, salt, oregano, and pepper; cover and cook on low for 8 hours.

2. Transfer the turkey to a cutting board. Shred the meat, return to the slow cooker, cover, and cook for 20 minutes.

3. Preheat the oven to 425°F. Grease a sheet pan with olive oil.

4. Turn off the slow cooker. Spoon 2 or 3 tablespoons of the turkey down the middle of a tortilla. Top with 2 tablespoons of cheese, then roll up and place on the sheet pan, seam-side down. Repeat with the remaining tortillas, turkey, and cheese.

5. Put the sheet pan in the oven and bake, turning the taquitos once, until crispy, for 12 to 16 minutes. Remove from the oven.

6. **To make the crema:** In a blender, combine the avocados, sour cream, cilantro, salt, pepper, cumin, lime juice, and lime zest. Blend until smooth.

7. Serve the taquitos with shredded lettuce, sour cream, and the avocado crema.

Red Wine–Braised Turkey Legs

PREP TIME: 1 HOUR / **COOK TIME:** 3 HOURS / **YIELD:** 4 SERVINGS

Braising in red wine is a classic French technique. A long and slow braise turns the turkey legs' connective tissue into gelatin, leaving the meat extremely tender and moist. Plus, braising makes overcooking almost impossible.

2 wild turkey legs, thighs attached

1 tablespoon kosher salt, plus more to taste

1 teaspoon freshly ground black pepper, plus more to taste

2 to 3 tablespoons olive oil

1 large onion, coarsely chopped

3 stalks celery, coarsely chopped

2 large carrots, coarsely chopped

2 medium cloves garlic, coarsely chopped

5 sprigs thyme

2 sprigs rosemary

2½ cups dry red wine, divided

2 bay leaves

3 to 4 cups beef broth

2 tablespoons unsalted butter

2 tablespoons all-purpose flour

1 cup heavy cream

1 tablespoon chopped fresh chives, for garnish

1 tablespoon chopped fresh parsley, for garnish

1. Preheat the oven to 275°F.

2. Season the turkey legs with the salt and pepper.

3. In a large Dutch oven, heat 2 tablespoons of olive oil over medium-high heat until hot.

4. Add the turkey legs, skin-side down. Cook, without moving (moving can rip the skin), until the skin is a deep golden brown, for 8 or 9 minutes; flip and cook the other side until browned, for about 5 minutes. Transfer to a plate.

5. Add 1 tablespoon of olive oil to the pot if needed. Add the onion, celery, carrots, garlic, thyme, and rosemary. Cook, stirring frequently, until the vegetables are golden brown, for about 10 minutes.

6. Add 1¼ cups of wine and, using a wooden spoon, scrape up the browned bits from the bottom of the pot.

7. Add the remaining 1¼ cups of wine and cook until reduced, for about 5 minutes.

8. Return the turkey and any accumulated juices to the pot, nestling the legs into the vegetables.

9. Add the bay leaves and enough broth so that the skin of the turkey legs is peeking out, but the rest of the legs is covered.

10. Put the pot in the oven and roast until the turkey is tender, for 2 to 2½ hours. Remove from the oven.

CONTINUED >

11. Transfer the legs to a serving platter. Strain the vegetables through a fine-mesh strainer into a medium bowl. Reserve the braising liquid and discard the solids.

12. To make the roux, in a medium saucepan, melt the butter over medium-high heat.

13. Whisk in the flour until smooth. Continue to whisk until the roux is slightly golden, for about 2 minutes.

14. Slowly whisk in the cream, about 3 tablespoons at a time, until all the cream is incorporated; this will prevent clumping.

15. Whisk in the reserved braising liquid and bring to a boil. Season with salt and pepper. Remove from the heat.

16. Serve the turkey legs with the sauce, garnished with the chives and parsley.

Coffee-Rubbed Smoked Wild Turkey

PREP TIME: 15 MINUTES, PLUS 12 TO 14 HOURS TO BRINE / **COOK TIME:** 6 TO 8 HOURS
YIELD: 4 TO 6 SERVINGS

Wild turkey is most definitely different from farm-raised turkey and must be treated as such. I always brine my wild turkey before cooking, no matter how I'm planning to cook it. Don't skip the brining process in this recipe because the turkey needs the extra moisture before hitting the smoker.

1 (2-pound) boneless wild
  turkey breast
½ recipe Classic Lemon-Herb
  Brine (page 241)
¼ cup Coffee Rub (page 246)

1. In a large stockpot, submerge the turkey breast in the brine and refrigerate for 12 to 14 hours.

2. Set an electric smoker to 180°F.

3. Remove the turkey from the brine, rinse with water, and pat dry using paper towels.

4. Sprinkle the Coffee Rub all over the turkey.

5. Put the turkey in the smoker and smoke using hickory wood (see page 4) until the internal temperature of the turkey reaches 160°F, for 6 to 8 hours. Using a spray bottle filled with water, spray the inside of the smoker with 3 or 4 squirts of water every 45 minutes. Doing so will help keep the exterior of the turkey from becoming tough.

6. Remove from the smoker. Transfer to a serving platter and let rest until the internal temperature of the turkey reaches 165°F. Slice and serve.

Christmas Roast Turkey

PREP TIME: 10 MINUTES, PLUS 24 HOURS TO BRINE / **COOK TIME:** 2 TO 3 HOURS, PLUS 25 MINUTES TO REST
YIELD: 6 TO 8 SERVINGS

Here's the perfect recipe for a Christmas turkey; this will be the one you pass down to your kids. The key to this turkey is brining it for 24 hours. You can use any flavor bacon you like; I prefer hickory-smoked.

1 (10- to 15-pound) wild turkey

1 recipe Classic Lemon-Herb Brine
(page 241)

Kosher salt

Freshly ground black pepper

2 onions, quartered

1 lemon, quartered

1 head garlic, skin on, cut
horizontally

8 sprigs thyme

5 sprigs rosemary

8 tablespoons (1 stick) butter,
softened

¼ cup olive oil

8 to 10 strips
hickory-smoked bacon

1. In a stockpot large enough to hold the turkey, submerge the turkey in the brine and refrigerate for 24 hours.

2. Preheat the oven to 425°F

3. Remove the turkey from the brine, rinse with water, and pat dry. Season the cavity with salt and pepper.

4. Fill the cavity with the onions, lemon, garlic, thyme, and rosemary.

5. Place the turkey, breast-side up, on a roasting rack in a large roasting pan.

6. Spread the butter and olive oil over the skin. If there is an opening under the skin and breast, insert some butter underneath the skin, making sure not to rip the skin.

7. Put the roasting pan in the oven and roast for 15 minutes.

8. Reduce the oven temperature to 350°F.

9. Arrange the bacon over the breast meat (this will help prevent the breast skin from burning). Roast until the internal temperature of the turkey reaches 155°F, for 2 to 3 hours. (For every pound, roast for 12 minutes.) Be sure to check the turkey every 20 minutes during the last hour of cooking.

10. Remove from the oven. Cover with aluminum foil, and let rest until the internal temperature rises to 165°F, for about 25 minutes. Carve the turkey and serve on a warm serving platter.

Wild Turkey and Apple Sausage

PREP TIME: 15 MINUTES / **COOK TIME:** 10 MINUTES / **YIELD:** 8 SERVINGS

OTHER GAME YOU CAN USE: WILD BOAR

Wild turkey is mostly prized for the breast and leg meat, but I have found grinding it to be pretty fantastic. Wild turkey is lean, even leaner than farm-raised, so the addition of fat is necessary in wild turkey sausage. This sausage recipe will definitely change the way you prepare your wild turkey harvest.

1 pound cold, ground wild turkey meat (see page 6)

3 tablespoons cold bacon fat

1 cup shredded apple, preferably Granny Smith

¼ cup unseasoned bread crumbs

½ teaspoon dried sage

½ teaspoon freshly ground black pepper

¼ teaspoon kosher salt

¼ teaspoon paprika

⅛ teaspoon ground nutmeg

Natural sausage casings (optional), for stuffing

Nonstick cooking spray, for greasing

1. In a large bowl, combine the turkey, bacon fat, apple, bread crumbs, sage, pepper, salt, paprika, and nutmeg. Mix well using your hands. Shape into 8 (½-inch-thick) patties or stuff into natural sausage casings (see page 6). If not cooking immediately, store the sausage in an airtight container in the refrigerator for up to 6 days or freeze for 3 months.

2. To cook the patties, preheat the broiler on high. Grease a sheet pan with nonstick cooking spray.

3. Put the patties on the prepared sheet pan. Broil 5 inches away from the heat source, turning once, until no longer pink in the center, for about 10 minutes. Remove from the broiler. Serve immediately.

CHAPTER 7

Game Fish

Fishing is my favorite form of hunting. Catching a trout on the fly is no easy feat, but when you do, it's nothing but pure joy. Holding your breath for three plus minutes to dive down and lie on the ocean's bottom to spear a single fish is hands down the most rewarding form of hunting. No matter how you catch your fish, it's always a delicious reward. Some of the best meals I have ever had were prepared on a boat, where I was devouring the freshest fish possible while still in a wetsuit. I've included some of my favorite boat meals in this chapter, as well as other favorites.

← Korean BBQ-Style Marinated Mahi Mahi with Charred Romaine, page 215

Freshwater Fish

Freshwater fish have meat that is more delicate than that of saltwater fish, thus making small fish like trout great for panfrying whole while at camp, or salt-baking back home. Freshwater fish do not have the briny flavors that saltwater fish tend to have. They are slightly sweet in flavor, which makes them a great choice for anyone who doesn't like that "fishy" taste. Freshwater fish work well when fried for tacos or turned into fish sticks. And because of their mildness, they partner well with all kinds of flavors. Be aware, freshwater fish have much smaller bones than saltwater fish, so you need to take more care when filleting them.

Saltwater Fish

Whether you're fishing inshore or offshore or spearfishing, the ocean provides a wealth of beautiful, clean protein. Saltwater fish are easily my favorite fish to eat because they have a much stronger taste than freshwater fish, the salt water imbuing them with an almost briny flavor.

The flavor and texture of saltwater fish can vary. For instance, grouper is very mild, with a chunky, flaked meat that takes well to marinades or dressings. Red snapper is nutty, sweet, and great for grilling whole, served with fresh herbs, or eaten raw as sashimi or in ceviche. Sea bass is very mild; it's a perfect choice to serve to those who say they don't like fish. Mahi mahi is very similar in texture to swordfish: firm and meaty, but milder in taste. Tuna is the fan favorite. It is great eaten raw, slow-poached, or grilled. Tuna, salmon, and bluefish have stronger flavor profiles, yet are extremely tender.

I've included salmon under Saltwater Fish even though they are anadramous, meaning they live part of their lives in both freshwater and saltwater. The saltwater category makes sense to me for salmon as it shares qualities with those saltwater fish that are oilier and meatier.

FRESHWATER FISH

Catfish Po'boy with Asian-Style Slaw and Sriracha Remoulade

PREP TIME: 30 MINUTES / **COOK TIME:** 20 MINUTES / **YIELD:** 4 SERVINGS

I'm taking the classic po'boy to a whole new level with this recipe, a mash-up between my love for the traditional po'boy and the classic Vietnamese sandwich, the bánh mì. It's the best of both worlds with its beautiful slaw and a kicked-up remoulade.

FOR THE REMOULADE:

1 cup mayonnaise

3 tablespoons sriracha

1 tablespoon ketchup

4 scallions, green and white parts, thinly sliced

2 tablespoons chopped fresh parsley

FOR THE SLAW:

½ head napa cabbage, thinly sliced

1 bell pepper, cut into matchsticks

1 small carrot, grated

6 scallions, green and white parts, thinly sliced

¼ cup distilled white vinegar

2 tablespoons chopped fresh cilantro

2 tablespoons chopped fresh mint

1 tablespoon soy sauce

Juice of 1 lime

1. **To make the remoulade:** In a small bowl, whisk together the mayonnaise, sriracha, ketchup, scallions, and parsley.

2. **To make the slaw:** In a medium bowl, stir together the cabbage, bell pepper, carrot, scallions, vinegar, cilantro, mint, and soy sauce until well combined.

3. Stir in the lime juice.

4. **To make the catfish:** In a shallow dish, combine the panko bread crumbs, plain bread crumbs, milk powder, ¼ cup of flour, the salt, garlic powder, thyme, cayenne pepper, ginger, and onion powder.

5. In another shallow dish, beat the eggs.

6. Put the remaining ¼ cup of flour in another shallow dish.

7. Dredge the catfish in the plain flour, then dip in the eggs, and dredge in the bread crumb mixture.

8. In a large skillet, heat ½ inch of vegetable oil over high heat until hot.

9. Fry 2 fillets at a time in the hot oil, flipping once, until crispy, golden brown, and cooked through, for about 4 minutes per batch. Turn off the heat.

FOR THE CATFISH:

1 cup panko bread crumbs

½ cup plain bread crumbs

¼ cup milk powder

½ cup all-purpose
   flour, divided

1 teaspoon kosher salt

1 teaspoon garlic powder

½ teaspoon dried thyme

¼ teaspoon cayenne pepper

¼ teaspoon ground ginger

¼ teaspoon onion powder

4 large eggs

8 (5- to 8-ounce) catfish fillets

Vegetable oil, for frying

8 hero rolls, split

8 lime wedges

10. To serve, spread the inside of the rolls with the remoulade, top each with a catfish fillet and some slaw.

11. Squeeze the lime wedges on top, and serve.

Butter-Baked Garlic Catfish

PREP TIME: 10 MINUTES / **COOK TIME:** 20 MINUTES / **YIELD:** 4 SERVINGS

OTHER FISH YOU CAN USE: TROUT, PANFISH

Butter-baked garlic catfish is every bit as decadent and delicious as it sounds. Julia Child said, "With enough butter, anything is good," and this recipe delivers buttery garlic goodness. It's like garlic bread, but with fish. Yes, it's that amazing and yet simple to make.

4 (6- to 8-ounce) catfish fillets, each cut into quarters

1 tablespoon kosher salt

½ teaspoon freshly ground black pepper

1½ cups (3 sticks) unsalted butter, melted

3 tablespoons minced garlic

2 tablespoons dried fines herbes

Juice of 2 lemons

4 bay leaves

2 sprigs rosemary

1. Preheat the oven to 350°F.

2. Arrange the catfish in a single layer in a 9-by-13-inch baking dish. Season with the salt and pepper.

3. Pour the butter over the catfish.

4. Add the garlic, fines herbes, lemon juice, bay leaves, and rosemary.

5. Put the baking dish in the oven and bake until the catfish is opaque in the center, for about 20 minutes. Remove from the oven.

Chimichurri-Rubbed Catfish with Mango Salsa

PREP TIME: 20 MINUTES / **COOK TIME:** 15 MINUTES / **YIELD:** 4 SERVINGS

OTHER FISH YOU CAN USE: SALMON, MAHI MAHI, PIKE, WALLEYE

Chimichurri is like a brighter, more citrusy version of a pesto. The flavors of the rub and the salsa help liven up catfish, which can sometimes be "muddy." Try adding some diced avocado or pineapple to the salsa to change things up; you won't regret it.

3 ripe mangos, peeled, pitted, and diced

1 medium bell pepper, finely diced

½ cup red onion, finely diced

¼ cup chopped fresh cilantro

¼ cup freshly squeezed lime juice

1 jalapeño, seeded and minced

1¼ teaspoons kosher salt, divided

4 (7- to 8-ounce) catfish fillets

¾ teaspoon freshly ground black pepper

3 tablespoons Chimichurri Rub (page 252)

½ cup all-purpose flour

3 tablespoons olive oil

2 tablespoons unsalted butter

1. To make the mango salsa, in a medium bowl, combine the mangos, bell pepper, onion, cilantro, lime juice, jalapeño, and ¼ teaspoon of salt.

2. Using a paper towel, pat the catfish dry. Season with the remaining 1 teaspoon of salt and the pepper.

3. Sprinkle the catfish with the rub and lightly pat it into the flesh.

4. Put the flour in a shallow dish.

5. Dredge the catfish in the flour and transfer to a sheet pan.

6. In a large skillet, heat the olive oil and butter over medium-high heat.

7. Once the butter has melted, add 2 fillets at a time and cook until a golden crust forms, for 4 or 5 minutes; flip and cook until cooked through, for 1 minute. Remove from the heat.

8. Transfer the catfish to a serving platter and top with the mango salsa.

Pecan-Crusted Bourbon Catfish

PREP TIME: 15 MINUTES / **COOK TIME:** 20 MINUTES / **YIELD:** 4 SERVINGS

OTHER FISH YOU CAN USE: TROUT

Is it "pee-can" or "pi-con"? Whichever one you say, I say try this recipe. It doesn't get more Southern than Bourbon, pecans, and catfish. Use any Bourbon you like; it doesn't have to be fancy. I like to serve this with a side of grits or grilled vegetables.

1 cup finely chopped pecans

½ cup panko bread crumbs

1 teaspoon kosher salt

½ teaspoon freshly ground black pepper

4 (4-ounce) catfish fillets

1 teaspoon Cajun Rub (page 247)

½ cup buttermilk

3 tablespoons Bourbon

1 teaspoon honey

1. Preheat the oven to 350°F.

2. In a shallow dish, stir together the pecans, bread crumbs, salt, and pepper.

3. Season the catfish with the Cajun Rub.

4. In another shallow dish, whisk together the buttermilk, Bourbon, and honey.

5. Dip the catfish in the buttermilk mixture, then dredge in the pecan mixture. Gently press to adhere. Transfer to a sheet pan.

6. Put the sheet pan in the oven and bake until the catfish is opaque in the center, for 15 to 20 minutes. Remove from the oven.

Fried Panfish Wontons with Sweet-and-Spicy Sauce

PREP TIME: 45 MINUTES / **COOK TIME:** 35 MINUTES / **YIELD:** 25 TO 30 WONTONS

OTHER FISH YOU CAN USE: ANY FISH

There's no need to order takeout when you can now make wontons yourself. I love fried wontons; their crunchy texture and the soft insides speak to me. I remember, as a young adult fresh out of college, eating takeout wontons on the floor of my apartment because I didn't own a couch. They were my ultimate comfort food. Now I've taken them up a notch for a version I eat at my kitchen table.

½ cup soy sauce

½ cup rice vinegar

¼ cup sesame oil, plus
1 teaspoon

¼ cup packed light or dark
brown sugar

2 tablespoons sambal oelek or
sriracha

1 tablespoon chopped
fresh chives

1 teaspoon fish sauce

1 teaspoon grated or minced
fresh ginger

1 teaspoon cornstarch

⅛ teaspoon freshly ground
black pepper

8 to 10 ounces skinless panfish
fillets, cut into ½-inch cubes

30 wonton wrappers (from a
12-ounce package)

Vegetable oil, for frying

1. To make the sauce, in a small bowl, whisk together the soy sauce, vinegar, ¼ cup of sesame oil, the brown sugar, and sambal oelek.

2. In a medium bowl, whisk together the chives, fish sauce, remaining 1 teaspoon of sesame oil, the ginger, cornstarch, and pepper.

3. Stir the panfish into the medium bowl.

4. Fill another small bowl with water, then lay a wonton wrapper on a clean work surface.

5. Add ½ tablespoon of the fish filling to the middle of the wrapper. Dip your finger in the water and gently trace the outer edges of the wrapper. Fold over a corner of the wrapper to meet the opposite corner, making a triangle. Press the edges together to seal. Repeat with the remaining wrappers and filling.

6. Fill a 4-quart Dutch oven or saucepan halfway with vegetable oil. Heat to 350°F.

7. Fry 5 to 8 wontons at a time (too many wontons will lower the oil temperature) until golden brown, for 3 or 4 minutes per batch. Using a slotted spoon, transfer to a wire rack. Turn off the heat.

8. Serve the hot wontons with the sauce.

Broiled Panfish with Bacon Butter

PREP TIME: 10 MINUTES / **COOK TIME:** 5 MINUTES / **YIELD:** 3 TO 4 SERVINGS

OTHER FISH YOU CAN USE: TROUT

Broiling is an underrated cooking technique in home kitchens, for reasons I don't understand. I use my broiler as much as possible, especially for game. Its high heat creates a delicious outer crust. Although it's simple to broil, do not walk away from the oven when you're doing it. Your fish or meat can go from perfection to burnt in a matter of seconds.

8 strips bacon, cooked until crispy and crumbled

8 tablespoons (1 stick) unsalted butter, softened

¼ cup chopped fresh chives

¼ cup finely grated Parmesan cheese

1½ pounds skinless panfish fillets

1 teaspoon garlic powder

1. In a small bowl, stir together the bacon, butter, chives, and Parmesan cheese until well combined.

2. Preheat the broiler.

3. Put the panfish on a broiler pan. Season with the garlic powder. Brush with a generous coating of the bacon butter.

4. Broil the panfish about 5 inches from the heat source until browned and cooked through, for about 5 minutes. Keep an eye on it because it cooks very fast. Remove from the broiler. Serve immediately.

Pike Patties with Chive-Parsley Yogurt

PREP TIME: 30 MINUTES / **COOK TIME:** 35 MINUTES / **YIELD:** 4 SERVINGS
OTHER FISH YOU CAN USE: SALMON, WALLEYE, TROUT, ANY WHITE, FLAKY FISH

Fish cakes are all the rage now, don't you know? Okay, well they may not be the most popular dish on Instagram, but they will make you the most popular person in your family. These pike patties can be adjusted to use with a wide variety of fish, making this recipe extremely versatile. I like to double the recipe and freeze a batch. In an airtight bag, they can keep in the freezer for up to 3 months and can be panfried frozen.

1 cup whole milk

1 pound skinless pike fillets

1 large potato, cut into
medium-size cubes

1 large shallot, minced

1 tablespoon grated or minced
fresh ginger

½ jalapeño, finely diced

2 teaspoons chopped fresh
tarragon

2 teaspoons chopped fresh mint

1 teaspoon kosher salt, plus more
to taste

1 teaspoon freshly ground
black pepper

2 tablespoons all-purpose flour

1 large egg

¼ cup sesame seeds

¼ cup panko bread crumbs

¾ cup vegetable oil

1 cup whole-milk Greek yogurt

1 teaspoon chopped fresh chives

1 teaspoon chopped fresh parsley

1. In a large skillet, bring the milk to a boil over medium-high heat.

2. Add the pike.

3. Reduce the heat to medium-low. Simmer until the pike has cooked through, for 8 minutes. Remove from the heat. Reserving the milk, strain the pike over a bowl. Transfer the pike to a large bowl. Return the milk to the skillet.

4. Add the potato, and bring to a boil.

5. Reduce the heat to medium-low. Simmer until the potato has cooked through, for 10 to 12 minutes. Drain.

6. Using 2 forks, flake the pike.

7. Add the potato, shallot, ginger, jalapeño, tarragon, mint, salt, and pepper to the flaked pike. Using your hands, mix everything together until it has a dough-like consistency. Divide into 4 patties about ¾ inch thick.

8. Spread the flour on a plate.

9. In a large shallow bowl, beat the egg.

10. On another plate, combine the sesame seeds and bread crumbs.

11. Dredge each patty in the flour, dip in the egg, then dredge in the bread crumb mixture.

CONTINUED >

12. In a large, nonstick high-sided skillet, heat the vegetable oil over medium heat.

13. Fry 2 patties at a time, turning once, until golden brown, for 4 to 6 minutes per batch. Transfer to a plate. Immediately season with salt. Turn off the heat.

14. In a small bowl, stir together the yogurt, chives, and parsley.

15. Serve the patties topped with the chive-parsley yogurt.

Cajun-Breaded Pike with Southern Corn Succotash

PREP TIME: 30 MINUTES / **COOK TIME:** 25 MINUTES / **YIELD:** 4 SERVINGS
OTHER FISH YOU CAN USE: WALLEYE

Pike may be a Northern fish, but there's no rule that says we can't put some Southern spin on it. This recipe is all about the crust. The addition of instant potatoes to the breading really takes this dish to the next level. But most important, it's a baked dish, which means it's easier to make.

FOR THE PIKE:

Nonstick cooking spray, for greasing

2 large eggs

1 tablespoon water

⅓ cup panko bread crumbs

⅓ cup instant potatoes

⅓ cup grated Parmesan cheese

2 tablespoons Cajun Rub (page 247)

1 teaspoon kosher salt

4 (4-ounce) skinless pike fillets

FOR THE SUCCOTASH:

Kosher salt

1 (16-ounce) bag frozen lima beans

6 strips bacon

1 medium onion, diced

⅓ cup diced red bell pepper

3 cups fresh or frozen corn kernels

1 pint cherry tomatoes, halved

1 tablespoon apple cider vinegar

1 teaspoon chopped fresh tarragon

1 teaspoon minced garlic

2 tablespoons unsalted butter

2 tablespoons chopped fresh chives

1. Preheat the oven to 425°F. Grease a large sheet pan with nonstick cooking spray.

2. **To make the pike:** In a shallow dish, beat together the eggs and water until smooth.

3. In another shallow dish, combine the bread crumbs, instant potatoes, Parmesan cheese, Cajun rub, and salt.

4. Dip the pike in the egg mixture to fully coat, then dredge in the bread crumb mixture. Place in a single layer on the prepared sheet pan.

5. Put the sheet pan in the oven and bake until the pike is opaque in the center, for 15 to 20 minutes. Remove from the oven.

6. **To make the succotash:** While the pike is baking, bring a pot of salted water to a boil over high heat.

CONTINUED >

7. Cook the lima beans as the package directs; reserving 1 cup of the cooking water, strain.

8. Line a plate with paper towels.

9. In a large skillet, cook the bacon over medium-high heat until crisp. Transfer to the prepared plate to drain, then chop into pieces.

10. Remove half of the rendered bacon fat from the skillet. Add the onion and bell pepper; cook until golden brown, for 2 minutes.

11. Add the lima beans, corn, tomatoes, vinegar, tarragon, garlic, and reserved cooking liquid.

12. Reduce the heat to medium. Cook for 5 to 8 minutes.

13. Stir in the butter and cook until melted.

14. Stir in the bacon. Remove from the heat.

15. Serve the pike topped with the succotash and garnished with the chives.

Pike with Chorizo and Cannellini Beans

PREP TIME: 15 MINUTES / **COOK TIME:** 30 MINUTES / **YIELD:** 4 SERVINGS

OTHER FISH YOU CAN USE: WALLEYE, TROUT

I've spent years in fine dining creating dishes with 50-plus ingredients, but nothing comforts the soul like a simple dish. This is one that you will keep coming back to.

2 tablespoons olive oil, divided

1 onion, finely diced

1 carrot, finely diced

1 stalk celery, finely diced

2 cloves garlic, minced

2 sprigs thyme

1 (15.5-ounce) can cannellini beans, drained and rinsed

1 cup chicken broth

4 ounces chorizo sausage, chopped

4 (4-ounce) skinless pike fillets

Kosher salt

Freshly ground black pepper

Grated zest of 1 lemon

¼ cup chopped fresh parsley

2 tablespoons freshly squeezed lemon juice

1. Preheat the oven to 350°F.

2. In a large nonstick skillet, heat 1 tablespoon of olive oil over medium-high heat.

3. Add the onion, carrot, and celery; cook until the onion is golden brown, for about 5 minutes.

4. Stir in the garlic and thyme; cook for 2 minutes.

5. Stir in the beans, broth, and chorizo; bring to a boil.

6. Reduce the heat to medium-low. Cover and simmer for 15 to 20 minutes. Remove from the heat.

7. While the mixture simmers, pat the pike dry with paper towels and place in a single layer on a sheet pan. Drizzle with the remaining 1 tablespoon of olive oil. Season with salt and pepper.

8. Sprinkle with the lemon zest.

9. Put the sheet pan in the oven and bake until the pike is opaque in the center, for 10 to 15 minutes. Remove from the oven.

10. Season the beans with salt and pepper. Stir in the parsley and lemon juice.

11. Divide the beans among 4 bowls, top each with a pike fillet, and serve immediately.

Mediterranean-Style Pike

PREP TIME: 10 MINUTES / **COOK TIME:** 30 MINUTES / **YIELD:** 4 SERVINGS

OTHER FISH YOU CAN USE: WALLEYE, TROUT

Only have one pan? No problem, this is the recipe for you. Be sure to use good-quality tomatoes and fresh herbs because they really make this dish sparkle.

½ cup extra-virgin olive oil, divided

6 roma tomatoes, chopped

1 onion, finely diced

1 tablespoon minced garlic

2 tablespoons chopped fresh basil

2 tablespoons capers, drained

Kosher salt

Freshly ground black pepper

4 (4-ounce) skinless pike fillets

1. In a medium skillet, heat all but 1 tablespoon of olive oil over medium heat.

2. Add the tomatoes and onion; cook until the onion is translucent, for 5 to 7 minutes.

3. Stir in the garlic and cook for 2 minutes. Remove from the heat.

4. Stir in the basil and capers. Season with salt and pepper. Pour into a bowl.

5. In the same skillet, heat the remaining 1 tablespoon of olive oil over medium-high heat.

6. Season the pike on both sides with salt and pepper. Once the pan is hot, add 2 fillets at a time and cook, flipping once, until golden brown on the outside and opaque in the center, for 6 to 8 minutes. Remove from the heat.

7. To serve, top the pike with the tomato mixture.

Smoked Trout

PREP TIME: 10 MINUTES, PLUS 1 HOUR TO BRINE / **COOK TIME:** 2 HOURS / **YIELD:** 6 SERVINGS
OTHER FISH YOU CAN USE: SALMON

Smoked trout is the perfect gathering dish. I like to serve my smoked trout with toasted baguette, cream cheese, thinly sliced red onions, and chives. You can also eat smoked trout cold or transform it into a dip or a spread. It's perfect in tea sandwiches . . . let's just say you have a lot of possibilities with smoked trout!

4 cups cool water

2 tablespoons kosher salt

2 tablespoons sugar

½ lemon, sliced

6 (6-ounce) skin-on trout fillets

1. To make the brine, in a shallow baking dish large enough to hold the trout, combine the water, salt, sugar, and lemon.

2. Place the trout, skin-side up, in the brine. Cover and refrigerate for 1 hour.

3. Set the smoker to 180°F.

4. Remove the trout from the brine. Using a paper towel, gently pat dry. Place the trout, skin-side down, in the smoker and smoke using alder wood, applewood, or pecan wood (see page 4) until the internal temperature of the trout reaches 145°F, for 1½ to 2 hours, depending on the thickness of the fillets. Remove from the smoker. Serve warm.

GAME TIP: If you make this with salmon, increase the smoke time another 20 to 30 minutes.

Trout Ceviche

PREP TIME: 15 MINUTES / **YIELD:** 4 SERVINGS

OTHER FISH YOU CAN USE: SALMON

Ceviche is a traditional South American dish, however, it should be a traditional dish for all fishermen. I know it is for me. It doesn't get any better than catching your own fish and preparing a fresh ceviche right after. No cooking equipment is needed other than a knife, a bowl, and a cutting board. Get creative with your ceviche; try adding different herbs or sweet fruits like mango and pineapple.

2 (4-ounce) skinless trout fillets, finely diced

1 red chile, seeded and minced

½ jalapeño, seeded and minced

1 large shallot, minced

1 bunch fresh cilantro, minced

1 ripe medium avocado, pitted, peeled, and finely diced

¼ small pineapple, cored, peeled, and finely diced

Grated zest of 1 lime

¼ cup freshly squeezed lime juice

2 tablespoons extra-virgin olive oil

Pinch sugar

Flaked sea salt or kosher salt

Tortilla chips, mini toasts, or crackers, for serving

1. Put the trout, chile, jalapeño, shallot, cilantro, avocado, pineapple, lime zest, lime juice, olive oil, and sugar in a large bowl. Season with salt. Toss together to fully combine. Let sit at room temperature for 5 to 10 minutes to let the flavors meld.

2. Serve the ceviche with tortilla chips, mini toasts, or crackers.

Cornmeal-Crusted Trout with Spiced Mandarin-Orange Jus

PREP TIME: 20 MINUTES / **COOK TIME:** 25 MINUTES / **YIELD:** 4 SERVINGS
OTHER FISH YOU CAN USE: CATFISH

It's time you stepped up your weekend fish fry—say goodbye to those lemon wedges and say hello to Mandarin-orange jus! This cornmeal-crusted trout is a classic. Some times you don't need to change a classic, but you can add to it. Mandarin oranges add the perfect amount of sweetness as well as the acid that fried foods need. Try this recipe with catfish and the sauce with other fried game meat, like venison.

1 (11-ounce) can
  mandarin oranges

¼ cup soy sauce

2 tablespoons grated fresh ginger

1 small shallot, minced

1 clove garlic, minced

⅛ teaspoon cayenne pepper

1 large egg

1 tablespoon water

1 cup yellow cornmeal

1 teaspoon garlic powder

1 teaspoon onion powder

1 teaspoon kosher salt

¼ teaspoon freshly ground
  black pepper

¼ teaspoon paprika

½ cup all-purpose flour

4 (4- to 6-ounce) skinless
  trout fillets

Vegetable oil, for frying

1. To make the jus, empty the can of mandarin oranges into a medium saucepan.

2. Add the soy sauce, ginger, shallot, garlic, and cayenne pepper; bring to a simmer over medium heat. Remove from the heat. Keep warm.

3. In a shallow bowl, beat together the egg and water.

4. In a shallow dish, whisk together the cornmeal, garlic powder, onion powder, salt, pepper, and paprika.

5. Put the flour on a large plate. Dredge each trout fillet in the flour, then dip in the egg, then dredge in the cornmeal mixture. Place in a single layer on a plate.

6. In a large skillet, heat 1 inch of vegetable oil over medium-high heat.

7. Once the oil is hot, fry 2 fillets at a time, turning once, until lightly browned, for 8 to 10 minutes per batch. Transfer to a plate. Turn off the heat.

8. Stir the jus; it should have thickened a bit. Top each fillet with the jus and serve.

Trout à la Meunière

PREP TIME: 10 MINUTES / **COOK TIME:** 20 MINUTES / **YIELD:** 4 SERVINGS
OTHER FISH YOU CAN USE: ANY WHITE FLAKY FISH

Sole à la meunière is a classic French dish; elegant, simple, and covered in butter. I replace sole with trout because my fly-fishing hobby supplies me with a surplus of it. I like to serve this on a bed of basmati rice because it sops up all the brown butter goodness.

9 tablespoons unsalted butter, divided

¼ cup minced shallots

3 tablespoons freshly squeezed lemon juice

½ cup all-purpose flour

1 teaspoon kosher salt

½ teaspoon freshly ground black pepper

¼ teaspoon cayenne pepper

4 (6-ounce) skin-on trout fillets

2 tablespoons olive oil, divided

¼ cup chopped fresh parsley

4 lemon wedges, for serving

1. Preheat the oven to 200°F.

2. To make the sauce, in a medium saucepan, melt 8 tablespoons of butter over medium-high heat.

3. Add the shallots and cook until tender, for 3 to 5 minutes. Remove from the heat.

4. Whisk in the lemon juice.

5. On a large, flat dish, combine the flour, salt, black pepper, and cayenne pepper.

6. Using paper towels, pat the trout dry. Dredge the fillets in the flour mixture, gently shaking off any excess.

7. Heat a large, nonstick skillet over medium-high heat. Pour in 1 tablespoon of olive oil and add the remaining 1 tablespoon of butter.

8. As soon as the butter melts and starts to sizzle, add 2 fillets, skin-side down. Cook until the skin is golden brown and crisp, for about 2 minutes; flip and cook until golden brown, for about 2 minutes. Transfer to a sheet pan and put in the oven to keep warm. Repeat with the remaining fillets. Turn off the heat.

9. Whisk the sauce and pour over the trout.

10. Sprinkle the trout with the parsley and serve with the lemon wedges.

Baked Salt-Crusted Whole Trout

PREP TIME: 15 MINUTES / **COOK TIME:** 35 MINUTES, PLUS 15 MINUTES TO REST / **YIELD:** 2 SERVINGS
OTHER FISH YOU CAN USE: SALMON

When baking in a salt crust, you're basically baking in an oven within the oven. The purpose of a salt crust is to retain moisture; it essentially allows the fish to steam inside while cooking evenly, which means a beautifully cooked fish. As the fish cooks, the salt perfectly seasons the flesh.

1 small bunch fresh parsley

1 small bunch fresh dill

2 lemons, zested and sliced

1 (16-ounce) box kosher salt, divided

3 large egg whites

1 (11- to 14-ounce) whole trout, cleaned

Freshly ground black pepper

1. Preheat the oven to 425°F.

2. Put the parsley, dill, lemon zest, and 1 cup of salt in a food processor. Pulse to combine. Transfer to a large bowl.

3. Add the remaining salt. Stir together.

4. Stir in the egg whites to form a paste-like texture.

5. Place a third of the salt mixture in a diagonal layer (the size of the trout) on a large sheet pan.

6. Place the trout on top of the salt.

7. Stuff the lemon slices in the cavity. Season the cavity with a bit of pepper.

8. Pour the remaining salt mixture over the trout, leaving the tip of the tail and the head exposed. Pat the salt mixture around the body to completely encase it.

9. Put the sheet pan in the oven and roast for 30 to 35 minutes. Remove from the oven. Let the trout rest inside the salt crust for 15 minutes.

10. Scrape off the salt. Transfer the trout to a serving platter and serve immediately.

GAME TIP: If you substitute a whole salmon, increase the oven temperature to 500°F and roast for 15 to 20 minutes.

Hot Walleye and Pimento Cheese Dip

PREP TIME: 20 MINUTES / **COOK TIME:** 35 MINUTES / **YIELD:** 12 SERVINGS

OTHER FISH YOU CAN USE: ANY WHITE, FLAKY FISH

If you've spent hours in the freezing cold fishing for walleye over ice, this is the perfect way to warm you back up. This is such a fun way to cook walleye—creamy and cheesy with a hint of spice. If you don't have walleye on hand, any other white, flaky fish will do! Serve with toasted bread slices, crackers, or celery sticks.

2 tablespoons unsalted butter

12 ounces skinless walleye fillets

1 small onion, finely diced

1 cup mayonnaise

1 cup shredded Cheddar cheese

4 ounces cream cheese, softened

2 tablespoons freshly squeezed lemon juice

1 tablespoon paprika

½ teaspoon garlic powder

¼ teaspoon cayenne pepper (optional)

1 small jalapeño, seeded and minced

1 (4-ounce) jar diced pimentos, drained

¼ cup chopped scallions, green and white parts

¼ cup chopped fresh parsley

½ cup panko bread crumbs

1 cup grated Parmesan cheese

1. Preheat the oven to 350°F.

2. In a large skillet, melt the butter over medium-high heat.

3. Add the walleye and onion; cook until the onion is translucent and the walleye has cooked through, for 5 to 7 minutes. Using a wooden spoon, gently flake apart the walleye and stir together with the onion and butter. Remove from the heat.

4. In a large bowl, stir together the mayonnaise, Cheddar cheese, cream cheese, lemon juice, paprika, garlic powder, cayenne pepper (if using), jalapeño, pimentos, scallions, and parsley until thoroughly combined. Spread evenly into a 9-inch baking dish.

5. Arrange the walleye and onion mixture over the cheese layer.

6. Sprinkle with the bread crumbs and Parmesan cheese.

7. Put the baking dish in the oven and bake until the dip is hot and bubbling, for about 25 minutes. Remove from the oven. Let cool for 5 minutes before serving.

Parmesan-Crusted Baked Walleye

PREP TIME: 10 MINUTES / **COOK TIME:** 15 MINUTES / **YIELD:** 4 SERVINGS
OTHER FISH YOU CAN USE: PIKE, SALMON, TROUT

Some say cheese doesn't go well with fish. I say you don't need that kind of negativity in your life! The addition of Parmesan in the breading not only gives this dish great salty umami flavor but also helps create a crunchy crust. If you're looking to feed your family a tasty meal that's fast and easy, give this one a try; it comes together in less than 30 minutes.

Nonstick cooking spray, for greasing

¾ cup panko bread crumbs

¾ cup finely grated Parmesan cheese

3 tablespoons unsalted butter, softened

3 tablespoons mayonnaise

2 tablespoons freshly squeezed lemon juice

1 teaspoon Worcestershire sauce

1 teaspoon kosher salt, plus more to taste

½ teaspoon freshly ground black pepper, plus more to taste

¼ teaspoon cayenne pepper

3 scallions, green and white parts, chopped

4 (4-ounce) skinless walleye fillets

2 tablespoons chopped fresh parsley

1. Preheat the oven to 425°F. Grease a 9-by-13-inch baking dish with nonstick cooking spray.

2. In a medium bowl, mix together the bread crumbs, Parmesan cheese, butter, mayonnaise, lemon juice, Worcestershire sauce, salt, black pepper, cayenne pepper, and scallions until well combined.

3. Using paper towels, pat the walleye dry. Lightly season with salt and pepper.

4. Arrange in a single layer in the prepared baking dish.

5. Top each fillet evenly with an equal amount of the bread crumb mixture.

6. Put the baking dish in the oven and bake until the walleye is just opaque in the center, for about 8 minutes.

7. Set the oven to broil. Broil for 2 or 3 minutes to crisp up the crust. Remove from the oven.

8. Garnish the walleye with the parsley and serve immediately.

Walleye Piccata

PREP TIME: 10 MINUTES / **COOK TIME:** 10 MINUTES / **YIELD:** 4 SERVINGS

OTHER FISH YOU CAN USE: PIKE, TROUT

This traditional Italian dish plays wells with fish. Walleye gets dredged in seasoned flour, sautéed in olive oil, and smothered in a tangy, lemon-butter pan sauce with salty capers. The flour not only helps create a light golden crust but also perfectly thickens the sauce as well.

4 (4-ounce) skinless
  walleye fillets

¼ teaspoon kosher salt, plus
  more to taste

¼ teaspoon freshly ground black
  pepper, plus more to taste

½ cup all-purpose flour

1 teaspoon garlic powder

½ teaspoon onion powder

2 tablespoons olive oil

½ cup white wine

Juice of 2 lemons

2 tablespoons capers, drained

3 tablespoons cold
  unsalted butter

2 tablespoons chopped
  fresh parsley

1. Using a paper towel, pat the walleye dry. Season with salt and pepper.

2. In a shallow dish, combine the flour, garlic powder, onion powder, salt, and pepper.

3. In a large sauté pan, heat the olive oil over medium-high heat.

4. Dredge the walleye in the flour mixture on both sides.

5. Add the walleye to the pan and fry, flipping once, until cooked through, for 4 to 6 minutes. Transfer to a serving plate.

6. Add the wine to the pan and cook, stirring, to reduce a bit, for 1 or 2 minutes.

7. Stir in the lemon juice and capers.

8. Add the butter and stir until fully incorporated and the sauce thickens slightly. Adjust the seasoning if needed. Remove from the heat.

9. Pour the sauce over the walleye and serve immediately, garnished with the parsley.

Grilled Whole Walleye with Charred Lemon Butter

PREP TIME: 10 MINUTES / **COOK TIME:** 20 MINUTES / **YIELD:** 8 SERVINGS

Grilling fish whole is my favorite way of cooking fish. When the bones and skin are cooked with the meat, they add more flavor to the dish. Let the fish come to room temperature before you start to grill it. When cold fish is put on the grill, it produces steam, which makes the skin stick to the grates.

1 (5- to 8-pound) walleye, cleaned

Olive oil, for brushing

½ teaspoon kosher salt, plus more to taste

Freshly ground black pepper

1 small bunch fresh parsley

1 clove garlic, crushed

2 lemons, halved

3 scallions, green and white parts, trimmed

4 tablespoons (½ stick) unsalted butter, softened

1 teaspoon grated lemon zest

1. Preheat the grill to 400°F.

2. Using paper towels, pat the walleye dry. Make 3 (2-inch-long) cuts on the skin on both sides.

3. Brush the skin and cavity with olive oil. Season with salt and pepper.

4. Stuff the cavity with the parsley and garlic.

5. Brush the grill grates with olive oil.

6. Place the walleye; lemons, cut-side down; and scallions on the grill directly over the fire. Cook until the walleye is lightly charred and releases from the grates, for about 10 minutes; flip and cook until the internal temperature of the walleye reaches 130°F, for about 10 minutes. Transfer to a serving platter. Cook the lemons and scallions until they are nicely charred, for about 10 minutes. Remove from the heat.

7. To make the charred lemon butter, squeeze the juice of the charred lemons into a small bowl; if bits of char come off, that's great.

8. Chop the scallions and add to the bowl.

9. Stir in the butter, lemon zest, and salt until well combined.

10. Serve the walleye whole with the charred lemon butter.

SALTWATER FISH

Smoked Bluefish Spread

PREP TIME: 25 MINUTES, PLUS 4 HOURS TO BRINE AND DRY / **COOK TIME:** 3 HOURS
YIELD: 4 TO 6 SERVINGS
OTHER FISH YOU CAN USE: TROUT, WALLEYE

Smoked fish spread or dip is a summer staple on the Georgia coast. Because bluefish are on the fatty side, their meat adds creaminess, making for a wonderful spread. If you don't have honey or soy sauce, or just want to try something different, marinate the bluefish in white wine, which helps cut the fattiness.

4 cups cold water

½ cup kosher salt

½ cup honey

½ cup soy sauce

1 pound skin-on bluefish fillets

6 ounces cream cheese, softened

3 tablespoons chopped fresh chives

3 tablespoons chopped fresh parsley

1 tablespoon chopped fresh tarragon

1 tablespoon minced garlic

2 tablespoons freshly squeezed lemon juice

1 tablespoon Worcestershire sauce

1 large shallot, minced

Toasted baguette slices, for serving

1. To make the brine, in a large baking dish, combine the water, salt, honey, and soy sauce. Stir until the salt and honey dissolve.

2. Add the bluefish, cover, and refrigerate for 1 hour.

3. Remove the bluefish from the brine. Rinse and pat dry, using paper towels. Transfer to a sheet pan and refrigerate, uncovered, for at least 3 hours.

4. Set an electric smoker to 200°F.

5. Place the bluefish, skin-side down, in the smoker and smoke using applewood, cherry wood, or alder wood (see page 4) for 3 hours. Remove from the smoker. Transfer to a platter. Let cool to room temperature.

6. Remove the skin from the bluefish and flake the meat into pieces.

7. In a large bowl, stir together the cream cheese, chives, parsley, tarragon, garlic, lemon juice, Worcestershire sauce, and shallot until well combined.

8. Gently fold in the bluefish pieces.

9. Serve the spread at room temperature with toasted baguette slices.

Fried Bluefish Burger with Creamy Slaw

PREP TIME: 25 MINUTES, PLUS 1 HOUR TO CHILL / **COOK TIME:** 10 MINUTES / **YIELD:** 4 SERVINGS
OTHER FISH YOU CAN USE: TROUT

Burgers aren't just for beef anymore. The crunchy fish, Cajun spice, and cool, creamy slaw hit all the right notes for an amazing burger. Plus, it's easy to make and perfect for an outdoor gathering.

FOR THE BURGERS:

1 pound cooked bluefish fillets, flaked into chunks

1½ cups panko bread crumbs

1 large egg, beaten

¼ cup mayonnaise

2 tablespoons chopped fresh parsley

1 tablespoon chopped fresh chives

1 tablespoon Cajun Rub (page 247)

1 teaspoon kosher salt

1 teaspoon grated lemon zest

½ cup vegetable oil

4 hamburger buns

Pickle chips, for serving (optional)

FOR THE SLAW:

1 head green cabbage, finely shredded

1 cup plain Greek yogurt

¼ cup chopped fresh chives

¼ cup chopped fresh cilantro

3 tablespoons distilled white vinegar

1 teaspoon kosher salt, plus more to taste

1 teaspoon freshly ground black pepper

½ teaspoon garlic powder

1. **To make the burgers:** In a large bowl, using your hands, combine the bluefish, bread crumbs, egg, mayonnaise, parsley, chives, Cajun Rub, salt, and lemon zest. Form into 4 patties and put on a sheet pan. Refrigerate for 1 hour to firm them up.

2. In a large skillet, heat the oil over medium-high heat until hot.

3. Add the bluefish patties and fry, flipping once, until golden brown, for 6 to 8 minutes. Remove from the heat. Season with salt.

4. **To make the slaw:** In a large bowl, combine the cabbage, yogurt, chives, cilantro, vinegar, salt, pepper, and garlic powder. Refrigerate until ready to serve.

5. To assemble the burgers, place a bluefish patty on the bottom of each bun, slather with a generous amount of slaw and pickle chips (if using), and cover with the bun tops. Serve immediately.

Vietnamese-Style Bluefish

PREP TIME: 10 MINUTES / **COOK TIME:** 15 MINUTES / **YIELD:** 4 SERVINGS

OTHER FISH YOU CAN USE: TROUT, SALMON

Vietnamese cuisine has a brilliant balance of aromatics, heat, sweetness, sourness, and savory. This recipe is a perfect beginner's introduction to Vietnamese flavors and can be used with other fish such as trout or salmon; just note that your cooking times will slightly increase with the thickness of the fish.

1 clove garlic, minced

⅓ cup packed light or dark brown sugar

3 tablespoons soy sauce

2 tablespoons fish sauce

2 tablespoons freshly squeezed lime juice

1 tablespoon grated lime zest

1 tablespoon vegetable oil

1 tablespoon rice vinegar

1 teaspoon kosher salt

1 teaspoon grated or minced fresh ginger

¼ teaspoon freshly ground black pepper

1½ pounds skin-on bluefish fillets

4 scallions, green and white parts, chopped

1 jalapeño, thinly sliced

¼ cup chopped fresh cilantro

2 tablespoons chopped fresh mint

Hot cooked white rice, for serving

1. In a large skillet, combine the garlic, brown sugar, soy sauce, fish sauce, lime juice, lime zest, vegetable oil, vinegar, salt, ginger, and pepper; bring to a simmer over medium-high heat. Cook until slightly syrupy, for about 2 minutes.

2. Place the bluefish, skin-side down, in the pan. Simmer, frequently basting with the sauce, for 2 or 3 minutes; flip and simmer, basting, until cooked through, for 2 or 3 minutes. Remove from the heat. Transfer the bluefish to a serving plate.

3. Garnish the bluefish with the scallions, jalapeño, cilantro, and mint; drizzle with the pan sauce. Serve with the rice.

Smokehouse-Rubbed Grilled Grouper with Corn Salad

PREP TIME: 15 MINUTES / **COOK TIME:** 30 MINUTES / **YIELD:** 2 SERVINGS

OTHER FISH YOU CAN USE: SALMON, WALLEYE

This is a dish with summertime vibes. My smokehouse rub is perfect for giving fish that touch of smokiness without overpowering its delicate flavor. The corn salad is light, fresh, and vibrant and super easy to make. Try adding diced mango or sprinkling Parmesan cheese on top.

5 ears corn, shucked

½ cup minced red onion

½ red bell pepper, minced

¼ cup chopped fresh cilantro

3 tablespoons apple cider vinegar

3 tablespoons extra-virgin
   olive oil

½ teaspoon kosher salt

½ teaspoon freshly ground
   black pepper

4 tablespoons (½ stick)
   unsalted butter

1 tablespoon minced garlic

2 (6-ounce) skin-on grouper fillets

2 tablespoons Smokehouse Rub
   (page 251)

1. Preheat the grill to 350°F to 400°F.

2. Bring a large pot of water to a boil over high heat. Fill a bowl with ice water.

3. Add the corn to the pot and cook for about 3 minutes. Remove from the heat. Drain and submerge in the ice water to stop the cooking. Drain and transfer to a cutting board. Cut the kernels off the cobs.

4. To make the salad, in a large bowl, stir the corn, onion, bell pepper, cilantro, vinegar, olive oil, salt, and pepper to combine.

5. In a small saucepan, melt the butter with the garlic. Remove from the heat.

6. Using a paper towel, pat the grouper dry. Sprinkle with the rub.

7. Place the grouper on the grill, skin-side down, directly over the fire. Close the lid and cook for 3 minutes, then brush with some of the garlic butter. Keep basting the grouper every 3 minutes until opaque in the center, for 12 to 15 minutes. Remove from the heat.

8. Serve the grouper fillets on top of the salad.

Classic Beer-Battered British Fried Fish with Spicy Tartar Sauce

PREP TIME: 30 MINUTES / **COOK TIME:** 15 MINUTES / **YIELD:** 6 SERVINGS
OTHER FISH YOU CAN USE: ANY LARGE-FLAKE WHITE FISH

When I was in London, I think I must have eaten my body weight in fish and chips. I was on a mission to bring back the most authentic version possible. After some trials and errors back home, this little gem emerged.

FOR THE SAUCE:

1 cup mayonnaise

5 tablespoons finely chopped dill pickles

3 scallions, green and white parts, finely chopped

3 tablespoons freshly squeezed lemon juice

2 tablespoons whole-grain mustard

1 teaspoon chopped fresh dill

1 teaspoon chopped fresh tarragon

1 teaspoon Worcestershire sauce

1 teaspoon sriracha

½ teaspoon kosher salt

½ teaspoon freshly ground black pepper

FOR THE FLOUR MIXTURE:

2 cups all-purpose flour

1 tablespoon kosher salt

1 tablespoon freshly ground black pepper

2 teaspoons garlic powder

2 teaspoons onion powder

1. **To make the sauce:** In a medium bowl, whisk together the mayonnaise, pickles, scallions, lemon juice, mustard, dill, tarragon, Worcestershire sauce, sriracha, salt, and pepper. (This can be made a day ahead and refrigerated for up to 7 days.)

2. **To make the flour mixture:** In a large bowl, whisk together the flour, salt, pepper, garlic powder, and onion powder.

3. **To make the batter:** In a medium bowl, whisk together the flour, paprika, and salt.

4. Whisk in the beer.

5. **To make the fish:** Fill a 6-quart, cast-iron Dutch oven or saucepan halfway with canola oil. Heat to 375°F. Set a wire rack over paper towels.

6. Dredge the grouper in the flour mixture to evenly coat, then dip in the batter, draining off any excess.

FOR THE BATTER:

3 cups all-purpose flour

3 tablespoons paprika

3 tablespoons kosher salt

1 (12-ounce) bottle lager beer

FOR THE FISH:

Vegetable oil, for frying

6 (6- to 8-ounce) skinless
    grouper fillets

Kosher salt

7. Fry 3 fillets at a time in the hot oil until the batter is golden brown and the fillets are trying to float to the top, for 5 to 7 minutes per batch. Using a slotted spoon, transfer to the prepared wire rack. Immediately season with salt. Turn off the heat.

8. Serve the fried grouper with the sauce.

Peruvian-Style Ceviche

PREP TIME: 25 MINUTES / **YIELD:** 4 SERVINGS

OTHER FISH YOU CAN USE: SEA BASS

I used to make this dish at a restaurant as a way to use up extra fish, but it soon turned into a menu staple. I love ceviche because it comes together quickly, is easy to make, and is always tasty. Peruvian ceviche includes sweet potato, which takes it to another level. Although traditional Peruvian ceviche uses ají amarillo chile paste, I've made the substitutions for you, so you can easily get everything at the grocery store.

1 large red onion, thinly sliced

1½ pounds skinless mahi mahi fillets

1 teaspoon kosher salt

1 tablespoon grated or minced fresh ginger

1 clove garlic, minced

1 jalapeño, seeded and finely diced

Juice of 8 limes

¼ cup fresh cilantro leaves

1 sweet potato, cooked and finely diced

Flaky sea salt

1. Submerge the onion in a bowl of ice water for 10 minutes, which will help tame the flavor a bit. Drain and spread out on a towel to soak up the excess water.

2. Cut the mahi mahi into strips around 1¼ inches by ¾ inch. Put in a large bowl.

3. Add the salt and mix well. Let sit for at least 2 minutes. This helps open the pores of the fish and lets it take on more flavors.

4. Add the ginger, garlic, jalapeño, and lime juice. Stir well to fully incorporate and let sit for 2 more minutes.

5. Add the onion, cilantro, and sweet potato. Gently stir together; you don't want to mash the sweet potato. Season with sea salt, then serve immediately.

Fried Mahi Mahi Tacos with Jalapeño Ranch

PREP TIME: 30 MINUTES / **COOK TIME:** 20 MINUTES / **YIELD:** 8 SERVINGS
OTHER FISH YOU CAN USE: ANY WHITE FLAKY FISH

If you are a fish taco lover, these are for you. I've made this recipe so many times trying to figure out the best batter, and I finally nailed it! Try using this recipe with salmon as well; it's delightful.

2 cups all-purpose flour

1 teaspoon kosher salt, plus more
   to taste

1 teaspoon garlic powder

1 teaspoon onion powder

½ teaspoon paprika

¼ teaspoon freshly ground
   black pepper

3 large eggs

¼ cup water

2 cups panko bread crumbs

4 cups vegetable oil

2 pounds skinless mahi mahi
   fillets, cut into 1-inch strips

24 corn tortillas, warmed

½ head Savoy cabbage, cored
   and shredded

⅓ cup packed fresh
   cilantro leaves

3 tablespoons chopped
   fresh chives

Pickled red onion, for garnish

3 limes, cut into wedges

1 recipe Jalapeño Ranch
   (page 262)

1. In a large bowl, whisk together the flour, salt, garlic powder, onion powder, paprika, and pepper.

2. In another large bowl, whisk together the eggs and water.

3. Put the bread crumbs in a third large bowl.

4. In a large, cast-iron Dutch oven, heat the vegetable oil to 375°F. Set a wire rack over paper towels.

5. Working in batches, dredge the mahi mahi in the flour mixture, then dip in the egg mixture, and dredge in the bread crumbs. Fry the mahi mahi in small batches in the hot oil until golden brown and cooked through, for 3 or 4 minutes per batch. Using a slotted spoon, transfer to the prepared wire rack. Season with a bit of salt. Turn off the heat.

6. To serve, stack 2 tortillas per taco. Divide the fried mahi mahi among the tortillas.

7. Top with the cabbage, cilantro, and chives.

8. Garnish each taco with the onion and top with a squeeze of lime juice and a dollop of Jalapeño Ranch.

Korean BBQ–Style Marinated Mahi Mahi with Charred Romaine

PREP TIME: 15 MINUTES, PLUS 45 MINUTES TO MARINATE / **COOK TIME:** 15 MINUTES / **YIELD:** 2 SERVINGS

OTHER FISH YOU CAN USE: PIKE, WALLEYE, CATFISH

Korean barbecue is a celebration of all things smoke, fire, and meat. Don't get me wrong, grilled kalbi is amazing, but I wanted to transfer those great Korean BBQ flavors to seafood. White fish is a perfect vehicle because it marinates quickly and takes on flavor well.

1 recipe Korean-Style BBQ Marinade (page 240)

2 (6-ounce) mahi mahi fillets

1 red bell pepper, seeded and halved

4 scallions, green and white parts, trimmed

1 head romaine lettuce, halved lengthwise

1 tablespoon olive oil

Sesame seeds, for garnish

1. In a medium bowl, combine the marinade and mahi mahi. Refrigerate for 45 minutes.

2. Preheat the grill to about 300°F, with an indirect setup (see page 3).

3. Remove the mahi mahi from the marinade. To make the sauce, pour the marinade into a medium saucepan. Bring to a boil. Cook for 5 minutes.

4. Reduce the heat to low. Simmer for 10 minutes. Remove from the heat.

5. While the sauce simmers, place the mahi mahi on the grill away from the fire, close the lid, and cook, turning once, until opaque in the center, for 10 to 14 minutes. Remove from the grill.

6. While the mahi mahi grills, place the bell pepper and scallions on the grill directly over the fire.

7. Brush the cut side of the romaine lettuce with the olive oil. Place, cut-side down, on the grill. Cook until the vegetables develop a bit of a char, for about 5 minutes. Remove from the heat.

8. Arrange each fillet on top of the romaine halves and garnish with sesame seeds. Serve with the bell pepper, scallions, and sauce alongside.

Salmon Gravlax

PREP TIME: 15 MINUTES, PLUS 24 HOURS TO CURE / **YIELD:** 10 TO 16 SERVINGS

This is an incredibly easy recipe for salmon gravlax. My suggestion is, because you will love it so much, to double the batch. That way you can freeze one for later; it keeps well in the freezer for up to 2 months. I love to serve my gravlax with toasted baguette slices, a mushroom cream sauce, and a lemon wedge. But I've often found that the gravlax is so good that it's great by itself.

1 tablespoon black peppercorns

1 cup kosher salt

1 cup sugar

1 cup chopped fresh dill, divided

1 (2-pound) skinless salmon fillet

1. Crush the peppercorns in a mortar and pestle or put them in a plastic bag and crush using a cast-iron skillet.

2. To make the cure, in a medium bowl, combine the crushed peppercorns, salt, sugar, and about ¾ cup of dill.

3. Place 2 large pieces of plastic wrap on a work surface slightly overlapping each other. Spread half of the cure in the middle of the plastic wrap in the shape of the salmon fillet.

4. Place the salmon on the cure, then top with the remaining cure.

5. Wrap the salmon in the plastic wrap and transfer to a 9-by-13-inch baking dish. Top with something flat, such as a small cutting board, and then put 3 (14-ounce) cans on top. You want to weigh down the salmon. Refrigerate for 12 hours.

6. Drain and discard any liquid in the dish; flip and refrigerate for 12 more hours.

7. Unwrap the salmon, scrape off the cure, and rinse with water. Pat dry.

8. Sprinkle the remaining ¼ cup of dill over the salmon for garnish. Slice thinly on an angle, making sure to not cut through the skin (you don't want to eat the skin).

Easy Sheet-Pan Salade Niçoise with Salmon

PREP TIME: 25 MINUTES / **COOK TIME:** 35 MINUTES / **YIELD:** 4 SERVINGS
OTHER FISH YOU CAN USE: TROUT

Salade Niçoise is kind of a French version of a Cobb salad in terms of iconic salads. Although I have written this recipe with the classic ingredients, I like to use whatever vegetables are in season, like roasted corn, avocado, asparagus, or squash. Cooking everything on a sheet pan makes life a bit easier.

FOR THE SALAD:

1 pound baby Yukon Gold
  potatoes, halved

3 tablespoons olive oil, divided

2 teaspoons kosher salt, divided

1 teaspoon freshly ground black
  pepper, divided

2 large eggs

6 ounces haricots verts, trimmed

4 (6-ounce) skinless salmon fillets

5 ounces tender mix salad greens

1 cup cherry tomatoes

½ cup pitted Niçoise olives

1. Preheat the oven to 400°F.

2. **To make the salad:** Put the potatoes on a sheet pan. Drizzle with 1 tablespoon of olive oil. Season with 1 teaspoon of salt and ½ teaspoon of pepper. Gently roll the potatoes in the oil to fully coat them.

3. Put the sheet pan in the oven and bake the potatoes for 20 minutes.

4. While the potatoes bake, bring a medium saucepan of water to a boil over high heat.

5. Add the eggs and cook for exactly 6 minutes. Drain, let cool, then peel and cut into quarters.

6. Once the potatoes have baked for 20 minutes, add the haricots verts to the sheet pan.

7. Make room in the center of the sheet pan and add the salmon.

8. Season the haricots verts and salmon with the remaining 1 teaspoon of salt and ½ teaspoon of pepper.

9. Drizzle the haricots verts, salmon, and potatoes with the remaining 2 tablespoons of olive oil.

CONTINUED >

FOR THE DRESSING:

2 tablespoons
  red-wine vinegar

1 tablespoon freshly squeezed
  lemon juice

1 small shallot, minced

1 teaspoon minced garlic

2 teaspoons Dijon mustard

¼ cup extra-virgin olive oil

Kosher salt

Freshly ground black pepper

10. Return the sheet pan to the oven and bake until the salmon has cooked through and the potatoes are tender, for about 15 minutes. Remove from the oven.

11. **To make the dressing:** In a small bowl, whisk together the vinegar, lemon juice, shallot, garlic, and mustard.

12. Slowly whisk in the olive oil. Season with salt and pepper.

13. To serve, put the greens in a large, shallow serving bowl and toss with the dressing to coat. Place the salmon fillets in the middle of the bowl and arrange the roasted vegetables around them.

14. Top with the eggs, tomatoes, and olives. Serve immediately.

Salmon Sashimi Bowl

PREP TIME: 15 MINUTES / **YIELD:** 2 SERVINGS

OTHER FISH YOU CAN USE: TUNA, SNAPPER

This recipe is a good example of what you can create with simple ingredients on hand. If you are a person who gets "hangry," this recipe is great because it comes together quickly and will leave you completely satisfied.

¼ cup soy sauce

1 teaspoon rice vinegar

1 teaspoon sesame oil

1 teaspoon sambal oelek or
   sriracha (optional)

2 cups hot cooked white rice

1 pound salmon fillets, cut into
   ¼-inch-thick slices

½ ripe avocado, peeled
   and sliced

½ English cucumber, thinly sliced

3 scallions, green and white
   parts, thinly sliced

Sesame seeds, for garnish

Pickled ginger, for serving

1. In a small bowl, whisk together the soy sauce, vinegar, sesame oil, and sambal oelek (if using).

2. Divide the rice between 2 bowls. Top each equally with the salmon, soy sauce mixture, avocado, cucumber, and scallions.

3. Garnish the bowls with sesame seeds and serve with pickled ginger.

Panko-Crusted Salmon with Pea Purée

PREP TIME: 20 MINUTES / **COOK TIME:** 20 MINUTES / **YIELD:** 4 SERVINGS

OTHER FISH YOU CAN USE: MAHI MAHI

There are a lot of things I have learned in my fine dining career. Among them is the importance of texture. Here, the crusty garlic bread crumbs, meaty salmon, and smooth pea purée make a beautiful combination.

2 tablespoons vegetable oil

⅔ cup panko bread crumbs

2 tablespoons minced
   fresh parsley

2 tablespoons chopped
   fresh chives

2 tablespoons olive oil

1 clove garlic, minced

1 teaspoon grated lemon zest

1 teaspoon kosher salt, divided

½ teaspoon freshly ground
   black pepper

4 (6-ounce) skin-on salmon fillets

2 tablespoons Dijon mustard

1 (10-ounce) bag frozen peas

½ cup heavy cream

Juice of ½ lemon

1. Preheat the oven to 425°F. Brush a sheet pan with the vegetable oil.

2. In a small bowl, stir together the bread crumbs, parsley, chives, olive oil, garlic, lemon zest, ½ teaspoon of salt, and the pepper.

3. Place the salmon, skin-side down, on the prepared sheet pan.

4. Brush the tops of the fillets with the mustard.

5. Gently press one-fourth of the bread crumb mixture on top of each fillet to cover.

6. Put the sheet pan in the oven and bake until the internal temperature of the salmon reaches 145°F, for 7 to 9 minutes. Remove from the oven. Transfer to a platter, cover with aluminum foil, and let rest for 5 to 10 minutes.

7. While the salmon rests, to make the pea purée, bring a large saucepan filled halfway with water to a boil over high heat.

8. Add the peas and cook for 3 or 4 minutes. Drain and transfer to a blender.

9. Add the cream and lemon juice; process until smooth.

10. Serve the salmon with the pea purée.

Crispy-Skinned Salmon with Sauce Vierge

PREP TIME: 15 MINUTES, PLUS 1 TO 2 HOURS TO MARINATE / **COOK TIME:** 10 MINUTES / **YIELD:** 2 SERVINGS
OTHER FISH YOU CAN USE: MAHI MAHI, SNAPPER, TROUT, TUNA

You'll sound like a total chef when you present your guests with this dish. Sauce vierge is typically served with shellfish in the south of France, but I haven't found a type of fish I didn't like paired with it. Try making the sauce with different combinations of herbs, like tarragon or cilantro with parsley and basil. This is a classic dish you'll want to master.

3 large ripe tomatoes, preferably heirloom, coarsely chopped

1 cup extra-virgin olive oil

Juice of 1 lemon

2 tablespoons chopped fresh basil

2 tablespoons chopped fresh chives

2 tablespoons chopped fresh parsley

1 teaspoon minced garlic

⅛ teaspoon ground coriander

2 (6-ounce) skin-on salmon fillets

Kosher salt

Freshly ground black pepper

3 tablespoons unsalted butter, softened

1. To make the sauce, in a medium bowl, combine the tomatoes, olive oil, lemon juice, basil, chives, parsley, garlic, and coriander. Cover and let sit at room temperature for 1 or 2 hours for the flavors to develop.

2. Preheat the broiler on high.

3. Using a paper towel, pat the salmon dry. Season with salt and pepper. Place on a sheet pan, skin-side up.

4. Rub the salmon with the butter. Broil 5 inches from the heat source until the skin is crispy and the flesh is opaque in the center, for 7 or 8 minutes. Remove from the broiler.

5. Serve the salmon with the sauce.

Cedar Plank Salmon with Everything Rub

PREP TIME: 10 MINUTES / **COOK TIME:** 25 MINUTES / **YIELD:** 4 SERVINGS

OTHER FISH YOU CAN USE: ANY WHITE FLAKY FISH, WALLEYE

Grilling food directly on a charred cedar plank imbues it with a smoky, earthy flavor. Doing so allows the extracts from the wood to transfer to the surface of the fish, an element that smoking alone just can't bring. The best tip I can give is to thoroughly soak the plank in water; otherwise, your fish will go up in flames along with the plank!

1 pound skin-on salmon fillets

3 tablespoons Everything Rub (page 253)

1 cedar plank, soaked in water for at least 1 hour

1 lemon, cut into wedges

1. Preheat the grill to 400°F to 450°F.

2. Sprinkle the salmon evenly with the rub.

3. Remove the soaked plank from the water and pat dry using a towel.

4. Place the plank on the grill grates and close the lid. Lightly char the plank for about 7 minutes.

5. Turn the plank over and place the salmon, skin-side down, on the charred plank. Close the lid and cook until the internal temperature of the salmon reaches 140°F, for about 15 minutes. Remove the plank to a heatproof surface.

6. Serve the salmon with the lemon wedges.

Hot-Smoked Salmon Fillet

PREP TIME: 15 MINUTES, PLUS 20 HOURS TO BRINE AND DRY / **COOK TIME:** 3 TO 5 HOURS
YIELD: 12 SERVINGS

Hot-smoked salmon is a signature preparation of the Pacific Northwest. Keep in mind that hot-smoked salmon does not have to be consumed warm; it's also delicious chilled.

1 quart cold water

⅓ cup kosher salt, plus
   1 teaspoon

2 (2-pound) salmon fillets

2 tablespoons packed light or
   dark brown sugar

1 tablespoon Cajun Rub
   (page 247)

¼ teaspoon freshly ground
   black pepper

1. To make the brine, in a large, flat plastic container with a lid, combine the water and ⅓ cup of salt, stirring until the salt dissolves.

2. Add the salmon, skin-side up. Cover and refrigerate for 8 hours.

3. Remove the salmon from the brine. Rinse well with cold water and pat dry using paper towels. Set a wire rack over a large sheet pan.

4. Place the salmon on the rack, skin-side down. Refrigerate, uncovered, for 8 to 12 hours. A film (called the pellicle) will form on the surface; it will help the smoke stick to the salmon.

5. Set an electric smoker to 180°F.

6. In a small bowl, combine the brown sugar, Cajun Rub, pepper, and the remaining 1 teaspoon of salt.

7. Sprinkle the salmon evenly with the mixture.

8. Place the salmon in the smoker, skin-side down, and smoke using alder wood (see page 4) until the internal temperature of the salmon reaches 135°F to 140°F, for 3 to 5 hours. Remove from the smoker. Serve hot or wrap tightly with plastic wrap and refrigerate for up to 12 days.

Candied Salmon Jerky

PREP TIME: 15 MINUTES, PLUS AT LEAST 12 HOURS TO CURE / **COOK TIME:** 3 TO 4 HOURS
YIELD: 50 PIECES

Move over, venison jerky. There's a new player in town and it's salmon. This is just as delicious, if not more so, than your typical jerky; a sweet yet savory snack that is going to be your next addiction. I use a dehydrator for this recipe, but if you don't have one, use a conventional oven at 170°F for 2 to 3 hours.

1½ cups packed light or dark brown sugar

⅓ cup kosher salt

1½ teaspoons garlic powder

1½ teaspoons onion powder

1 teaspoon cayenne pepper

½ teaspoon freshly ground white pepper

2 to 3 pounds skinless salmon fillets, cut into ½-inch-thick strips

¼ cup maple syrup

1. To make the cure, in a medium bowl, combine the brown sugar, salt, garlic powder, onion powder, cayenne pepper, and white pepper.

2. Place some of the cure on the bottom of a 9-by-13-inch baking dish.

3. Set the salmon strips on top. Sprinkle the remaining cure over the salmon strips. Using your hands, gently press to coat all the strips with the sugar mixture. Cover and refrigerate for 12 to 18 hours.

4. Set a dehydrator to 145°F.

5. Remove the salmon strips from the cure, carefully scraping off as much of it as possible. Place on the dehydrator trays so they do not touch. Dehydrate for 3 to 4 hours, basting the salmon pieces with the maple syrup every hour. Your finished jerky should be pliable like leather and should fray and crack slightly at the point at which you bend it. Remove from the dehydrator.

STORING: Refrigerate in an airtight container for up to 3 months or store at room temperature for up to 1 month.

Sea Bass in Coconut Cream

PREP TIME: 20 MINUTES / **COOK TIME:** 25 MINUTES / **YIELD:** 4 TO 6 SERVINGS

OTHER FISH YOU CAN USE: ANY WHITE FLAKY FISH

Sea bass is a hearty fish, meaning it's not as soft and delicate in texture as some others, which gives it the ability to stand up to longer cooking methods. So, if you want to plan ahead, you can also make this dish in the slow cooker; just place all the ingredients in the slow cooker and cook on high for 4 hours.

3 tablespoons olive oil

1 red onion, thinly sliced

1 large red bell pepper, thinly sliced

3 cloves garlic, minced

1 tablespoon minced fresh ginger

2 teaspoons ground cumin

2 teaspoons sambal oelek or sriracha

Juice of 1 lime

1 (28-ounce) can crushed tomatoes, preferably San Marzano

1 (13.6-ounce) can full-fat coconut cream

1½ pounds skinless sea bass fillets

Kosher salt

Freshly ground black pepper

3 cups hot cooked basmati rice

¼ cup chopped fresh cilantro

1. In a large skillet, heat the olive oil over medium-high heat.

2. Add the onion and bell pepper; cook until the onion is translucent, for about 4 minutes.

3. Stir in the garlic, ginger, cumin, sambal oelek, and lime juice; cook for 2 minutes.

4. Add the tomatoes and coconut cream; stir to combine.

5. Season the sea bass with salt and pepper. Nestle it into the sauce until just about completely covered.

6. Reduce the heat to medium. Simmer until the sea bass has cooked through, for about 15 minutes. Remove from the heat.

7. Serve the sea bass in large pieces over the rice, garnished with the cilantro.

Pan-Seared Sea Bass with Avocado Salsa

PREP TIME: 10 MINUTES, PLUS 15 MINUTES TO MARINATE / **COOK TIME:** 10 MINUTES

YIELD: 4 SERVINGS

OTHER FISH YOU CAN USE: SALMON, MAHI MAHI, WALLEYE

A taste of California on a plate, this recipe is simple and lets the fresh ingredients shine. In this recipe, the sea bass gets a quick marinade, but we don't toss the marinade out. Instead, after placing the fillets in the pan, we also pour the marinade into the pan to give the fish another chance to take on more flavor.

3 tablespoons unsalted butter, melted

4 tablespoons freshly squeezed lime juice, divided

3 tablespoons soy sauce

2 tablespoons olive oil

1 tablespoon grated or minced fresh ginger

2 cloves garlic, coarsely chopped

4 (7-ounce) sea bass fillets

2 large ripe avocados, pitted, peeled, and finely diced

¼ red onion, minced

½ cup diced mango

½ red bell pepper, minced

1 tablespoon minced fresh cilantro

1 teaspoon minced jalapeño

Kosher salt

Freshly ground black pepper

2 tablespoons vegetable oil

1. In a shallow dish, combine the butter, 3 tablespoons of lime juice, the soy sauce, olive oil, ginger, and garlic.

2. Put the sea bass in the dish, turning several times to fully coat. Let marinate, skin-side up, for 15 minutes.

3. While the sea bass marinates, to make the salsa, put the avocados, onion, mango, bell pepper, cilantro, jalapeño, and the remaining 1 tablespoon of lime juice in a medium bowl. Season with salt and pepper. Toss to combine.

4. In a large skillet, heat the vegetable oil over medium-high heat.

5. Add the sea bass, skin-side down, then add the marinade. Cook, flipping once, until you can easily flake the fish with a fork, for 8 to 10 minutes. Remove from the heat.

6. Serve the sea bass immediately, topped with the salsa.

Fried Snapper with Peruvian-Style Green Sauce and Baked Fries

PREP TIME: 20 MINUTES / **COOK TIME:** 35 MINUTES / **YIELD:** 4 SERVINGS

OTHER FISH YOU CAN USE: SEA BASS, PIKE, WALLEYE, MAHI MAHI

My dad used to take me to a tiny Peruvian restaurant in Los Angeles. It was totally off the beaten path and completely worth it. That's where I discovered that Peruvians love fries and green sauce. Green sauce is addictive and literally can be put on anything—it really shines with fried fish and potatoes.

½ cup all-purpose flour

1 teaspoon kosher salt, plus more to taste

1 teaspoon garlic powder

1 teaspoon onion powder

½ teaspoon freshly ground black pepper, plus more to taste

¼ teaspoon paprika

2 russet potatoes, cut into ½-inch wedges

1 large onion, coarsely chopped

3 tablespoons olive oil

3 cups vegetable oil

4 (6-ounce) skinless red snapper fillets

Peruvian-Style Green Sauce (page 259), for serving

1. Preheat the oven to 400°F.

2. In a large, shallow bowl, whisk together the flour, salt, garlic powder, onion powder, pepper, and paprika.

3. Put the potatoes and onion on a sheet pan. Drizzle with the olive oil. Season with salt and pepper. Roll the potatoes on the sheet pan to thoroughly coat.

4. Put the sheet pan in the oven and bake until the potatoes are golden brown and fork-tender, for 35 minutes. Remove from the oven.

5. While the potatoes are cooking, in a 4-quart Dutch oven or heavy saucepan, heat the vegetable oil to 275°F to 300°F. Set a wire rack over paper towels.

6. Gently dredge the snapper in the flour mixture to coat on both sides. Fry 1 fillet at a time in the hot oil, flipping once, until cooked through and golden brown, for about 6 minutes per fillet. Transfer to the prepared wire rack. Turn off the heat.

7. Serve the snapper with the roasted potatoes and onion with the sauce on the side.

Crème Fraîche Baked Snapper

PREP TIME: 15 MINUTES / **COOK TIME:** 15 MINUTES / **YIELD:** 4 SERVINGS
OTHER FISH YOU CAN USE: MAHI MAHI, PIKE, SEA BASS, BLUEFISH, SALMON

If you are looking for an exceptional fish dish that is also easy, this is it. This one-pan dish produces beautifully cooked fish. Your guests will think you spent hours cooking, when really it only took 30 minutes. Make sure to not overcook the fillets; having them a bit underdone is best.

4 (8-ounce) skin-on red snapper fillets

1 teaspoon kosher salt, plus more to taste

¼ teaspoon freshly ground black pepper, plus more to taste

1 cup crème fraîche

3 tablespoons Dijon mustard

2 tablespoons minced shallots

2 tablespoons chopped fresh dill

2 tablespoons chopped fresh parsley

2 teaspoons capers, drained

1. Preheat the oven to 425°F. Line a sheet pan with parchment paper.

2. Arrange the snapper, skin-side down, on the prepared sheet pan. Season with salt and pepper.

3. In a medium bowl, combine the crème fraîche, mustard, shallots, dill, parsley, capers, salt, and pepper. Spoon over the snapper to completely cover.

4. Put the sheet pan in the oven and bake until the snapper is just opaque in the center, for 10 to 12 minutes, depending on the thickness. Remove from the oven.

5. Serve the snapper immediately, topped with the sauce.

Snapper Crudo

PREP TIME: 15 MINUTES / **YIELD:** 4 SERVINGS

OTHER FISH YOU CAN USE: TUNA, MAHI MAHI

I spearfish a lot and the best meals are the ones eaten on the boat prepared with fish you've just harvested yourself. I always bring the ingredients for this recipe on a fishing trip. It's simple, elegant, and delicious.

2 tablespoons freshly squeezed orange juice

2 tablespoons soy sauce

1 tablespoon sesame oil

1 tablespoon freshly squeezed lime juice

1 teaspoon grated lemon zest

8 ounces snapper fillets, cut into ¼-inch-thick slices

2 jalapeños, seeded and thinly sliced

1 tablespoon chopped fresh cilantro

Flaked sea salt

1. In a small bowl, whisk together the orange juice, soy sauce, sesame oil, lime juice, and lemon zest.

2. Arrange the snapper on a serving platter and drizzle with the sauce.

3. Top with the jalapeños, cilantro, and sea salt; serve immediately.

Tuna Tataki

PREP TIME: 5 MINUTES / **COOK TIME:** 1 MINUTE / **YIELD:** 2 SERVINGS

OTHER FISH YOU CAN USE: SALMON

Japanese cuisine is a wonderful example of how simple ingredients create beautiful dishes. This isn't at all complicated, but the results are amazing. I have yet to spear my dream tuna, but when I do, this will be the first dish I make with it. Until then, I get my tuna loins from my fellow spearfishing friends.

2 tablespoons vegetable oil

8 ounces ahi tuna loin

3 tablespoons ponzu

1 tablespoon chopped scallion, green and white parts

2 teaspoons soy sauce

1 teaspoon grated or minced fresh ginger

1 teaspoon sesame seeds

½ lemon

1 jalapeño, julienned (optional)

1. In a nonstick frying pan, heat the oil over high heat.

2. Add the tuna loin and sear for about 30 seconds per side. Remove from the heat.

3. In a small bowl, stir together the ponzu, scallion, soy sauce, and ginger.

4. Cut the tuna into ¼-inch-thick slices and arrange on a serving plate.

5. Drizzle with the sauce and sprinkle with the sesame seeds.

6. Top with a squeeze of the lemon and the jalapeño (if using).

Ahi Tuna Poke Bowl

PREP TIME: 10 MINUTES, PLUS 30 MINUTES TO MARINATE / **YIELD:** 4 SERVINGS

OTHER FISH YOU CAN USE: SALMON

Hawaii is my one true love. I would love nothing more than to spearfish all day while eating pineapple and poke. The best poke I ever had was from a well-known restaurant in Maui. This recipe is my take on a simple poke. But feel free to make it your own, adding chopped pineapple, fried onions, avocado, or edamame to your bowl; they all are fantastic in this recipe.

½ cup soy sauce

⅓ cup thinly sliced scallions, green and white parts

1 tablespoon freshly squeezed lime juice

2 teaspoons sesame oil

1 teaspoon rice vinegar

1 teaspoon sriracha (optional)

1 pound ahi tuna steaks, cut into ½-inch cubes

Hot cooked sushi rice, for serving

⅓ cup diced sweet onion

1 teaspoon toasted sesame seeds

1. In a large bowl, whisk together the soy sauce, scallions, lime juice, sesame oil, vinegar, and sriracha (if using).

2. Add the tuna and gently stir to fully coat. Cover and refrigerate for 30 minutes.

3. Serve the tuna on top of rice, sprinkled with the onion and sesame seeds.

Marinades, Brines, Rubs, Sauces, and Stocks

Marinades, brines, rubs, and sauces can take your meal to the next level. Marinades and brines are especially important for wild game because these animals have much less fat than their farmed counterparts, which can result in toughness if they are not cooked properly. Brines introduce moisture to the meat. Marinades add flavor and can help break down muscle fiber, making the game more tender. Rubs are sprinkled on prior to cooking to help create a tasty crust. Some of the recipes you'll find in this chapter are called for in recipes elsewhere in the book, but the majority are bonus recipes you can use to experiment with.

← Korean-Style BBQ Marinade, page 240

MARINADES & BRINES

Pomegranate Molasses Marinade

PREP TIME: 5 MINUTES / **COOK TIME:** 5 MINUTES
YIELD: ABOUT 5 CUPS
USE WITH: VENISON, ELK, MOOSE, BEAR,
WILD BOAR, UPLAND GAME BIRDS

The acid from the pomegranate juice helps tenderize the meat, while the molasses brings a deep, almost smoky hint of flavor.

4 cups pomegranate juice

¾ cup chopped fresh mint

½ cup light molasses

¼ cup freshly squeezed
   lemon juice

¼ cup olive oil

5 cloves garlic, minced

2 teaspoons kosher salt

1 teaspoon freshly ground
   black pepper

In a large saucepan, whisk together the pomegranate juice, mint, molasses, lemon juice, olive oil, garlic, salt, and pepper over medium heat. Bring to a simmer. Cook, whisking occasionally, until the molasses has dissolved. Remove from the heat. Let cool. Once the liquid is at room temperature, use immediately to marinate game for 6 to 8 hours, or store in the refrigerator for up to 5 days.

Yogurt Marinade

PREP TIME: 10 MINUTES

YIELD: ABOUT 2½ CUPS

USE WITH: ALL WILD GAME AND FISH

If you can master one marinade, it should be this one. You can create so many flavor variations with this recipe. The great thing about yogurt is that the enzymes in it help tenderize wild game and ensure that moisture is not lost. It also creates an instant sauce.

BASIC YOGURT MARINADE:

2 cups whole-milk plain Greek yogurt

3 cloves garlic, minced

2 tablespoons freshly squeezed lemon juice

1 teaspoon kosher salt

½ teaspoon freshly ground black pepper

FOR INDIAN-STYLE, ADD:

2 teaspoons ground cumin

1 teaspoon ground coriander

1 teaspoon ground turmeric

½ teaspoon ground allspice

FOR SRIRACHA-LIME, ADD:

3 tablespoons sriracha

2 tablespoons freshly squeezed lime juice

Grated zest of 1 lime

FOR LEMON-HERB, ADD:

3 tablespoons minced fresh parsley

1 tablespoon minced fresh dill

1 tablespoon chopped fresh chives

Grated zest of 1 lemon

In a medium bowl, whisk together the yogurt, garlic, lemon juice, salt, and pepper until well combined. Mix in the additional flavorings (if using) until well combined. Use immediately to marinate game and fish for 6 to 48 hours, or store in an airtight container in the refrigerator for up to 4 days.

Herb-Lemon Marinade

PREP TIME: 10 MINUTES

YIELD: ABOUT 1 CUP

USE WITH: WILD BOAR, WATERFOWL, UPLAND GAME BIRDS

If you can find them, Meyer lemons bring a sweet, floral, yet not-too-sour lemon flavor to this marinade without overpowering the meat. I particularly like it with fish and quail.

½ cup freshly squeezed lemon juice, preferably from Meyer lemons

½ cup olive oil

2 tablespoons sugar

1 tablespoon grated lemon zest

1½ teaspoons kosher salt

1 teaspoon Dijon mustard

½ teaspoon freshly ground black pepper

In a medium bowl, whisk together the lemon juice, olive oil, sugar, lemon zest, salt, mustard, and pepper until well combined. Use immediately to marinate fish for 1 hour, small cuts of meat for 4 hours, and larger cuts for up to 6 hours, or store in an airtight container in the refrigerator for up to 5 days.

Balsamic Marinade

PREP TIME: 5 MINUTES

YIELD: ABOUT 1 CUP

USE WITH: VENISON, ELK, MOOSE, BEAR, WATERFOWL, UPLAND GAME BIRDS

Balsamic vinegar packs a beautiful punch of tart yet sweet flavor that pairs well with dark-meat wild game meats. The added bonus of this recipe is you can use it as a salad dressing. You can also change it up by using one of the many flavored balsamic vinegars now available.

½ cup extra-virgin olive oil

½ cup balsamic vinegar

2 cloves garlic, minced

1 tablespoon Dijon mustard

1 tablespoon minced fresh rosemary

1 teaspoon kosher salt

½ teaspoon freshly ground black pepper

In a small bowl, whisk together the olive oil, vinegar, garlic, mustard, rosemary, salt, and pepper until well combined. Use immediately to marinate game for 2 to 4 hours, or store in an airtight container in the refrigerator for up to 1 week.

Buttermilk Marinade

PREP TIME: 10 MINUTES
YIELD: ABOUT 6¼ CUPS
USE WITH: ALL WILD GAME

Buttermilk is a chef's secret weapon. Restaurants will marinate chicken, fish, and red meats in it overnight to give a subtle tanginess. The good bacteria in buttermilk also help break down proteins, which makes it a perfect tenderizer.

6 cups buttermilk

Grated zest of 1 lemon

1 tablespoon chopped
  fresh dill

1 tablespoon kosher salt

1 teaspoon freshly ground
  black pepper

⅛ teaspoon ground allspice

In a large bowl, whisk together the buttermilk, lemon zest, dill, salt, pepper, and allspice until well combined. Use immediately to marinate game meats for 12 to 48 hours, or store in an airtight container in the refrigerator for up to 5 days.

Korean-Style BBQ Marinade

PREP TIME: 15 MINUTES / **COOK TIME:** 2 MINUTES
YIELD: ABOUT 2¼ CUPS
USE WITH: VENISON, ELK, MOOSE, BEAR,
WATERFOWL, UPLAND GAME BIRDS

The soy sauce in this marinade will impart great umami flavor to whatever game you use it with. One caution: because of the marinade's high salt content, be careful not to over-marinate, or you may end up with a very salty final result.

1 cup soy sauce

1 cup chopped scallions, green and white parts

3 tablespoons sugar

2 tablespoons freshly squeezed lime juice

2 tablespoons minced garlic

1 tablespoon sesame oil

1 teaspoon grated or minced fresh ginger or 2 teaspoons ground ginger

1 teaspoon freshly ground black pepper

1 teaspoon red pepper flakes or Korean chile powder

In a medium bowl, whisk together the soy sauce, scallions, sugar, lime juice, garlic, sesame oil, ginger, black pepper, and red pepper flakes until well combined. Use immediately to marinate game for 1 to 4 hours, or store in an airtight container in the refrigerator for up to 7 days.

Classic
Lemon-Herb Brine

PREP TIME: 20 MINUTES / **COOK TIME:** 30 MINUTES

YIELD: ABOUT 1 GALLON

USE WITH: WILD BOAR, WATERFOWL, UPLAND GAME BIRDS

Want to amaze people with your awesome wild turkey or tremendously moist boar? Be sure to brine them.

2 quarts water

1 cup kosher salt

½ cup packed light or dark brown sugar

¼ cup honey

12 bay leaves

2 heads garlic, cut crosswise in half, skin on

2 tablespoons black peppercorns

5 sprigs rosemary

1 small bunch fresh dill

1 small bunch fresh thyme

1 cinnamon stick

4 lemons, cut crosswise in half

3 oranges, cut crosswise in half

8 cups ice

1. In a large stockpot, combine the water, salt, brown sugar, honey, bay leaves, garlic, black peppercorns, rosemary, dill, thyme, and cinnamon stick.

2. Squeeze the lemon juice into the pot and add the lemon rinds.

3. Repeat with the oranges. Cook over high heat, stirring frequently, until the sugar and honey dissolve. Remove from the heat.

4. Stir in the ice. Let cool completely before using. Add the proteins and soak, covered, in the brine in the refrigerator for up to 24 hours.

Maple Brine

PREP TIME: 10 MINUTES / **COOK TIME:** 15 MINUTES
YIELD: ABOUT ½ GALLON
USE WITH: VENISON, ELK, MOOSE, BEAR,
WILD BOAR, WATERFOWL, UPLAND GAME BIRDS, FISH

I created this brine after a hunt in Canada because I was so inspired by all things maple. Maple has a great sweet, smoky flavor and is perfectly balanced with the salt. Don't be afraid to use this brine on all proteins.

2 quarts water

1 cup packed light or dark
   brown sugar

1 cup maple syrup

½ cup kosher salt

¼ cup soy sauce

8 cloves garlic, crushed

10 fresh sage leaves

4 bay leaves

4 sprigs thyme

1 teaspoon black
   peppercorns

In a large stockpot, combine the water, brown sugar, maple syrup, salt, soy sauce, garlic, sage, bay leaves, thyme, and black peppercorns over medium-high heat; stir frequently until the sugar has dissolved, about 10 minutes after the mixture starts to simmer. Remove from the heat. Let cool to room temperature. Add the proteins and soak completely covered in the brine in the refrigerator up to 24 hours.

Wild Boar Brine

PREP TIME: 10 MINUTES
YIELD: ABOUT 6 ½ CUPS

Brining your wild boar is a great way to ensure a tender and moist outcome. Unlike farmed pork, wild boar has a tough texture, but a simple brine can make all the difference.

6 cups water

¼ cup apple cider vinegar

¼ cup packed light or dark
   brown sugar

2 tablespoons kosher salt

1 teaspoon dried thyme

1 teaspoon onion powder

1 teaspoon whole
   juniper berries

1 teaspoon pink peppercorns

¼ teaspoon red
   pepper flakes

In a large bowl, whisk together the water, vinegar, brown sugar, salt, thyme, onion powder, juniper berries, peppercorns, and red pepper flakes until the salt and sugar have dissolved. Add the boar and soak completely covered in the brine in the refrigerator for up to 24 hours.

Citrus–Soy Sauce Brine

PREP TIME: 10 MINUTES

YIELD: ABOUT 9 CUPS

USE WITH: ALL WILD GAME

Soy and citrus are a wonderful combination that not only helps tenderize the meat, but also imparts a beautiful salty, tart flavor to wild game.

8 cups water, divided

½ cup packed light or dark brown sugar

½ cup kosher salt

½ cup freshly squeezed lemon juice, rinds reserved

¼ cup freshly squeezed lime juice, rinds reserved

¼ soy sauce

⅛ teaspoon red pepper flakes

1. In a large saucepan, whisk together 2 cups of water, the brown sugar, salt, lemon juice, lime juice, and soy sauce; bring to a simmer over medium heat and stir until the sugar and salt have dissolved. Remove from the heat. Pour into a large bowl.

2. Stir in the remaining 6 cups of water, the lemon rinds, lime rinds, and red pepper flakes. Let cool to room temperature. Add the proteins and soak completely covered in the brine in the refrigerator for up to 24 hours.

RUBS

Coffee Rub

PREP TIME: 5 MINUTES
YIELD: ABOUT ¾ CUP
USE WITH: VENISON, ELK, MOOSE, BEAR, WILD BOAR

This rub's robust flavor pairs nicely with game.

2 tablespoons kosher salt

2 tablespoons
espresso powder

2 tablespoons garlic powder

2 tablespoons
smoked paprika

1 tablespoon freshly ground
black pepper

1 tablespoon ground
coriander

1 tablespoon onion powder

1 teaspoon chili powder

½ teaspoon cayenne pepper

In a small bowl, whisk together the salt, espresso powder, garlic powder, paprika, pepper, coriander, onion powder, chili powder, and cayenne pepper. Store in an airtight container in a dry place for up to 1 month. To use, sprinkle 2 teaspoons per pound all over the meat and lightly press to adhere.

Cajun Rub

PREP TIME: 5 MINUTES

YIELD: ABOUT ⅔ CUP

USE WITH: ALL WILD GAME AND FISH

This Cajun rub harkens back to its French roots with the inclusion of warm spices like nutmeg, taking this rub to a whole new level.

2 tablespoons paprika

2 tablespoons kosher salt

1 tablespoon sugar

1 tablespoon garlic powder

1 tablespoon onion powder

1 tablespoon chili powder

1 tablespoon dried thyme

1 tablespoon freshly ground
   black pepper

1 teaspoon red pepper flakes

½ teaspoon ground allspice

¼ teaspoon ground nutmeg

¼ teaspoon ground cloves

In a small bowl, whisk together the paprika, salt, sugar, garlic powder, onion powder, chili powder, thyme, black pepper, red pepper flakes, allspice, nutmeg, and cloves. Store in an airtight container in a dry place for up to 1 month. To use, sprinkle 2 teaspoons per pound all over the meat and lightly press to adhere.

Indian-Style Spice Rub

PREP TIME: 5 MINUTES

YIELD: ABOUT ¾ CUP

USE WITH: ALL WILD GAME AND FISH

Indian food has a complex level of flavors achieved through the melding of multiple spices. Some of my favorite dishes use this spice blend.

3 tablespoons kosher salt

2 tablespoons packed light or dark brown sugar

2 tablespoons ground cumin

1 tablespoon ground coriander

1 tablespoon paprika

1 tablespoon ground ginger

1 tablespoon ground turmeric

2 teaspoons ground cardamom

1 teaspoon freshly ground black pepper

1 teaspoon ground cinnamon

½ teaspoon garam masala

In a small bowl, whisk together the salt, brown sugar, cumin, coriander, paprika, ginger, turmeric, cardamom, pepper, cinnamon, and garam masala. Store in an airtight container in a dry place for up to 1 month. To use, sprinkle 2 teaspoons per pound all over the meat and lightly press to adhere.

All-Purpose Seafood Rub

PREP TIME: 5 MINUTES

YIELD: ABOUT ½ CUP

USE WITH: ALL FISH

From trout to scallops, this rub does it all! Consider doubling the recipe because you will quickly find a ton of uses for it.

3 tablespoons kosher salt

4 teaspoons garlic powder

1 tablespoon celery salt

1 tablespoon freshly ground
   black pepper

2 teaspoons ground ginger

2 teaspoons paprika

1 teaspoon dry mustard

1 teaspoon dried basil

½ teaspoon ground allspice

½ teaspoon cayenne pepper

½ teaspoon ground nutmeg

In a small bowl, whisk together the kosher salt, garlic powder, celery salt, black pepper, ginger, paprika, mustard, basil, allspice, cayenne pepper, and nutmeg. Store in an airtight container in a dry place for up to 1 month. To use, sprinkle 2 teaspoons per pound all over the fish and lightly press to adhere.

Chili-Lime Rub

PREP TIME: 10 MINUTES

YIELD: ABOUT ⅓ CUP

USE WITH: ALL WILD GAME AND FISH

The streets of Mexico City inspired this blend, particularly my memories of eating chunks of mango sprinkled with the hot-tart seasoning Tajín, made from ground chiles, salt, and dehydrated lime juice. This rub will bring a little heat to your protein!

2 tablespoons kosher salt

2 tablespoons chili powder

1 teaspoon ground cumin

1 teaspoon cayenne pepper

½ teaspoon garlic powder

½ teaspoon onion powder

½ teaspoon ground coriander

½ teaspoon chipotle powder

½ teaspoon sugar

Grated zest of 2 limes

In a small bowl, whisk together the salt, chili powder, cumin, cayenne pepper, garlic powder, onion powder, coriander, chipotle powder, sugar, and lime zest. Store in an airtight container in a dry place for up to 1 month. To use, sprinkle 2 teaspoons per pound all over the meat and lightly press to adhere.

Smokehouse Rub

PREP TIME: 5 MINUTES
YIELD: ABOUT ½ CUP
USE WITH: ALL WILD GAME

This recipe delivers that great smokehouse crust that everyone loves. If you want to turn this into a marinade or braising liquid, add 1 tablespoon to your favorite beer.

3 tablespoons smoked sea salt

1 tablespoon garlic powder

1 tablespoon packed light or dark brown sugar

1 tablespoon onion powder

1 tablespoon freshly ground black pepper

1 teaspoon yellow mustard

1 teaspoon dried thyme

½ teaspoon smoked paprika

In a small bowl, whisk together the salt, garlic powder, brown sugar, onion powder, pepper, mustard, thyme, and paprika. Store in an airtight container in a dry place for up to 1 month. To use, sprinkle 2 teaspoons per pound all over the meat and lightly press to adhere.

Chimichurri Rub

PREP TIME: 5 MINUTES

YIELD: ABOUT 1 CUP

USE WITH: ALL WILD GAME

Based on the Argentinian fresh herb sauce, this rub is a great alternative when you don't have fresh herbs on hand.

3 tablespoons dried basil

3 tablespoons dried oregano

2 tablespoons dried parsley

2 tablespoons dried thyme

2 tablespoons kosher salt

1 tablespoon paprika

1 tablespoon freshly ground black pepper

2 teaspoons garlic powder

1 teaspoon red pepper flakes

Grated zest of 1 lime

Grated zest of 1 lemon

In a small bowl, whisk together the basil, oregano, parsley, thyme, salt, paprika, black pepper, garlic powder, red pepper flakes, lime zest, and lemon zest. Store in an airtight container in a dry place for up to 1 month. To use, sprinkle 2 teaspoons per pound all over the meat and lightly press to adhere.

Everything Rub

PREP TIME: 5 MINUTES

YIELD: ½ CUP

USE WITH: ALL WILD GAME

Here's my version of that delicious combination of flavors you find on an everything bagel. Sprinkle it on anything and everything, from veggies to eggs to bear!

2 tablespoons kosher salt

2 tablespoons poppy seeds

1 tablespoon white
sesame seeds

1 tablespoon black
sesame seeds

1 tablespoon dried
minced garlic

1 tablespoon dried
minced onion

1 tablespoon paprika

1 teaspoon dried basil

1 teaspoon dried oregano

½ teaspoon dried thyme

In a small bowl, whisk together the salt, poppy seeds, white sesame seeds, black sesame seeds, minced garlic, minced onion, paprika, basil, oregano, and thyme. Store in an airtight container in a dry place for up to 1 month. To use, sprinkle 2 teaspoons per pound all over the meat and lightly press to adhere.

Taco Seasoning

PREP TIME: 2 MINUTES / **YIELD:** ½ CUP

USE WITH: ALL WILD GAME

Tacos are a staple in any household. I use this seasoning on everything, including vegetables. Yes, you can get store-bought, but making your own is so much cheaper and results in way better flavor.

3 tablespoons chili powder

1 tablespoon ground cumin

1 tablespoon garlic powder

1 tablespoon smoked
  paprika

1½ teaspoons dried oregano

1½ teaspoons onion powder

¾ teaspoon kosher salt

¾ teaspoon freshly ground
  black pepper

¾ teaspoon red pepper
  flakes

In a small jar, combine the chili powder, cumin, garlic powder, paprika, oregano, onion powder, salt, black pepper, and red pepper flakes. Shake to mix together. Use immediately or store sealed in the jar for up to 1 year.

SAUCES & STOCKS

Brown Butter–Caper Sauce

PREP TIME: 5 MINUTES / **COOK TIME:** 10 MINUTES

YIELD: ABOUT ¾ CUP

USE WITH: ALL WILD GAME

If you are ever in a pinch for a sauce, make brown butter! This easy sauce is a great one to master, since it can be a canvas for many flavorings, like chives, shallots, ginger, scallions, and more.

8 tablespoons (1 stick) unsalted butter

2 cloves garlic, minced

2 tablespoons coarse-grain mustard

2 tablespoons capers, drained

2 tablespoons chopped fresh parsley

¼ teaspoon kosher salt

⅛ teaspoon freshly ground black pepper

1. In a small saucepan, melt the butter over medium-high heat.

2. Reduce the heat to medium-low. Cook until the butter is fragrant and caramel in color, for about 5 minutes. Keep an eye on it; you don't want it to turn black. Remove from the heat.

3. Stir in the garlic, mustard, capers, parsley, salt, and pepper. Serve immediately.

Aïoli

PREP TIME: 15 MINUTES / **YIELD:** ½ CUP

USE WITH: ALL WILD GAME

If you master one sauce, let it be aïoli. Enjoy the classic version or one of the many flavor variations.

FOR CLASSIC AÏOLI:

2 cloves garlic, peeled

Pinch kosher salt

1 large egg yolk

2 teaspoons freshly squeezed lemon juice

½ teaspoon Dijon mustard

4 tablespoons extra-virgin olive oil, divided

3 tablespoons vegetable oil

FOR HERBED AÏOLI, ADD:

2 tablespoons minced fresh tarragon

2 tablespoons minced fresh basil

2 tablespoons minced fresh parsley

2 tablespoons minced fresh cilantro

FOR LEMON-DILL AÏOLI, ADD:

3 tablespoons minced fresh dill

Grated zest of 1 lemon

FOR SRIRACHA AÏOLI, ADD:

2 tablespoons sriracha

Grated zest of 1 lime

FOR HONEY-BASIL AÏOLI, ADD:

3 tablespoons minced fresh basil

2 tablespoons honey

1. **To make Classic Aïoli:** Mince the garlic with the salt, using the knife to create a paste.

2. In a small bowl, whisk together the egg yolk, lemon juice, and mustard.

3. Whisk in about 1 tablespoon of olive oil.

4. While constantly whisking, add a couple drops of olive oil at a time to the yolk mixture, until the remaining 3 tablespoons of olive oil have been incorporated.

5. Continue with the vegetable oil. Whisk constantly until the mixture emulsifies or thickens. If your emulsion breaks (meaning the oil separates), stop adding oil and whisk harder until the mixture comes together again, then continue adding the oil.

6. Serve as is or stir in the ingredients for your preferred flavoring.

Chimichurri

PREP TIME: 10 MINUTES, PLUS 20 MINUTES
FOR THE FLAVORS TO MELD
YIELD: ABOUT 1 ¼ CUPS

USE WITH: ALL WILD GAME AND FISH

Chimichurri is an all-star player because it can be used as a sauce, marinade, salad dressing, and even as a baste for your proteins on the grill.

½ cup chopped fresh parsley

½ cup olive oil

3 tablespoons
  red-wine vinegar

4 cloves garlic, minced

2 Anaheim chiles, diced

1 teaspoon kosher salt

¾ teaspoon dried oregano

½ teaspoon freshly ground
  black pepper

1. For a more rustic and traditional-style chimichurri, in a small bowl, whisk together the parsley, olive oil, vinegar, garlic, chiles, salt, oregano, and pepper. For a smoother style, use a food processor and pulse until the desired texture is reached.

2. Let rest for 20 minutes for the flavors to meld.

Peruvian-Style Green Sauce

PREP TIME: 10 MINUTES
YIELD: ABOUT 4¼ CUPS
USE WITH: ALL WILD GAME AND FISH

If you are a hot sauce aficionado, this sauce is for you! You can spice it up by adding more jalapeño peppers or keep it mild to be enjoyed by all.

2 cups packed fresh cilantro

1 cup coarsely chopped iceberg lettuce

¾ cup mayonnaise

⅓ cup grated Parmesan cheese

1½ tablespoons freshly squeezed lime juice

½ teaspoon kosher salt, plus more to taste

¼ teaspoon freshly ground black pepper, plus more to taste

1 jalapeño, seeded and coarsely chopped

3 cloves garlic, coarsely chopped

¼ cup extra-virgin olive oil, plus more as needed

In a food processor, combine the cilantro, lettuce, mayonnaise, Parmesan cheese, lime juice, salt, pepper, jalapeño, garlic, and olive oil. Blend until the cilantro is in very tiny pieces and the sauce is smooth. Adjust the seasonings if needed. If the flavor is too intense, add more olive oil. Store in an airtight container in the refrigerator for up to 1 week.

Thai-Inspired Peanut Sauce

PREP TIME: 5 MINUTES

YIELD: ABOUT 1 CUP

USE WITH: ALL WILD GAME AND FISH

Beware of this sauce! Why? Because you can easily eat it all in one sitting. It's the boss and can be used as a salad dressing, as a dipping sauce, for satay, and even straight up with some ramen noodles.

½ cup peanut butter

2 tablespoons soy sauce

1½ tablespoons grated fresh ginger

1 tablespoon rice vinegar

1 tablespoon freshly squeezed lime juice

2 teaspoons sambal oelek or sriracha

3 cloves garlic, coarsely chopped

3 tablespoons chicken broth or water

1. In a food processor, combine the peanut butter, soy sauce, ginger, vinegar, lime juice, sambal oelek, and garlic; blend until the sauce is almost smooth.

2. Add the broth 1 tablespoon at a time, pulsing between additions, until the desired consistency is reached. For a dressing, add more broth; for a dip, use less broth. Store in an airtight container in the refrigerator for up to 1 week.

Yum Yum Sauce

PREP TIME: 5 MINUTES

YIELD: ABOUT 1 ⅓ CUPS

USE WITH: ALL WILD GAME AND FISH

You know that kick-ass sauce that is always served at hibachi restaurants? The one you dip everything from your steak to your veggie tempura in? Here it is in all its easy-to-make glory.

1 cup mayonnaise

2 tablespoons unsalted butter, melted

2 tablespoons water

1 tablespoon tomato paste

1 tablespoon honey

½ teaspoon garlic powder

½ teaspoon paprika

In a medium bowl, whisk together the mayonnaise, butter, water, tomato paste, honey, garlic powder, and paprika until well combined. Store in an airtight container in the refrigerator for up to 1 month.

Jalapeño Ranch

PREP TIME: 5 MINUTES

YIELD: ABOUT 1 ¼ CUPS

USE WITH: ALL WILD GAME MEATS AND FISH

This is the ultimate taco topping, pizza sauce, and French-fry dipping sauce. But it's also pretty dang fantastic on freshly grilled venison as well.

1 cup sour cream

⅓ cup chopped fresh cilantro

¼ cup chopped fresh chives

¼ cup chopped fresh parsley

2 tablespoons freshly squeezed lime juice

1½ teaspoons garlic powder

1 teaspoon onion powder

1 teaspoon kosher salt

1 teaspoon freshly ground black pepper

1 jalapeño, seeded and chopped

In a food processor, combine the sour cream, cilantro, chives, parsley, lime juice, garlic powder, onion powder, salt, pepper, and jalapeño; blend until everything is smooth and creamy. Store in an airtight container in the refrigerator for up to 7 days.

Bri's House Asian-Style Sauce

PREP TIME: 5 MINUTES

YIELD: ABOUT 1 ¼ CUPS

USE WITH: ALL WILD GAME

This is a super simple sauce that's wonderful on all types of meat and can even be used as a salad dressing or drizzled over roasted vegetables. It is beautiful over raw and cooked fish as well.

½ cup soy sauce

¼ cup rice vinegar

¼ cup freshly squeezed lime juice

2 tablespoons sambal oelek or sriracha

1 tablespoon sesame oil

2 teaspoons packed light or dark brown sugar

In a medium bowl, whisk together the soy sauce, vinegar, lime juice, sambal oelek, sesame oil, and brown sugar until well combined. Store in an airtight container in the refrigerator for up to 3 weeks.

Venison Stock

PREP TIME: 25 MINUTES / **COOK TIME:** 7 TO 9 HOURS / **YIELD:** 2 QUARTS

The darker the roast, the more flavor you get, and the color of your stock is determined by how well you brown your bones. Those brown roasted parts are what give this stock its depth of flavor. Use this in venison recipes or to replace beef stock when needed.

5 to 8 pounds venison bones (can have some meat left on the bone)

¼ cup safflower oil

Kosher salt

3 large onions, cut into chunks

4 medium carrots, cut into chunks

3 stalks celery, cut into chunks

1 bunch fresh parsley

3 bay leaves

1. Preheat the oven to 400°F.

2. Put the bones on a sheet pan. Drizzle with the safflower oil. Season with salt.

3. Put the sheet pan in the oven and roast until the bones are a deep brown color, for about 1 hour. Remove from the oven.

4. Put the roasted bones, onions, carrots, celery, parsley, and bay leaves in a large stockpot. Fill the stockpot with water until everything is just covered. Bring to a simmer over medium-low heat. Cover and simmer for 6 to 8 hours. If there is a buildup of scum on the top, use a slotted spoon to remove it while the stock simmers. Remove from the heat.

5. Set a colander over a clean pot. Reserving the liquid, strain and discard the bones and vegetables. Let the stock cool to room temperature. Store in an airtight container in the refrigerator for up to 5 days. Or freeze in an airtight container for up to 2 months.

Venison Demi-Glace

PREP TIME: 20 MINUTES / **COOK TIME:** 2 HOURS
YIELD: 2 CUPS
USE WITH: ANY BIG GAME

Demi-glace is stock reduced until it's almost a thick syrup. The beautiful thing about demi-glace is you can use it to season soup and sauces. You only need a little amount, about 1 tablespoon, to give any sauce a huge punch of umami flavor. As a French-trained chef, this is my secret weapon for enhancing dishes.

2 cups Venison Stock
(page 264)
1 large onion,
coarsely chopped
2 stalks celery,
coarsely chopped

1 tablespoon tomato paste
6 sprigs parsley
2 sprigs thyme
1 teaspoon black
peppercorns

1. In a large pot, combine the stock, onion, celery, tomato paste, parsley, thyme, and peppercorns; bring to a boil over high heat.

2. Reduce the heat to medium. Simmer until half the liquid has evaporated. Remove from the heat.

3. Set a colander over a clean bowl. Reserving the liquid, strain and discard the vegetables. Let the demi-glace cool to room temperature. Store in an airtight container in the refrigerator for up to 7 days. Or freeze in an airtight container for up to 3 months.

MEASUREMENT CONVERSIONS

Volume Equivalents	U.S. Standard	U.S. Standard (ounces)	Metric (approximate)
Liquid	2 tablespoons	1 fl. oz.	30 mL
	¼ cup	2 fl. oz.	60 mL
	½ cup	4 fl. oz.	120 mL
	1 cup	8 fl. oz.	240 mL
	1½ cups	12 fl. oz.	355 mL
	2 cups or 1 pint	16 fl. oz.	475 mL
	4 cups or 1 quart	32 fl. oz.	1 L
	1 gallon	128 fl. oz.	4 L
Dry	⅛ teaspoon	–	0.5 mL
	¼ teaspoon	–	1 mL
	½ teaspoon	–	2 mL
	¾ teaspoon	–	4 mL
	1 teaspoon	–	5 mL
	1 tablespoon	–	15 mL
	¼ cup	–	59 mL
	⅓ cup	–	79 mL
	½ cup	–	118 mL
	⅔ cup	–	156 mL
	¾ cup	–	177 mL
	1 cup	–	235 mL
	2 cups or 1 pint	–	475 mL
	3 cups	–	700 mL
	4 cups or 1 quart	–	1 L
	½ gallon	–	2 L
	1 gallon	–	4 L

Oven Temperatures

Fahrenheit	Celsius (approximate)
250°F	120°C
300°F	150°C
325°F	165°C
350°F	180°C
375°F	190°C
400°F	200°C
425°F	220°C
450°F	230°C

Weight Equivalents

U.S. Standard	Metric (approximate)
½ ounce	15 g
1 ounce	30 g
2 ounces	60 g
4 ounces	115 g
8 ounces	225 g
12 ounces	340 g
16 ounces or 1 pound	455 g

INDEX

ACKNOWLEDGMENTS

Writing a book is harder than I thought, but it's more rewarding than I ever imagined. None of this would have been possible if Joe Cho hadn't found me and believed that I could do this. So, thank you, Joe, for going to bat for me, having my back, and believing in me.

I'm eternally grateful for Pam Kingsley, my editor who forever changed the way I write a recipe, who gave me the right guidance, and, most of all, put up with me as I learned this whole book-writing process. Thank you, Pam, for all you have done for me and this book.

I'd like to give a big bear hug and thank you to my dad. Thank you for giving me the gift of the outdoors, making me fearless beyond your liking, and for supporting me through this crazy thing we call life. Thank you for all the little moments that now play a huge role in my life, like taking me scuba diving for the first time. It has led me to the most beautiful memories I will ever have. Thank you for all the adventures in the desert motorcycle riding. Thank you for all the long talks while deep-sea fishing. Most of all, thank you for every jam session in the car while rocking out to the Beach Boys. I hold all those moments close to my heart. You're the reason I'm never afraid to try because I know my dad will always have my back.

Thank you to my Mama, who once told me that my craziness was because I was missing chemicals in my brain but who loved me beyond measure anyway. Thank you for all the prayers I made you say while I was off swimming with sharks or bear hunting. Thank you for teaching me compassion and making me want a better world for humans and animals. You're the reason for my kind heart.

Thank you to my husband, Ryan; this book is for you because of you. Because it's you who puts up with every crazy idea I have and always responds with an even crazier idea. You pushed me like no one else to pursue my passions; you support every dream I have, and you are my biggest fan. Thank you for being my best friend and for always watching the baby while I go hunting!

Thank you to my daughter, Mila, for making me a mommy. You bring so much joy to my life. I can only hope I make you as proud of me as I am of you, my sweet girl.

And most of all, thank you to my publisher, Callisto Media!

ABOUT THE AUTHOR

Born and raised in sunny California, **Bri Van Scotter** grew up riding horses and racing dirt bikes. When it was time to head to college, she understood the value of a university degree. So, she chose California State University, Fullerton. After graduation, her degree landed her a job at a large retailer, however, that meant she would sit in a cubicle all day. Not keen on that kind of life, Bri got a job as a hostess at a local restaurant. Having a huge passion for cooking and baking, Bri quickly ended up in the pastry department. Baking desserts at the restaurant became something she looked forward to every day. It was then she decided to head to culinary school. She went on to graduate from The Culinary Institute of America in Napa, California with a degree in Culinary Arts, and then got an additional degree from The Art Institute of Orange County, California.

Bri has worked in some of the most prestigious restaurants in the U.S. as both an Executive Chef and Executive Pastry Chef. But it wasn't until a move to Georgia that she discovered her love for hunting. Her husband bought her a bow, which he thought would be just for fun, but which ended up changing her career. Six months later, she was in a tree stand on opening day getting her first doe. After her first harvest, she noticed there was a lack of wild game recipes. So, she created Wilderness to Table, a website dedicated to self-harvested wild game recipes.

Her blog caught the eye of a producer and was turned into a television show that is now available on Amazon Prime and iTunes. Bri has appeared on news segments, gives cooking demonstrations, and is an advocate for hunting and conservation. Bri now travels the world to hunt. She is an avid upland bird shooter and can always be seen with her bird dog by her side.

To learn more about Bri, head to WildernesstoTable.com or visit her on Instagram at @wildernesstotable. There she shares more wild game recipes and a look into her world as an avid hunter, scuba diver, spearfisher, free diver, and traveler.

CPSIA information can be obtained
at www.ICGtesting.com
Printed in the USA
JSHW071958210423
40493JS00002B/2